Ageing and Effecting I
Care in China

MW00509329

Recognizing rapidly ageing population is one key concern faced by cities and the challenge it would present to healthcare system, this book looks at ageing in China's population as well as the delivery and financing of long-term care (LTC) in China.

The book compares key features of long-term care insurance (LTCI) schemes in 15 pilot cities and evaluates the sustainability of various financing models adopted by the cities in the LTCI schemes. The book uses an interpretive case study approach to give an in-depth look into the LTC models in three pilot cities – Qingdao, Nantong, and Shanghai. The three cities represent three different models of financing and delivering LTC. To assess how effective the LTC models in these three cities are, the book uses five criteria, including utilization of medical resources, cost, equity, quality of care, and sustainability. Also, the authors discuss how the financing and delivery of LTC can be improved in China, the impact of the 2019 coronavirus disease (COVID-19) pandemic on older adults in need of LTC in the country, and the implications of China's LTCI reform for other countries.

The book will be a useful reference to scholars and policymakers who look at urban ageing and healthcare costs and delivery.

Sabrina Ching Yuen Luk is Assistant Professor in Public Policy and Global Affairs, Nanyang Technological University, Singapore. Her research areas include healthy ageing, healthcare and long-term care reforms, smart cities, and crisis leadership and management.

Hui Zhang is Associate Professor in the Department of Health Policy and Management, School of Public Health, Sun Yat-sen University of China. She holds a PhD in Health Economics from The Hong Kong Polytechnic University. Her research interests are healthcare financing, health insurance reform, and cost-effectiveness analysis.

Peter P. Yuen is Dean of the College of Professional and Continuing Education of The Hong Kong Polytechnic University (PolyU) and Professor in the Department of Management and Marketing of PolyU. He is a founding Fellow of the Hong Kong College of Health Services Executives and an Honorary Fellow of the Australian College of Health Services Management.

Routledge Studies in the Modern World Economy

For more information about this series, please visit: www.routledge.com/
Routledge-Studies-in-the-Modern-World-Economy/book-series/SE0432

Ageing and Effecting Long-term Care in China

Sabrina Ching Yuen Luk, Hui Zhang and Peter P. Yuen

Routledge
Taylor & Francis Group

LONDON AND NEW YORK

First published 2022
by Routledge
2 Park Square, Milton Park, Abingdon, Oxon OX14 4RN

and by Routledge
605 Third Avenue, New York, NY 10158

Routledge is an imprint of the Taylor & Francis Group, an informa business

© 2022 Sabrina Ching Yuen Luk, Hui Zhang and Peter P. Yuen

British Library Cataloguing-in-Publication Data
A catalogue record for this book is available from the British Library

Library of Congress Cataloging-in-Publication Data
A catalog record for this book has been requested.

ISBN: 978-0-367-17499-6 (hbk)
ISBN: 978-1-032-18538-5 (pbk)
ISBN: 978-0-429-05719-9 (ebk)

DOI: 10.4324/9780429057199

Typeset in Galliard
by Apex CoVantage, LLC

Contents

Tables

Preface

This book is the result of three years' hard work. I decided to write this book together with Professor Yuen and Professor Zhang in summer 2018 because the financing and delivery of long-term care (LTC) in China have been underexplored and have not been understood completely. China is one of the world's fastest ageing countries and has the world's largest ageing population. A rapidly ageing population has led to the growing demand for LTC in the country. But China is getting old before getting rich (*wei fu xian lao*). Hence, many people face financial hardship when they get old due to having limited economic resources. This raises concern over how older adults with physical and cognitive impairments can get proper and sufficient help and services.

In 2016, the Chinese government implemented a pilot long-term care insurance (LTCI) reform in the country. A total of 15 cities were selected to implement the LTCI scheme. Local governments were given discretion to determine the source of finance, contribution rate, the insured population, and insurance benefits in accordance with their socio-economic conditions. It would be timely and meaningful for us to examine whether the implementation of LTCI helps meet the specific needs of older adults with physical disability or dementia. It would also be useful for scholars, political leaders, and policymakers to learn from the reform experience of China if they plan to advocate and implement LTC reform in their countries or cities.

While I bear much of the responsibility to write this book, Professor Yuen provides inputs to Chapters 4 and 8, and Professor Zhang provides inputs to Chapter 4. I adopt an interpretive case study approach in this book to obtain in-depth investigation of the LTC models in three pilot cities – Qingdao, Nantong, and Shanghai – representing three different models of financing and delivering LTC. I make use of lots of tables to help illustrate LTCI schemes, LTC needs assessment standard, and different types of LTC service packages in these three cities. Lots of Chinese materials (e.g. books, journal articles, government documents and reports, newspaper reports) that have not been found in the existing Western studies are also used to help illustrate the financing and delivery of LTC in China.

At present, most of the pilot cities, when funding LTCI schemes, heavily rely on money transferred from the employment-based and resident-based health insurance schemes. This may affect the financial sustainability of LTCI in the long run. For readers who are interested in knowing more about health insurance reforms in China, you are welcome to read my earlier work titled *Financing Healthcare in China: Towards Universal Health Insurance* (2017, Abingdon, Oxon; New York: Routledge). For readers who are interested in knowing LTCI reform experience of other Asian countries or how the LTCI reform experience of China is different from that in other Asian countries, you are welcome to read my previous work titled *Ageing, Long-term Care Insurance and Healthcare Finance in Asia* (2020, Abingdon, Oxon; New York, NY: Routledge).

I hope that this book can provide some valuable insights into some of the key issues of LTCI reform in China.

Sabrina Ching Yuen Luk
Summer 2021, Singapore

Abbreviations

AD	Alzheimer's Disease
ADLs	Activities of Daily Living
BI	Barthel Index
BMI	Basic Medical Insurance
BPSD	Behavioural and Psychological Symptoms of Dementia
CAWA	Chinese Aging Well Association
CCTV	Closed-circuit Television
CEC	Central Economic City
CHARLS	China Health and Retirement Longitudinal Study
CLHLS	Chinese Longitudinal Healthy Longevity Surveys
CNCA	China National Committee on Aging
COCs	Coastal Open Cities
COPD	Chronic Obstructive Pulmonary Disease
COVID-19	The 2019 Coronavirus Diseases
CRCA	China Research Centre on Ageing
EoL	End-of-life
EUR	Euro
FEA	Federal Employment Agency
GDP	Gross Domestic Product
HAMD	Hamilton Depression Rating Scale
HIS	Hachinski Ischemic Score
IADLs	Instrumental Activities of Daily Living
IT	Information Technology
LTC	Long-term Care
LTCI	Long-term Care Insurance
MCA	Ministry of Civil Affairs
MLSS	Ministry of Labor and Social Security
MMSE	Mini-mental State Examination
MoCA	Montreal Cognitive Assessment
MOHRSS	Ministry of Human Resources and Social Security
MSA	Medical Savings Account
NETDA	Nantong Economic and Technological Development Area
NHFPC	National Health and Family Planning Commission

NGOs	Non-governmental Organizations
OECD	Organisation for Economic Co-operation and Development
OOP	Out-of-pocket
QoL	Quality of Life
PICC	Peripherally Inserted Central Catheter
PWD	People with dementia
RMB	Renminbi
ROK	Republic of Korea
SDGs	Sustainable Development Goals
SDG3	Sustainable Development Goal 3
SDL	Self-directed Learning
SMIE	Social Medical Insurance for Employee
SMIR	Social Medical Insurance for Resident
SPF	Social Pooling Fund
TFR	Total Fertility Rate
UEBMI	Urban Employee Basic Medical Insurance
URBMI	Urban Resident Basic Medical Insurance
URRBMI	Urban and Rural Resident Basic Medical Insurance
UK	the United Kingdom
UN	United Nations
US	the United States
VAD	Vascular Dementia
WMLs	White Matter Lesions

1   Understanding long-term care

Introduction

This book is about the financing and delivery of long-term care (LTC) in China. China is the most populous country in the world, with a population experiencing one of the fastest speeds of ageing that mankind has ever experienced. It has lifted more than 800 million people out of poverty through over three decades of economic reforms and openingup (World Bank n.d.). Economic growth has brought about improved living standards for the population (Yao 2000) and rapid nutritional improvement (Wang *et al.* 1993). Health status among older adults – especially women – is also improving with rising educational attainment and better medical care (Population Reference Bureau 2020). The combination of increasing life expectancy and declining birth rates has accelerated the ageing process in China (Lu and Liu 2019: 25). From 2001 to 2018, the annual growth rate of the elderly population aged 65 and above in China reached 3.28 percent, which significantly exceeded the annual growth rate of 0.66 percent for the total population (Lu and Liu 2019: 25). Rapid population ageing has profoundly affected socio-economic development and put great pressure on systems that develop healthcare and LTC (Lu and Liu 2019: 25–6).

China is a huge country. Different cities and regions of this country vary with socio-economic, cultural, and health status. Some of them are currently experimenting with new models to finance and deliver LTC. The success or failure of different LTC financing models within China will be of great interest not only to the population of China, but also to academics, public policymakers, and care providers throughout the world. Population ageing is a global phenomenon. Many countries are also facing challenges in implementing fair, responsive, and sustainable LTC policies (Colombo *et al.* 2011: 3). This book attempts to shed some light on this grand challenge.

This introductory chapter examines what LTC is, the importance of LTC, major LTC issues around the world, different types of LTC financing, and the challenges of providing and financing LTC in China. It presents the analytical perspective, methodology, and structure of the book.

DOI: 10.4324/9780429057199-1

Definition of long-term care

LTC, also known as aged care or social care (Roberts 2017; Yuen 2018), refers to a broad range of services needed by individuals with 'physical, cognitive, or mental disability or condition that results in functional impairment and dependence on others for an extended period of time' (O'Shaughnessy *et al*. 2007: 3). It 'supports older adults in two distinct realms: activities of daily living (ADLs) and instrumental activities of daily living (IADLs)' (Agency for Healthcare Research and Quality 2011: 1). ADLs refer to 'skills required to manage one's basic physical needs including personal hygiene or grooming, dressing, toileting, transferring or ambulating, and eating' (Edemekong *et al*. 2020). IADLs refer to activities which allow an individual to live independently in a community, including cooking, cleaning, doing laundry, transportation, and managing finances (Guo and Sapra 2020). LTC services vary widely in their frequency, intensity, and cost (Agency for Healthcare Research and Quality 2011: 1; O'Shaughnessy *et al*. 2007: 3), 'depending on an individual's underlying conditions, the severity of his or her disabilities, and the location in which services are provided' (O'Shaughnessy *et al*. 2007: 3).

There is a rising demand for LTC and 'the need for increased access to effective long-term care is becoming a pressing issue in practically all societies' (World Health Organization 2003: 227). It is widely recognized that LTC can achieve gains in health and contribute to alleviating suffering, reducing comfort, improving the limitations caused by disability and disease, maintaining the best possible levels of functioning and the best possible quality of life (QoL) (World Health Organization 2003: 231).

Delivery of LTC

Most formal LTC 'is provided through organized service providers that operate in specific settings' (Wunderlich and Kohler 2001: 41). Non-residential service providers include home care and hospice care agencies (Wunderlich and Kohler 2001: 41), day care centres, dementia day care centres, and community-based day rehabilitation centres for older adults. Institutional providers include nursing homes, rehabilitation hospitals, LTC units of acute care hospitals, group homes, assisted living facilities (Wunderlich and Kohler 2001: 41–51), and personal care homes (O'Shaughnessy *et al*. 2007). Organized service providers are operated by the government, private for-profit organizations, corporate chains, or non-governmental organizations (NGOs). Many formal caregivers are trained, licensed, and qualified professionals employed by care provider organizations (Ghibelli *et al*. 2017: 13). They 'have contracts specifying care responsibilities, are paid and entitled to social rights and working regulations' (Ghibelli *et al*. 2017: 13).

Nevertheless, informal caregivers, mostly family members or friends, comprise the backbone of LTC provision in most countries (Coleman and Pandya 2002; Ghibelli *et al*. 2017: 3). They perform various care tasks such as personal care and help with IADLs although they are not paid and are not usually trained to provide such care tasks (Ghibelli *et al.* 2017: 3). '[N]early all individuals needing assistance receive some amount of informal care from loved ones in addition to or in place of formal services' (Mommaerts 2015). Changing demographic patterns and other societal changes, however, are reducing the availability of family carers. Family planning efforts in many countries have resulted in the tendency of having smaller household size. 'The mean average household size across the 153 countries or areas is 4.0 persons per household and the median is 3.8 persons per household' (United Nations 2019a: 3). The smallest average household sizes in Eastern and South-Eastern Asia are observed in Japan (2.4 persons per household), Republic of Korea (ROK) (2.9), and Hong Kong (2.9) (United Nations 2019a: 5). Meanwhile, other societal changes – such as rising childlessness, decreased co-residence of older adults with their children and families, rising female participation in the formal labour market, higher divorce rates, and a decline in willingness to care – also reduce the availability of family carers, leading to a growing demand for paid care (Colombo *et al.* 2011: 65).

'LTC is a highly labour-intensive sector, which consists of a range of medical, personal care and assistance services' (OECD 2020a: 18). In recent years, however, the number of formal LTC workers has stagnated or even decreased in many countries (Colombo *et al.* 2011; OECD 2019a, 2020a). In threequarters of Organisation for Economic Co-operation and Development (OECD) countries, for example, growth in the number of LTC workers has been outpaced by the growth in numbers of older adults between 2011 and 2016 (OECD 2020a: 10). 'There is a worsening shortage of competent, committed, paid long-term care workers who are able to meet the needs of older adults' (Stone and Harahan 2010: 109). Low recruitment and retention of workers in the LTC sector is due to low wages, onerous working condition, less career promotion prospects, and the physical and mental stress of the job (OECD 2020a: 10). 'LTC jobs suffer from a lack of status and recognition' (OECD 2020a: 50) because the majority of LTC workers do not hold tertiary education (OECD 2019a: 234). The median hourly wage for LTC workers (i.e. nurses and personal carers) across 11 OECD countries was Euro (EUR) 9 per hour, compared to EUR 14 for hospital workers in the same occupation (OECD 2020a: 20). 'The average tenure is two years lower in the LTC workforce than in the overall workforce' (OECD 2020a: 15). LTC requires workers to deliver more complex care (e.g. health condition monitoring, case management, communication with professionals and families) than generally portrayed (OECD 2020a: 14). However, LTC workers do not receive sufficient training on geriatric conditions and interpersonal skills to provide care that meets quality criteria (OECD 2020a). Having physical health problems such as back pain when lifting patients (OECD 2020a: 22) and exposure to health risks such as anxiety, burnout, and depression (OECD 2020a: 10) are common among LTC workers. To raise efficiency in the LTC sector, some countries such as Norway and the Netherlands utilize assistive technology to assist care workers in their job and enhance care quality (OECD 2020a: 11–2).

Importance of LTC

As a result of longer life expectancy, the size and proportion of older adults are increasing in almost every country (United Nations 2019b: 1). 'Globally, a person aged 65 years in 2015–2020 could expect to live, on average, an additional 17 years' (United Nations 2019b: 1). The number of persons aged 80 years or above was 'projected to increase more than threefold between 2017 and 2050, rising from 137 million to 425 million' (United Nations 2017: 1). In 2019, there were over 700 million persons aged 65 years or above in the world (United Nations 2019b). The number of such older persons has been projected to double in 30 years' time (United Nations 2019b). The percentage of persons aged 65 years was projected to increase from 9 percent in 2019 to 16 percent by 2050 – one in six people in the world will be aged 65 years or older (United Nations 2019b: 1). The increase in life expectancy is coupled with the decrease in fertility rate in many countries. At present, 'close to half of all people globally live in a country or area where lifetime fertility is below 2.1 live births per woman' (United Nations 2019c: 2). Projections indicate that in 2050, the number of persons aged 60 and above will surpass the number of youth aged 10–24 years (2.1 billion vs 2.0 billion) (United Nations 2017: 1). In the same year, 'it is expected that nearly 8 in 10 of the world's older persons will be living in the developing regions' (United Nations 2017: 1).

The rapid ageing of population has driven governments around the world to 'design innovative policies and public services specifically targeted to older persons, including policies addressing housing, employment, health care, infrastructure and social protection, among others' (United Nations 2017: 2). It is also 'expected to be accompanied by an increase in the need for LTC services' (Costa-Font *et al.* 2017: 38). For most individuals, it is difficult to foresee whether LTC 'will be required in the future, and if so, the type, the duration and the cost of that care' (Colombo *et al.* 2011: 263). If they fail to pre-fund LTC services *ex ante* before the need arises (Costa-Font *et al.* 2017: 38), 'they themselves, their family, or the state end up facing potentially substantial costs *ex post*' (Costa-Font *et al.* 2017: 38). Ageing is often associated with poverty (Kwan and Walsh 2018). In 15 OECD countries, for example, 'older people are more likely to be income poor than the total population' (OECD 2019b: 186). In G20 countries, poverty rates among persons aged above 65 are high in China (39%) and India (23%) (OECD 2019b: 186). Causes of old age poverty include insufficient savings (United Nations, n.d.), inability to manage financial resource, forced retirement, increased cost of living (Khan *et al.* 2017), heavy financial burden of medical expenses (Legislative Council of the Hong Kong Special Administrative Region 2007), and 'the absence of social protection systems' (United Nations, n.d.). Without government support, many older adults and their family members will have to endure great financial hardship and suffering in the older adults' final journey of life. The need for government intervention is necessary.

In 2015, world leaders agreed to 17 Sustainable Development Goals (SDGs) set up by the United Nations (UN) to end extreme poverty, promote prosperity, and address a range of social needs such as health and equality by 2030 ('Sustainable Development Goals' n.d.). 'To ensure progress towards implementing the SDGs, it is essential to prepare for the economic and social transformations associated with ageing and old age' (United Nations Development Programme 2017: 17). This is due to the fact that ageing cuts across 'the goals on poverty eradication, good health, gender equality, economic growth and decent work, reduced inequalities and sustainable cities' (United Nations Development Programme 2017: 7). Sustainable Development Goal 3 (SDG3) is about good health and well-being. Being able to finance and deliver LTC properly helps achieve good health and well-being of older adults.

LTC issues around the world

Expenditure rise

LTC demand expansion 'takes place in a gradual way, but expenditure on LTC has been rising even faster than that on general health care' (Costa-Font *et al.* 2017: 38). The annual growth rate in expenditure on LTC by government and compulsory insurance schemes was 4.6 percent between 2005 and 2015 across OECD countries (OECD 2017: 214). Spending growth stands out for the ROK (OECD 2017: 214). Spending on LTC in the ROK increased by more than 25 percent per year (in real terms) between 2005 and 2018 (OECD 2020b: 4). This led to the share of LTC in Gross Domestic Product (GDP) in the ROK growing sharply from 0.1 percent to 1 percent during the same period (OECD 2020b: 4). 'The Netherlands and Scandinavian countries (Denmark, Norway, and Sweden) are by far the highest spenders on LTC' (OECD 2020b: 1). They allocate about 3.5 percent or more of GDP to LTC because of having more developed formal LTC systems (OECD 2020b: 1). 'As populations age, growing demand for long-term care is expected, particularly when the baby boom generations reach old age after 2030' (OECD 2005: 3). Hence, expenditure on LTC is expected to increase at an accelerated rate in the coming years.

An increase in the number of people with dementia

'Dementia rates are growing at alarming proportion in all regions of the world and are related to population aging' (Rizzi *et al.* 2014: 908915). Dementia is defined as the deterioration in cognitive function beyond what might be expected from normal ageing, affecting memory, thinking, comprehension, orientation, language, calculation, learning capacity, and judgement, but not consciousness (World Health Organization 2020). 'Dementia results from a variety of diseases and injuries that primarily or secondarily affect the brain' (World Health Organization 2020). 'There are over 200 subtypes of dementia' (Dementia UK n.d.). But Alzheimer's disease (AD) is the most common form of dementia and may contribute to 60–70 percent of cases, according to Queensland Brain Institute ('Types of dementia' n.d.). Worldwide, around 50 million people have dementia, with around 10 million new cases every year (World Health Organization 2020). The number of people with dementia (PWD) is projected to reach 82 million in 2030 and 152 million in 2050 (World Health Organization 2020).

'Despite billions of dollars spent on research into dementia-related disorders, there is still no cure or even substantially disease-modifying treatment for dementia' (OECD 2019a: 224). Dementia typically progresses in three stages: early (or 'mild'), middle (or 'moderate'), and late (or 'severe') ('Stages of Alzheimer's & Dementia' 2020). 'As dementia progresses, a person will need more help and, at some point, will need a lot of support with daily living' ('The progression and stages of dementia' n.d.). The majority of PWD cared for at home are supported by 'spouses or life partners, followed by children and children-in-law, in majority women' (Seidel and Thyrian 2019: 655). 'Caregiving is known to be accompanied by burden for the caregiver' (Seidel and Thyrian 2019: 655). Dementia caregiving severely burdens the physical, psychological, financial, and social world of caregivers providing informal care to older PWD due to disruptive behaviours of PWD, changes in personality as dementia progresses, and inadequacies in caregiver social support (Messinger-Rapport *et al.* 2006). Globally, the cost of dementia increased from US$604 billion in 2010 to US$818 billion in 2015, representing an increase of 35.4 percent (Alzheimer's Disease International 2015: 58). 'By 2030, it is estimated that the global cost of dementia could grow to US$2 trillion, which could overwhelm health and social care systems' (El-Hayek *et al.* 2019: 324). But epidemiological studies have shown that ageing without dementia is achievable when there are intervention strategies to promote healthy lifestyles (e.g. a balanced diet, physical activity, and no smoking), maintain vascular health, and increase cognitive reserve (e.g. engage in mentally stimulating activities) (Qiu and Fratiglioni 2018: 938–9).

Barriers to access end-of-life (EoL) care

The use of LTC facilities as a site for EoL care for older adults is likely to increase due to the pressure to decrease hospital costs (Brazil *et al.* 2004: 85). EoL care refers to 'care given in the period leading up to death' (Razmaria 2016: 115) to maintain 'the quality of life and comfort of the patient, and their family, through management of pain and other physical, psychosocial and spiritual morbidities' (Mistry *et al.* 2015: e007492). At present, there is insufficient access to EoL care. Particularly, EoL care for older adults is often suboptimal (Burns 2010). Quality of Death Index, which measures the current environment for EoL care services in 40 countries, shows that most developing countries rank poorly, mainly due to lack of money and recognition in government policy for EoL care (American Academy of Actuaries 2017). The bottom of the overall ranking includes Mexico, China, Brazil, Uganda, and India (American Academy of Actuaries 2017). Barriers to accessing EoL care include lack of political will, lack of government support for EoL care, poor education and training of staff, lack of evidence for and monitoring of EoL care (Worldwide Hospice Palliative Care Alliance 2015: 14), and psychological, social, cultural, and financial barriers (Worldwide Palliative

Care Alliance 2014: 31). Population ageing represents a global challenge for future EoL care (Bone *et al.* 2018: 329). How to improve older adults' access to EoL care, how to provide high-quality EoL care, and how to ensure adequate resources, bed capacity, and training of staff in EoL care in LTC facilities are important issues that need to be addressed properly (Bone 2018).

Allocating and balancing responsibilities

Different historical and cultural contexts have rendered the allocation of responsibilities for delivering and financing LTC complicated and highly heterogeneous. The debate on LTC tends to focus on:

- Which type of LTC should be put under the bureaucracy for healthcare and which type of LTC should be put under the bureaucracy for social care;
- The balance between residential and home-based/community-based LTC;
- The balance between public, not-for-profit, and private provision of LTC;
- The balance between formal and informal care;
- The balance between government subsidy and individual/family resources in paying for LTC;
- Whether LTC financing should be separate or a part of the healthcare financing system;
- Whether LTC financing should be tax-based or insurance-based;
- Whether support should be in cash or in kind.

LTC financing

A country/region's LTC services are financed by a mix of funding sources: taxes, compulsory insurance, voluntary insurance, out-of-pocket (OOP) payments, and donations. The size of each of the sources varies from jurisdiction to jurisdiction. Elaborations on each of the sources are provided in the following.

Taxes

'Taxation is, by and large, the most important source of government revenue in nearly all countries' (Ortiz-Ospina and Roser n.d.). Tax revenues are raised through a mix of individual income taxes, corporate income taxes, property taxes, consumption taxes, and social insurance taxes (Enache 2021: 2). LTC services under a tax-based system 'can be provided directly by government units or through NGOs' (Yuen 2018: 12). Universal coverage is common although some services such as personal care in the United Kingdom (UK) are limited to certain care recipients through means testing (Yuen 2018: 12). Long waiting time for LTC services is also quite common due to underfunding (Yuen 2018: 12). Countries or cities using a tax-based model include Denmark, Finland, Norway, Sweden (Colombo *et al.* 2011: 220), Australia, New Zealand, the UK, and Hong Kong (Yuen 2018: 11). However, relying on tax revenues to pay for

LTC services is problematic for countries with an ageing population (Yuen 2018) because 'revenues from social contributions linked primarily to the labour market are expected to decline substantially' (Cylus *et al.* 2019: 7) as a result of a shrinking workforce (Yuen 2018). Some form of tax broadening such as levying special taxes on either individuals or businesses might be necessary in order to help pay for the ever-increasing LTC expenses (Yuen 2018: 8). Another policy option is to expand the tax revenue base by increasing the number of contributors to the system through raising the retirement age or allowing more immigration (Cylus *et al.* 2019: 15). The contribution rates of taxation can also be increased to generate additional resources (Cylus *et al.* 2019: 17).

Compulsory insurance

LTC can be financed by a stand-alone compulsory social insurance programme. Service coverage under this financing model 'is generally comprehensive – not just in reaching the entire population needing care, but also with respect to the scope of the covered services' (Colombo *et al.* 2011: 220). Countries using this model include Germany and Japan. Germany enacted a social insurance programme for LTC in 1994, which provided for 'extensive nursing home and home-care benefits for people of all ages without regard to financial status' (Cuellar and Wiener 2000: 10). It required employers and employees to equally share the LTC insurance premium that was fixed by law at 1.7 percent of salary (Cuellar and Wiener 2000: 10). Japan implemented a public social insurance programme for LTC in 2000. Insured people aged 65 years or above (Category 1) and insured persons aged between 40 and 64 years (Category 2) with a certification for LTC service needs can utilize in-home services, community-based services, and facility services according to their care needs (Yamada and Arai 2020: 174–6). The universal social insurance schemes in both Germany and Japan are 'typically organized as pay-as-you-go systems' (Eling 2020: 39), 'meaning that today's working generation finances the costs of today's beneficiaries' (Eling 2020: 39). In addition, LTC can be financed by a universal mandatory social health insurance scheme (Schut and Van Den Berg 2012: 103). The Netherlands was the first country implementing a universal mandatory social health insurance scheme to cover various LTC services including nursing home care, institutionalized care, home healthcare, and family care for eligible care recipients (Schut and Van Den Berg 2012: 104).

Voluntary insurance

Voluntary private long-term care insurance (LTCI) 'is a financial contract whereby the insurer agrees to provide covered benefits in exchange for regular premium payments by the policyholder' (Johnson and Uccello 2005: 3). 'Policyholders cannot collect benefits until their disabilities reach the levels specified in their contracts' (Johnson and Uccello 2005: 3). The cost and adequacy of policies vary by how much they pay, for how long, when they start paying benefits, and the types of services they cover (Johnson and Uccello 2005: 3). Private LTCI coverage 'rises with wealth, because wealthier people are better able to afford coverage than those with less wealth' (Johnson 2016: 3). Voluntary private LTCI can protect one's income and assets against the risk of needing LTC and provide more choices regarding the care received (Colombo *et al.* 2011: 247). A study found that private LTCI can affect patterns of care utilization (Li and Jensen 2011). Private LTCI 'significantly increases the demand for nursing home care, especially among very disabled seniors, whose needs for assistance are many' (Li and Jensen 2011: 48). It also 'enables moderately disabled older adults to avoid or at least postpone nursing home entry, making it possible for them to remain at home instead' (Li and Jensen 2011: 48). However, the problems of affordability, adverse selection (Johnson and Uccello 2005: 5), the availability of cheaper substitutes (e.g. public LTC insurance), unpaid care provided directly by family members, and financial transfers from children may undermine the private insurance market (Brown and Finkelstein 2007: 1968). Even for the United States (US), where private health insurance is the dominant form of financing for healthcare, only 4 percent of LTC costs are paid by private insurance (Brown and Finkelstein 2007: 1968).

OOP payment/co-payment

OOP payments associated with LTC or co-payment 'are defined as beneficiary participation in the cost of a service' (Del Pozo-Rubio *et al.* 2020: 295). It has the functions of 'curtailing excessive demand, known as moral hazard' (Del Pozo-Rubio *et al.* 2020: 295) and 'reducing costs by raising additional financial resources' (Del Pozo-Rubio *et al.* 2020: 295). Most systems require some cost-sharing on LTC benefits (Yuen 2018: 9). 'Cost-sharing in universal systems either comes as a fixed percentage of cost, or as the difference between the benefit and actual spending' (OECD 2005: 25). In the Netherlands, however, income-related co-payments are required for most LTC services covered by the universal mandatory social health insurance scheme (Schut and Van Den Berg 2012: 105). 'The burden of private expenditure in nursing homes can be substantial for individual households' (OECD 2005: 29), contributing to 30 percent or more of total spending in countries such as the UK, the US, and Germany (OECD 2005: 29). Hence, OOP payment may increase the risk of poverty (OECD 2020c). 'LTC costs can be impoverishing for moderately and severely disabled LTC users, even for those who were not poor before the onset of disability' (Colombo *et al.* 2011: 29). In OECD countries, where overall total public LTC spending is higher, older LTC recipients tend to be at an estimated lower risk of poverty after receiving public support (OECD 2020c: 5).

Donations

LTC can also be funded by charitable donations. Many not-for-profit nursing homes or nursing homes with charitable status heavily rely on donations to expand and sustain their services because government subsidy alone is insufficient to support their work ('Donation' n.d.). Donations can be raised by a nursing home's charitable foundation (Tunney 2020) or come from the general public. For example, a study estimated that 9 percent of total LTC spending in Singapore in 2015 came from charitable donations (Graham and Bilger 2017: 376). Nowadays, many nursing homes receive public donations via online platforms. Donations can be made through VISA, Mastercard, or other electronic fund transfer services.

A global review of the finance of LTC finds that two thirds of the financing is done through taxes and OOP payments, while the rest of the financing is organized in universal social insurance schemes such as those implemented in Germany or Japan (Eling 2020: 39).

Challenges of providing and financing LTC in China

'China has the largest and most rapidly ageing population in the world' (United Nations Economic and Social Commission for Asia and the Pacific 2015: 4). This 'will significantly increase demands for LTC and will generate significant public expenditure due to increasing disability trends' (Xu and Chen 2019: 3530). Traditionally, adult children take care of their elder parents as a fulfilment of filial piety (*xiao*) (Zhan and Montgomery 2003: 226). Filial piety is a Confucian concept 'including concern for parental health, financially supporting parents, fulfilling the housing needs of parents, and respect for parental authority' (Lai 2010: 202). However, 'demographic shifts and socioeconomic changes are eroding this tradition' (Yang *et al.* 2016: 1393). The so-called 4–2–1 family structure (i.e. four grandparents, two parents, and one child) as a result of the one-child policy and the marriage of two only children (Jiang and Sa´nchez-Barricarte 2011: 126) leaves 'a great burden on each young person to provide old age support' (Ebenstein 2014: 304) due to having no siblings to share the responsibilities (Zhan and Montgomery 2003: 212). Besides, intense rural–urban migration for more job opportunities and higher incomes (Lu and Xia 2016) 'has further aggravated the instability and deficiency of LTC provision by families' (United Nations Economic and Social Commission for Asia and the Pacific 2015: 4). Hence, 'families may not continue to be the mainstay of elder care' (Feng *et al.* 2012: 2765), which leads to 'increased demand for LTC support from society and government at all levels' (United Nations Economic and Social Commission for Asia and the Pacific 2015: 4).

'In 2011, for the first time, the government incorporated the construction of a social aged care service system into its specialized planning' (Du *et al.* 2021: 137). However, the supply of LTC services in rural areas still lags behind that in urban areas due to the geographical environment, poorer economic conditions, and the social culture (Du *et al.* 2021: 143). Meanwhile, shortage of elder care workers and their lack of professional and comprehensive LTC training affect quality of care for older adults (United Nations Economic and Social Commission for Asia and the Pacific 2015: 14–5). The pilot LTCI reform, launched in

15 cities in the country in 2016, has enriched LTC service provision (Du *et al.* 2021) and provided financial support for disabled older adults in need of LTC. However, there is concern over the financial stability and sustainability of LTCI in the long run since the funding of the LTCI system has yet to be independent from the medical insurance system.

Analytical perspective, methodology, and structure of the book

This study adopts a demand–supply perspective to examine the delivery and financing of LTC in China. It uses secondary data including books, book chapters, journal articles, international reports, statistical yearbooks, newspaper reports, and websites. Some of the Chinese literature, newspaper reports, and government publications used in this study have never appeared in previous Western studies. The demand for LTC is affected by demographic transformations, health status of older adults, and personal wealth. Chapter 2 examines how a large and growing ageing population at an accelerated pace in China, multiple chronic conditions among older adults, the prevalence of old-age disability and dementia in the country, and the phenomenon of 'getting old before getting rich' affect the demand for LTC. The supply of LTC for older adults is determined by the capacity of family members to provide care, support for informal carers, and the availability of LTC institutions and formal caregivers. Chapter 3 examines how changes in the living arrangement of older adults, the national policy on developing LTC delivery and financing systems, and support for informal carers of older adults with disability or dementia affect the supply of LTC for older adults in China. Chapter 4 examines the pilot LTCI schemes in 15 cities in China in detail. It evaluates the sustainability of various financing models adopted by the 15 cities in the LTCI schemes. The LTC model in three pilot cities – Qingdao, Nantong, and Shanghai – representing three different models of financing and delivering LTC are analysed in Chapters 5, 6, and 7 respectively in greater depth in terms of the system's performance in utilization of medical resources, cost, equity, quality of care, and sustainability. The final chapter recapitulates the development of LTC financing and delivery in China. Recommendations for the Chinese government to improve the financing and delivery of LTC and implications of China's LTCI reform for other countries are made towards the end.

References

Agency for Healthcare Research and Quality (2011) *Long-Term Care for Older Adults: A Comparative Effectiveness Review of Institutional versus Home and Community-Based Care.* Online. Available HTTP: https://effectivehealthcare.ahrq.gov/sites/default/files/pdf/long-term-care-adults_research-protocol.pdf (accessed 7 July 2021).

Alzheimer's Disease International (2015) *World Alzheimer Report 2015: The Global Impact of Dementia.* Online. Available HTTP: www.alz.co.uk/research/WorldAlzheimer Report2015.pdf (accessed 1 December 2020).

American Academy of Actuaries (2017) *End-of-Life Care in an Aging World: A Global Perspective*. Washington, DC. Online. Available HTTP: www.actuary.org/end-of-life-care (accessed 1 December 2020).

Bone, A. (2018) *How Will Population Ageing Affect Future End of Life Care?* Online. Available HTTP: https://blog.oup.com/2018/04/population-ageing-future-care/ (accessed 4 July 2021).

Bone, A. E., Gomes, B., Etkind, S. N., Verne, J., Murtagh, F. E. M., Evans, C. J. and Higginson, I. J. (2018) 'What Is the Impact of Population Ageing on the Future Provision of End-of-Life Care? Population-Based Projections of Place of Death', *Palliative Medicine*, 32 (2): 329–36.

Brazil, K., McAiney, C., Caron-O'Brien, M., Kelley, M. L., O'Krafka, P. and Sturdy-Smith, C. (2004) 'Quality End-of-Life Care in Long-Term Care Facilities: Service Providers' Perspective', *Journal of Palliative Care*, 20 (2): 85–92.

Brown, J. R. and Finkelstein, A. (2007) 'Why Is the Market for Long-Term Care Insurance So Small?', *Journal of Public Economics*, 91(10): 1967–91.

Burns, E. (2010) *Palliative and End of Life Care for Older People*. Online. Available HTTP: www.bgs.org.uk/resources/palliative-care (accessed 4 July 2021).

Coleman, B. and Pandya, S. M. (2002) *Family Caregiving and Long-Term Care*. Online. Available HTTP: https://assets.aarp.org/rgcenter/il/fs91_ltc.pdf (accessed 6 July 2021).

Colombo, F., Llena-Nozal, A., Mercier, J. and Tjadens, F. (2011) *Help Wanted?: Providing and Paying for Long-Term Care*. Paris: OECD Publishing. Online. Available HTTP: https://ec.europa.eu/health/sites/health/files/state/docs/oecd_help-wanted_en.pdf (accessed 7 July 2021).

Costa-Font, J., Courbage, C. and Zweifel, P. (2017) 'Policy Dilemmas in Financing Long-Term Care in Europe', *Global Policy*, 8 (Supplement 2): 38–45.

Cuellar, A. E. and Wiener, J. M. (2000) 'Can Social Insurance for Long-Term Care Work? The Experience of Germany', *Health Affairs*, 19 (3): 8–25.

Cylus, J., Roubal, T., Ong, P. and Barber, S. (2019) *Sustainable Health Financing with an Ageing Population: Implications of Different Revenue Raising Mechanisms and Policy Options*. World Health Organization, Regional Office for Europe. Online. Available HTTP: https://apps.who.int/iris/handle/10665/331977 (accessed 5 July 2021).

Del Pozo-Rubio, R., Pardo-García, I. and Escribano-Sotos, F. (2020) 'Financial Catastrophism Inherent with Out-of-Pocket Payments in Long Term Care for Households: A Latent Impoverishment', *International Journal of Environmental Research and Public Health*, 17: 295.

Dementia UK (n.d.) *What Is Dementia?* Online. Available HTTP: www.dementiauk.org/get-support/diagnosis-and-next-steps/what-is-dementia/ (accessed 5 July 2021).

Donation (n.d.) Online. Available HTTP: www.sanh.org.sg/donation/ (accessed 6 July 2021).

Du, P., Dong, T. and Ji, J. (2021) 'Current Status of the Long-Term Care Security System for Older Adults in China', *Research on Aging*, 43 (3–4): 136–46.

Ebenstein, A. (2014) 'Fertility and Population in Developing Countries', in A. J. Culyer (ed.) *Encyclopedia of Health Economics*, Burlington: Elsevier Science, pp. 300–8.

Edemekong, P. F., Bomgaars, D. L., Sukumaran, S. and Levy, S. B. (2020) *Activities of Daily Living*. Online. Available HTTP: www.ncbi.nlm.nih.gov/books/NBK470404/ (accessed 7 July 2021).

El-Hayek, Y. H., Wiley, R. E., Khoury, C. P., Daya, R. P., Ballard, C., Evans, A. R., Karran, M., Molinuevo, J. L., Norton, M. and Atri, A. (2019) 'Tip of the Iceberg: Assessing the Global Socioeconomic Costs of Alzheimer's Disease and Related Dementias and Strategic Implications for Stakeholders', *Journal of Alzheimer's Disease*, 70 (2): 323–41.

Eling, M. (2020) 'Financing Long-Term Care: Some Ideas from Switzerland Comment on "Financing Long-Term Care: Lessons from Japan"', *International Journal of Health Policy and Management*, 9 (1): 39–41.

Enache, C. (2021) *Sources of Government Revenue in the OECD*. Online. Available HTTP: https://files.taxfoundation.org/20210210172143/Sources-of-Government-Revenue-in-the-OECD-2021.pdf (accessed 5 July 2021).

Feng, Z., Liu, C., Guan, X. and Mor, V. (2012) 'China's Rapidly Aging Population Creates Policy Challenges in Shaping a Viable Long-Term Care System', *Health Affairs*, 31 (12): 2764–73.

Ghibelli, P., Barbieri, D., Fernandez, J. and Knapp, M. (2017) *The Role of Public and Private Actors in Delivering and Resourcing Long-Term Care Services*. Online. Available HTTP: https://ec.europa.eu/research/participants/documents/downloadPublic?documentIds=080166e5b03cff53&appId=PPGMS (accessed 6 July 2021).

Graham, W. C. K. and Bilger, M. (2017) 'Financing Long-Term Services and Supports: Ideas from Singapore', *The Milbank Quarterly*, 95 (2): 358–407.

Guo, H. J. and Sapra, A. (2020) *Instrumental Activity of Daily Living*. Online. Available HTTP: www.ncbi.nlm.nih.gov/books/NBK553126/ (accessed 7 July 2021).

Jiang, Q. and Sa´nchez-Barricarte, J. J. (2011) 'The 4-2-1 Family Structure in China: A Survival Analysis Based on Life Tables', *European Journal of Ageing*, 8 (2): 119–27.

Johnson, R. W. (2016) *Who Is Covered by Private Long-Term Care Insurance?* Online. Available HTTP: www.urban.org/sites/default/files/publication/83146/2000881-Who-Is-Covered-by-Private-Long-Term-Care-Insurance.pdf (accessed 5 July 2021).

Johnson, R. W. and Uccello, C. E. (2005) *Is Private Long-Term Care Insurance the Answer?* Online. Available HTTP: www.urban.org/sites/default/files/publication/42851/1000795-Is-Private-Long-Term-Care-Insurance-the-Answer-.PDF (accessed 5 July 2021).

Khan, N., Khan, S., Leng, O. T. S., Chen, T. B. and Vergara, R. G. (2017) 'Explore the Factors That Influence Elderly Poverty', *Journal of Southeast Asian Research*, Article ID 938459, DOI: 10.5171/2017. 938459. Online. Available HTTP: https://ibimapublishing.com/articles/JSAR/2017/938459/938459-1.pdf (accessed 5 July 2021).

Kwan, C. and Walsh, C. A. (2018) 'Old Age Poverty: A Scoping Review of the Literature', *Cogent Social Sciences*, 4 (1): 1478479. Online. Available HTTP: https://doi.org/10.1080/23311886.2018.1478479 (accessed 26 March 2021).

Lai, D. W. L. (2010) 'Filial Piety, Caregiving Appraisal, and Caregiving Burden', *Research on Aging*, 32 (2): 200–23.

Legislative Council of the Hong Kong Special Administrative Region (2007) *Report on Elderly in Poverty*. Online. Available HTTP: www.legco.gov.hk/yr06-07/english/hc/papers/hc0608cb2-2048-e.pdf (accessed 6 October 2020).

Li, Y. and Jensen, G. A. (2011) 'The Impact of Private Long-Term Care Insurance on the Use of Long-Term Care', *Inquiry*, 48: 34–50.

Lu, J. and Liu, Q. (2019) 'Four Decades of Studies on Population Aging in China', *China Population and Development Studies*, 3: 24–36. Online. Available HTTP: https://link.springer.com/content/pdf/10.1007/s42379-019-00027-4.pdf (accessed 3 October 2020).

Lu, M. and Xia, Y. (2016) *Migration in the People's Republic of China*. Online. Available HTTP: www.adb.org/sites/default/files/publication/191876/adbi-wp593.pdf (accessed 8 July 2021).

Messinger-Rapport, B. J., McCallum, T. J. and Hujer, M. E. (2006) *Impact of Dementia Caregiving on the Caregiver in the Continuum of Care*. Online. Available HTTP: www.hmpgloballearningnetwork.com/site/altc/article/dementia-caregiving (accessed 4 July 2021).

Mistry, B., Bainbridge, D., Bryant, D., Toyofuku, S. T. and Seow, H. (2015) 'What Matters Most for End-of-Life Care? Perspectives from Community-Based Palliative Care Providers and Administrators', *BMJ Open*, 5: e007492.

Mommaerts, C. (2015) *Funding Long-Term Care: Cash Benefits for Informal Care*. Online. Available HTTP: https://isps.yale.edu/news/blog/2015/01/funding-long-term-care-cash-benefits-for-informal-care (accessed 4 July 2021).

OECD (2005) *Long-Term Care for Older People*. Online. Available HTTP: https://read.oecd-ilibrary.org/social-issues-migration-health/long-term-care-for-older-people_9789264015852-en#page1 (accessed 6 July 2021).

OECD (2017) *Health at a Glance 2017: OECD Indicators*. Online. Available HTTP: www.health.gov.il/publicationsfiles/healthataglance2017.pdf (accessed 4 July 2021).

OECD (2019a) *Health at a Glance 2019: OECD Indicators*. Paris: OECD Publishing. Online. Available HTTP: https://doi.org/10.1787/4dd50c09-en (accessed 3 October 2020).

OECD (2019b) *Pensions at a Glance 2019: OECD and G20 Indicators*. Paris: OECD Publishing. Online. Available HTTP: www.oecd-ilibrary.org/docserver/b6d3dcfc-en.pdf?expires=1605355136&id=id&accname=guest&checksum=0DCEDB35FF52D8B4018982F4BA1D715E (accessed 6 December 2020).

OECD (2020a) *Who Cares? Attracting and Retaining Care Workers for the Elderly*. OECD Health Policy Studies. Paris: OECD Publishing. Online. Available HTTP: https://doi.org/10.1787/92c0ef68-en (accessed 30 June 2021).

OECD (2020b) *Spending on Long-Term Care*. Online. Available HTTP: www.oecd.org/health/health-systems/Spending-on-long-term-care-Brief-November-2020.pdf (accessed 7 July 2021).

OECD (2020c) *Affordability of Long-Term Care Services among Older People in the OECD and the EU: Social Protection for Long-Term Care in Old Age*. Online. Available HTTP: www.oecd.org/health/health-systems/Affordability-of-long-term-care-services-among-older-people-in-the-OECD-and-the-EU.pdf (accessed 5 July 2021).

Ortiz-Ospina, E. and Roser, M. (n.d.) *Taxation*. Online. Available HTTP: https://ourworldindata.org/taxation (accessed 5 July 2021).

O'Shaughnessy, C., Stone, J., Gabe, T. and Shrestha, L. B. (2007) *Long-Term Care: Consumers, Providers, Payers, and Programs*. Online. Available HTTP: www.everycrsreport.com/files/20070315_RL33919_e1951d0bd61be6b997521ff91443b90f845398f0.pdf (accessed 7 July 2021).

Population Reference Bureau (2020) *What Can We Learn from the World's Largest Population of Older People?* Online. Available HTTP: Available at www.prb.org/

wp-content/uploads/2020/07/TRA39-2020-health-aging-China.pdf (accessed 3 October 2020).

The Progression and Stages of Dementia (n.d.) Online. Available HTTP: www. alzheimers.org.uk/about-dementia/symptoms-and-diagnosis/how-dementia-progresses/progression-stages-dementia (accessed 4 July 2021).

Qiu, C. and Fratiglioni, L. (2018) 'Aging without Dementia Is Achievable: Current Evidence from Epidemiological Research', *Journal of Alzheimer's Disease*, 62: 933–42.

Razmaria, A. A. (2016) 'End-of-Life Care', *JAMA*, 316 (1): 115.

Rizzi, L., Rosset, I. and Roriz-Cruz, M. (2014) 'Global Epidemiology of Dementia: Alzheimer's and Vascular Types', *BioMed Research International*, 2014: 908915.

Roberts, K. (2017) *International Aged Care: A Quick Guide*. Online. Available HTTP: https://parlinfo.aph.gov.au/parlInfo/download/library/prspub/5363034/upload_binary/5363034.pdf (accessed 7 July 2021).

Schut, F. T. and Van Den Berg, B. (2012) 'Long-Term Care Insurance in the Netherlands', in J. Costa-Font and C. Courbage (eds.) *Financing Long-Term Care in Europe: Institutions, Markets and Models*, London, UK: Palgrave Macmillan, pp. 103–24.

Seidel, D. and Thyrian, J. R. (2019) 'Burden of Caring for People with Dementia: Comparing Family Caregivers and Professional Caregivers: A Descriptive Study', *Journal of Multidisciplinary Healthcare*, 12: 655–63.

Stages of Alzheimer's & Dementia: Durations & Scales Used to Measure Progression (GDS, FAST & CDR) (2020) Online. Available HTTP: www.dementiacarecentral. com (accessed 4 July 2021).

Stone, R. and Harahan, M. F. (2010) 'Improving the Long-Term Care Workforce Serving Older Adults', *Health Affairs*, 29 (1): 109–15.

Sustainable Development Goals (n.d.) Online. Available HTTP: https://unric.org/en/united-nations-sustainable-development-goals/ (accessed 4 July 2021).

Tunney, J. (2020) *Not-for-Profit Long-Term Care Homes Face Uncertain Future after 2020*. Online. Available HTTP: www.cbc.ca/news/canada/ottawa/long-term-care-homes-not-for-profit-1.5855329 (accessed 6 July 2021).

Types of dementia (n.d.) Online. Available HTTP: https://qbi.uq.edu.au/brain/dementia/types-dementia (accessed 4 March 2020).

United Nations (2017) *World Population Ageing 2017 Highlights*. Online. Available HTTP: www.un.org/en/development/desa/population/publications/pdf/ageing/WPA2017_Highlights.pdf (accessed 1 December 2020).

United Nations (2019a) *Patterns and Trends in Household Size and Composition: Evidence from a United Nations Dataset*. Online. Available HTTP: www.un.org/en/development/desa/population/publications/pdf/ageing/household_size_and_composition_technical_report.pdf (accessed 4 December 2020).

United Nations (2019b) *World Population Ageing 2019 Highlights*. Online. Available HTTP: www.un.org/en/development/desa/population/publications/pdf/ageing/WorldPopulationAgeing2019-Highlights.pdf (accessed 6 December 2020).

United Nations (2019c) *World Population Prospects 2019 Highlights*. Online. Available HTTP: https://population.un.org/wpp/Publications/Files/WPP2019_Highlights.pdf (accessed 6 December 2020).

United Nations (n.d.) *Income Poverty in Old Age: An Emerging Development Priority*. Online. Available HTTP: www.un.org/esa/socdev/ageing/documents/Poverty-IssuePaperAgeing.pdf (accessed 8 December 2020).

United Nations Development Programme (2017) *Ageing, Older Persons and the 2030 Agenda for Sustainable Development*. Online. Available HTTP: www.un.org/development/desa/ageing/wp-content/uploads/sites/24/2017/07/UNDP_AARP_HelpAge_International_AgeingOlderpersons-and-2030-Agenda-2.pdf (accessed 4 July 2021).

United Nations Economic and Social Commission for Asia and the Pacific (2015) *Long-Term Care for Older Persons in China*. Online. Available HTTP: www.unescap.org/sites/default/files/Long%20Term%20Care%20for%20older%20persons%20in%20China.pdf (accessed 7 July 2021).

Wang, Q., Jensen, H. H. and Johnson, S. R. (1993) *China's Nutrient Availability and Sources, 1950–91*. CARD Working Papers, 125. Online. Available HTTP: https://lib.dr.iastate.edu/cgi/viewcontent.cgi?article=1141&context=card_workingpapers (accessed 11 October 2020).

World Bank (n.d.) *China Overview*. Online. Available HTTP: www.worldbank.org/en/country/china/overview (accessed 7 July 2021).

World Health Organization (2003) *Key Policy Issues in Long-Term Care*. Online. Available HTTP: www.who.int/chp/knowledge/publications/policy_issues_ltc.pdf (accessed 7 July 2021).

World Health Organization (2020) *Dementia*. Online. Available HTTP: www.who.int/news-room/fact-sheets/detail/dementia (accessed 3 July 2021).

Worldwide Hospice Palliative Care Alliance (2015) *Palliative Care and the Global Goal for Health Report*. Online. Available HTTP: www.thewhpca.org/resources/item/palliative-care-and-the-global-goal-for-health-report-2 (accessed 7 December 2020).

Worldwide Palliative Care Alliance (2014) *Global Atlas of Palliative Care at the End of Life*. Online. Available HTTP: www.who.int/nmh/Global_Atlas_of_Palliative_Care.pdf (accessed 7 December 2020).

Wunderlich, G. S. and Kohler, P. O. (eds.) (2001) *Improving the Quality of Long-Term Care*. Washington: National Academy of Sciences. Online. Available HTTP: www.ncbi.nlm.nih.gov/books/NBK224500/pdf/Bookshelf_NBK224500.pdf (accessed 7 July 2021).

Xu, X. and Chen, L. (2019) 'Projection of Long-Term Care Costs in China, 2020–2050: Based on the Bayesian Quantile Regression Method', *Sustainability*, 11: 3530.

Yao, S. (2000) 'Economic Development and Poverty Reduction in China over 20 Years of Reforms', *Economic Development and Cultural Change*, 48 (3): 447–74.

Yamada, M. and Arai, H. (2020) 'Long-Term Care System in Japan', *Annals of Geriatric Medicine and Research*, 24 (3): 174–80.

Yang, W., He, A. J., Fang, L. and Mossialos, E. (2016) 'Financing Institutional Long-Term Care for the Elderly in China: A Policy Evaluation of New Models', *Health Policy and Planning*, 31: 1391–1401.

Yuen, P. (2018) 'The Economics of Long-Term Care', in B. Fong, A. Ng and P. Yuen (eds.) *Sustainable Health and Long-Term Care Solutions for an Aging Population*, Hershey, PA, USA: IGI Global, pp. 1–18.

Zhan, H. J. and Montgomery, R. J. V. (2003) 'Gender and Elder Care in China: The Influence of Filial Piety and Structural Constraints', *Gender & Society*, 17 (2): 209–29.

2 Population ageing in China

Introduction

Over the past 70 years, China has undergone enormous demographic transformation. At present, China is the most populous country in the world. It had 1.41 billion people in 2020 (Albert 2021). China's population ages at an unprecedented speed and scale. Geographically speaking, the eastern coastal regions, Chongqing and Sichuan in the western region, and Anhui in the central region have higher ageing levels. Rural areas have higher ageing levels and more empty-nest elders than urban areas. People are getting old before getting rich. They may not have enough money and resources to support their living in old age. People are living longer, but many of them suffer from poorer health and dementia. Deterioration in physical and cognitive functions results in an increased level of dependency and reduced quality of life (QoL) in older adults.

Characteristics of ageing in China's population

There are six key characteristics of ageing in China's population: (1) ageing at an unprecedented speed; (2) ageing at an unprecedented scale; (3) geographical differences in the proportion of elderly population; (4) urban–rural differences in the proportion of elderly population; (5) the growth of empty-nest elders; and (6) the phenomenon of 'getting old before getting rich'.

Ageing at an unprecedented speed

First, 'China is one of the world's most aged countries and the speed of population ageing is among the fastest in the world' (Chi 2018a). In 1999, China met the United Nation's definition of an 'ageing society', with persons aged 65 and above making up more than 7 percent of its total population. It took China only 40 years to become an ageing society, while it took the United Kingdom (UK), the United States (US), and the Nordic countries more than 100 years to do so (Cai *et al.* 2012: 12). Since 2000, the speed of population ageing in China has surpassed that of the world (Chen and Chan 2011: 63). While it took the world 60 years (1950–2010) to experience a 3 percent increase in the ratio of those

DOI: 10.4324/9780429057199-2

aged 60 and above, it took only 10 years (2000–2010) for China to experience a 3.8 percent increase in the ratio of those aged 60 and above (Zhang W. 2012). According to the China National Committee on Aging (CNCA), China experienced a net increase of 110 million citizens aged over 60 during the period 1999–2017 (Xinhuanet 2018). Of this number, 2017 had seen the first annual increase of more than 10 million (Xinhuanet 2018). By 2026, China will become an 'aged society', with persons aged 65 and above making up more than 14 percent of its total population (China Daily 2019a). By 2047, China will become a 'super-aged society', with persons aged 65 and above making up more than 21 percent of its population (Wang 2017).

Ageing at an unprecedented scale

Second, China has the world's largest ageing population (China Daily 2019a). Using data from *China's Aging Statistics Compendium, 1953–2009* and *Tabulation on the 2010 Population Census of the People's Republic of China (Book I)*, the author calculated the number of elderly people aged 60 years and above and the proportion of elderly population aged 60 years and above to the total population in China. The result indicated that the number of elderly population and the proportion of elderly population to the total population have increased over the past 60 years. In 1953, the number of elderly people aged 60 years and above was about 41.5 million, which accounted for 7.3 percent of the total population. In 1982, the number of elderly people aged 60 years and above rose to about 76.6 million, which accounted for 7.6 percent of the total population. From 2000 to 2010, the number of elderly people aged 60 years and above rose from about 129.9 million to 177.5 million, which accounted for 10.5 percent and 13.3 percent respectively of the total population. At the end of 2011, China's population aged 60 years and above reached 185 million, which exceeded the sum of population aged 60 and above in Europe (Wang 2012). By 2018, China had 249 million people aged 60 and above, accounting for 17.9 percent of its total population (China Daily 2019a). By 2050, China's population aged 60 or above will touch 487 million, accounting for about 35 percent of its population (Chi 2018b).

In 2013, China had the world's largest number of oldest-old group aged 80 years or above, which were 23 million persons (United Nations 2013: 32). By the end of 2017, the total number of oldest-old people was 26 million, accounting for 1.8 percent of the country's total population (China Daily 2019a). The proportion of oldest-old people is projected to increase from 2 percent in 2025 to 8 percent in 2050, according to a report issued by Peking Union Medical College and Chinese Aging Well Association (CAWA) (China Daily 2019a).

The increase in the proportion of elderly population to the total population was related to rapid fertility decline and increased life expectancy. Rapid fertility decline was reflected in a decrease in the total fertility rate (TFR) over time. TFR refers to the average number of children born to a woman over her lifetime. In 1949, the TFR was an average of 6.14 births per woman (White 2006: 44). During the period of Great Leap Forward (1958–1961), the TFR precipitously dropped from an average of 5.68 births per woman in 1958 to an average of 3.29 births per woman in 1961 due to the devastating famine and economic dislocation (White 2006: 43–4). The TFR rebounded to an average of 7.5 births per woman in 1963 (White 2006: 51) but dropped quickly during the Cultural Revolution decade (1966–1976) due to the integration of an increasingly aggressive birth control programme into the economic planning process (White 2006: 57–60). The TFR dropped from an average of 6.26 births per woman in 1966 to 3.24 births per woman in 1976 (White 2006: 44).

The TFR has continued to drop further since the one-child policy was officially enforced in 1980 to curb fast population growth that was 'said to pose a serious threat to economic development and environmental sustainability' (Yan 2006: 3). It dropped from an average of 2.63 births per woman in 1981 to 2.01 births per woman in 1991 (White 2006: 44), which was below the replacement level of 2.1 births per woman. The demographic effects of below replacement fertility on a country accelerated the population ageing process and population decline because couples, on average, did not produce enough children to replace themselves. Since the early 1990s, the TFR has been below the replacement level. The two-child policy introduced in 2016 as an active response to address the challenge of an ageing population and balance population development has failed to spark a major baby boom in the nation (Phillips 2015; Gietel-Basten 2017). In 2017, China's fertility rate was 1.63 births per woman (The World Bank Group 2019). In 2018, new births in China were 15.23 million, which undercut 'the reading of 17.86 million in 2016 and 17.23 million in 2017, according to data from the National Bureau of Statistics' (Leng 2019). The nationwide birth figures for 2018 fell far short of the family planning authority's previous expectations of up to 20 million births under the two-child policy (Xin and Leng 2019). The underlying causes of low fertility include weak state support, high living costs (especially housing), family unfriendly working-time culture (Gietel-Basten 2017), and the lack of childcare (BBC News 2018).

Steady increase in life expectancy of both sexes is another reason for China to have a higher proportion of elderly population. In 1949, the average life expectancy in China was only 35 years (Xinhua News 2004). From 1960 to 1970, the average life expectancy rose from 43.5 years to 63 years (Tulchinsky and Varavikova 2014: 708; Zhang and Zhang 2012). From 1981 to 1990, the average life expectancy slightly increased from 67.8 years to 68.6 years (National Bureau of Statistics of China 2018). From 2000 to 2010, the average life expectancy increased from 71.4 years to 74.8 years (National Bureau of Statistics of China 2013: 101). In 2012, the average life expectancy reached 75 years (World Health Organization 2014: 60). In recent years, the average life expectancy has continued to increase. From 2015 to 2018, the average life expectancy increased from 76.3 years to 77 years (China Daily 2019b; National Health Commission of the People's Republic of China 2019). Meanwhile, females have longer life expectancy than males (Table 2.1). In 2015, the average life expectancy was 79.4 years for females and 73.6 years for males (National Bureau of Statistics of China

Table 2.1 Life expectancy at birth in China

Year	Total	Males	Females
1981	67.77	66.28	69.27
1990	68.55	66.84	70.47
1996	70.80	–	–
2000	71.40	69.63	73.33
2005	72.95	70.83	75.25
2010	74.83	72.38	77.37
2015	76.34	73.64	79.43

Source: China Statistical Yearbook 2018.

2018). The average life expectancy 'is expected to be at around 80 years by 2050' (World Health Organization 2015: 1). With rapid fertility decline and increased life expectancy, 'future cohorts of elderly can expect to have smaller numbers of living children – and fewer sources of familial support' (Chinese Academy of Social Sciences *et al.* 2011: 7).

Geographical differences in the proportion of elderly population

Third, there were differences in the proportion of elderly population among provinces, municipalities, and autonomous regions due to geographical differences in socio-economic development. Since the 1950s, the eastern coastal regions of China have had a higher level of ageing than the western regions of China. Besides, the eastern coastal regions of China have aged faster than the western regions of China. The study of Liu (1997), which ranked Chinese provinces from top to bottom by the proportion of elderly population aged 65 years and above in the first four population censuses of China (1953–1990), showed that most of the provinces in eastern China had a higher proportion of elderly population than the provinces in western China. In 1953, Shandong and Hebei provinces in eastern China, which had 6.31 percent and 6.24 percent respectively of elderly population aged 65 years and above, ranked first and second, while Gansu and Qinghai in western China, which had 3.09 percent and 2.82 percent respectively of elderly population aged 65 years and above, ranked twenty-fifth and twenty-sixth (Liu 1997: 34). In 1982, Shanghai (7.42%), Zhejiang (5.76%), Hebei (5.67%), Beijing (5.65%), and Shangdong (5.62%) in eastern China were the top five municipalities/provinces having high proportions of elderly population aged 65 and above (Liu 1997: 34). In 1990, municipalities and provinces in eastern China were still the top five places having high proportions of elderly population aged 65 and above. They were Shanghai (9.38%), Zhejiang (6.83%), Jiangsu (6.79%), Tianjin (6.46%), and Beijing (6.35%) (Liu 1997: 34). Liu (1997) argued that municipalities or provinces having high levels of ageing were due to having very low TFR.

Using the data obtained from *the 2000 Population Census of China*, the author calculated the proportion of elderly population aged 65 years and above by provinces and ranked the provinces from top to bottom. The result indicated that the top five places having a high proportion of elderly population were similar to the results in 1990. Shanghai (11.46%), Zhejiang (8.92%), Jiangsu (8.84%) were still the top three places having high proportions of elderly population, while Beijing (8.42%) and Tianjin (8.41%) ranked fourth and fifth respectively this time (Table 2.2).

Table 2.2 The proportion of population aged 65 and above to the total population of China in 2000

Province/ Municipality/ Autonomous region	Total population*	Population aged 65+**	Proportion of population aged 65+ to the total population**	Ranking
Beijing	13,569,194	1,142,864	8.42%	**4**
Tianjin	9,848,731	828,413	8.41%	**5**
Hebei	66,684,419	4,699,148	7.05%	14
Shanxi	32,471,242	2,055,048	6.33%	18
Inner Mongolia	23,323,347	1,284,647	5.51%	26
Liaoning	41,824,412	3,297,206	7.88%	8
Jilin	26,802,191	1,619,759	6.04%	23
Heilongjiang	36,237,576	2,015,344	5.56%	25
Shanghai	16,407,734	1,880,316	11.46%	1
Jiangsu	73,043,577	6,458,388	8.84%	3
Zhejiang	45,930,651	4,098,584	8.92%	2
Anhui	58,999,948	4,479,972	7.59%	9
Fujian	34,097,947	2,279,642	6.69%	16
Jiangxi	40,397,598	2,532,328	6.27%	19
Shandong	89,971,789	7,308,473	8.12%	6
Henan	91,236,854	6,482,364	7.10%	13
Hubei	59,508,870	3,818,701	6.42%	17
Hunan	63,274,173	4,726,550	7.47%	11
Guangdong	85,225,007	5,259,948	6.17%	20
Guangxi	43,854,538	3,202,960	7.30%	12
Hainan	7,559,035	509,531	6.74%	15
Chongqing	30,512,763	2,445,382	8.01%	7
Sichuan	82,348,296	6,229,433	7.56%	10
Guizhou	35,247,695	2,102,966	5.97%	24
Yunnan	42,360,089	2,580,293	6.09%	22
Tibet	2,616,329	124,282	4.75%	28
Shaanxi	35,365,072	2,175,962	6.15%	21
Gansu	25,124,282	1,307,498	5.20%	27
Qinghai	4,822,963	220,039	4.56%	30
Ningxia	5,486,393	245,501	4.47%	31
Xinjiang	18,459,511	862,480	4.67%	29

Note:

* The data are obtained from *Tabulation on the 2000 Population Census of the People's Republic of China (Book I)*, China Statistics Press, p. 134.
** This is the author's calculation using data from *Tabulation on the 2000 Population Census of the People's Republic of China (Book I)*, China Statistics Press, pp. 141–4.

However, the situation became quite different in 2010. Table 2.3 illustrates the author's calculation using data from *the 2010 Population Census of the People's Republic of China*. The result indicated that there was a huge difference in the top five places having high proportions of elderly population aged 65 and above. Some of the provinces in western and central China had higher proportions of elderly population. Chongqing (11.72%) and Sichuan (10.95%) in western China ranked first and second this time, which was followed by Jiangsu (10.88%), Liaoning (10.31%) in eastern China, and Anhui (10.23%) in central China. Chongqing and Sichuan were two of the largest labour-exporting provinces in China. These two provinces had a striking labour export with young, working-age labour force exploring employment opportunities in other provinces while leaving old-aged parents at home, which resulted in having a higher proportion of elderly population. Anhui province had a higher proportion of elderly population because of the generation of baby boomers born in the 1950s joining the ranks of China's older population (Anhui Ageing Commission Office 2008).

Besides, Table 2.3 indicated that, in 2010, 26 places (4 municipalities, 2 autonomous regions, and 20 provinces) in China had become an ageing society, with population aged 65 and above making up more than 7 percent of its total population. Only Guangdong, Xinjiang, Ningxia, Qinghai, and Tibet provinces were not ageing societies. Guangdong province had the largest number of floating population 'who live and work in areas other than their registered address' (World Health Organization 2013: 3). According to *the 2010 Population Census of the People's Republic of China*, the number of floating population in Guangdong was about 21.5 million (Population Census Office and Department of Population and Employment Statistics 2012a: 490). And 85.77 percent (about 18.4 million) of the floating population went to Guangdong province for work and doing businesses in the place (Population Census Office and Department of Population and Employment Statistics 2012a: 622). The floating population is young and belongs to working-age population, thereby decreasing the proportion of elderly population. According to *Report on China's Migrant Population Development 2015*, the proportion of work-age population aged between 15 and 59 accounted for 78 percent of the total number of floating population in China in 2014 (Southern Metropolis Daily 2015). Xinjiang, Ningxia, Qinghai, and Tibet were ranked in the bottom four in terms of the proportion of elderly population aged 65 years and above. Their proportions of elderly population aged 65 years and above were very low, which accounted for only 6.48 percent, 6.39 percent, 6.30 percent, and 5.09 percent respectively. They shared the common characteristics of being remote provinces located in the northwest and western parts of China with less developed economies. Besides, these four provinces implemented a second-child permit policy for peasants (Scharping 2003: 104) and granted 'privileges for even higher birth orders for some groups of their population' (Scharping 2003: 104). This can explain why the proportion of elderly population aged 65 years and above remained low in these places.

Table 2.3 The proportion of population aged 65 and above to the total population of China in 2010

Province/ Municipality/ Autonomous region	Total population*	Population aged 65+**	Proportion of population aged 65+ to the total population**	Ranking
Beijing	19,612,368	1,708,852	8.71%	13
Tianjin	12,938,693	1,102,388	8.52%	15
Hebei	71,854,210	5,919,738	8.24%	19
Shanxi	35,712,101	2,705,259	7.58%	25
Inner Mongolia	24,706,291	1,868,177	7.56%	26
Liaoning	43,746,323	4,509,441	10.31%	4
Jilin	27,452,815	2,301,838	8.38%	16
Heilongjiang	38,313,991	3,173,314	8.28%	18
Shanghai	23,019,196	2,331,313	10.13%	6
Jiangsu	78,660,941	8,558,646	10.88%	3
Zhejiang	54,426,891	5,081,675	9.34%	9
Anhui	59,500,468	6,084,548	10.23%	5
Fujian	36,894,217	2,912,130	7.89%	22
Jiangxi	44,567,797	3,388,301	7.60%	24
Shandong	95,792,719	9,429,686	9.84%	7
Henan	94,029,939	7,859,344	8.36%	17
Hubei	57,237,727	5,201,894	9.09%	11
Hunan	65,700,762	6,419,361	9.77%	8
Guangdong	104,320,459	7,086,150	6.79%	27
Guangxi	46,023,761	4,252,921	9.24%	10
Hainan	8,671,485	699,682	8.07%	21
Chongqing	28,846,170	3,381,468	11.72%	1
Sichuan	80,417,528	8,805,507	10.95%	2
Guizhou	34,748,556	3,026,181	8.71%	12
Yunnan	45,966,766	3,505,474	7.63%	23
Tibet	3,002,165	152,908	5.09%	31
Shaanxi	37,327,379	3,183,837	8.53%	14
Gansu	25,575,263	2,105,575	8.23%	20
Qinghai	5,626,723	354,684	6.30%	30
Ningxia	6,301,350	402,787	6.39%	29
Xinjiang	21,815,815	1,414,079	6.48%	28

Note:

* The data are obtained from *Tabulation on the 2010 Population Census of the People's Republic of China* (Book I), China Statistics Press, p. 115.

** This is the author's calculation using data from *Tabulation on the 2010 Population Census of the People's Republic of China* (Book I), China Statistics Press, pp. 120–2.

Urban–rural differences in the proportion of elderly population

Fourth, there were urban–rural differences in the proportion of elderly population in China. Ageing was faster in rural areas than in urban areas. From 1982 to 2010, rural areas had a higher proportion of population aged 60 years and above than urban areas. Table 2.4 illustrates the author's calculation using data from the 1982, 2000, and 2010 Population Census of China. It showed that in 1982, the proportion of elderly population aged 60 years and above was 7.77 percent in rural areas and 7.37 percent in urban areas. The rural–urban difference in the proportion of elderly population was only 0.4 percent. However, the urban–rural differences in the proportion of elderly population have widened over the past three decades. In 2010, the proportion of elderly population aged 60 years and above rose to 14.98 percent in rural areas while that of in urban areas rose to 11.47 percent. The rural–urban difference in the proportion of elderly population was 3.51 percent.

The reason why rural areas have higher proportions of elderly population than urban areas needs more explanation. Rural areas had higher fertility rate than urban areas because Chinese population with rural or agricultural household registration status could give birth to more than one child. In 2010, the TFR was 1.44 in rural areas but 0.88 in urban areas (China Economic Herald 2012). According to *the 2010 Population Census of China*, the number of births in rural areas was two times more than the number of births in urban areas. In 2010, the number of births in rural areas was 650,170, while the number of births in urban areas was only 315,041 (Population Census Office and Department of Population and Employment Statistics 2012b: 2027–33). However, 'a large-scale migration of younger workers from rural to urban areas' (Liu 2014: 305) for more and better job opportunities in non-agricultural fields resulted in accelerating population ageing in rural areas.

Growth of empty-nest elders

Fifth, the growth of empty-nest elders has become a very serious problem in China (Lu 2017). Empty-nest elders are older people left behind by their children to live alone (empty-nest singles) or live with a spouse (empty-nest couples) and who have no relatives living nearby to look after or accompany them (Zhou *et al.* 2015: 294; Luk and Preston 2016: 138). This is due to 'the massive out-migration of young people to cities for work' (Feng *et al.* 2012: 2765). In 2013, there were 100 million empty-nest elders, accounting for half of the total elderly population in the nation (Zhou *et al.* 2015). 'The empty nest phenomenon has been more severe in rural areas than in urban areas' (Gao *et al.* 2014: 1821). 'Moreover, there are more women as the sole members of the household than men' (Hu and Peng 2015: 9). It is because women in general live longer than men and are more likely to lose their spouse when they grow old (Hu and Peng 2015: 9). Empirical studies found that empty-nest elders are more vulnerable than non-empty-nest elders because of having poorer physical, psychological, and cognitive health (Gao *et al.* 2017). They have higher prevalence of chronic diseases (Liu and Guo 2008: 823), loneliness, depressive symptoms, mental disorders (Liu and Guo 2008; Wang *et al.* 2017; Zhang C. *et al.* 2019), and suffer more serious progression of white matter lesions (WMLs) and cognitive impairment (Duan

Table 2.4 The proportion of population aged 60 and above to the total population in urban and rural areas of China in 1982, 2000, and 2010

	1982		2000		2010	
	Urban	*Rural*	*Urban*	*Rural*	*Urban*	*Rural*
(a) No. of people aged 60+	10,702,060	61,977,195	29,420,070	85,568,096	46,313,673	99,303,297
(b) Proportion	7.37%	7.77%	10.05%	10.92%	11.47%	14.98%

Note: (a) and (b) are the author's calculation according to the data obtained from *1982 Population Census of China*, Beijing: The Statistical Publishing House, pp. 284–93, 304–13; *Tabulation on the 2000 Population Census of the People's Republic of China (Book I)*, Beijing: China Statistics Press, pp. 145–55, 167–77; and *Tabulation on the 2010 Population Census of the People's Republic of China (Book I)*, Beijing: China Statistics Press, pp. 123–30, 139–46.

et al. 2017). Besides, they have 'lower life satisfaction, lower income, poorer relationships with children, [and] less social support' (Liu and Guo 2008: 823). By 2030, the number of empty-nest elders is projected to reach over 200 million, and the proportion of empty nester elderly households will reach 90 percent in the nation (Wang 2018). How to better accommodate the needs of empty-nest elders will continue to be a daunting task for local governments.

The phenomenon of 'getting old before getting rich'

Sixth, China is getting old before getting rich (*wei fu xian lao*). This is a situation when population is ageing rapidly while the economy is still in development. Most industrialized countries got rich first before getting old (*xian fu hou lao*). 'In most industrialized countries, population ageing went hand-in-hand with economic growth in a gradual and natural manner' (Yan 2006: 6). But China had relatively low Gross Domestic Product (GDP) per capita compared to its Asian counterparts such as Singapore, Japan, and the Republic of Korea (ROK), which also encountered an ageing population (Zhang M. 2012). According to the data of the World Bank, the GDP per capita in China in 2014 was less than US$10,000, while the GDP per capita in Singapore, Japan, and the ROK were about US$56,000, US$36,000, and US$28,000 respectively (The World Bank 2015). These Asian countries 'can confront their ageing demography with the accumulated wealth of having become rich first' (Johnston 2012) while China fails to do so. Since the 1980s, old-age dependency ratio has increased. It increased from 8.0 percent in 1982 to 8.3 percent in 1990, 9.9 percent in 2000, 11.9 percent in 2010, and 15.86 percent in 2017 (National Bureau of Statistics of China 2016a, 2018). Rising old-age dependency ratio has put pressure on economic growth, healthcare system, and social security system.

Meanwhile, the number of working-age population aged between 16 and 59 years old has decreased since it peaked at 925 million in 2011 (Zhao 2016). The number of working-age population decreased from 922 million in 2012 to 910.96 million in 2015 and 897.29 million in 2018 (National Bureau of Statistics of China 2016b, 2019; Zhao 2016). The working-age population is expected to have a sharp decrease from 830 million in 2030 to 700 million by 2050, according to the Ministry of Human Resources and Social Security (Zhao 2016). The shrinking working-age population has three consequences. First, China faces the problem of labour shortage. It will increase the bargaining power of workers for higher wages and better benefits. This will drive up labour costs. Second, the shrinking working-age population is 'eroding the manufacturing and export competitiveness that helped fuel China's 30-year expansion' (South China Morning Post 2015). Demographic dividend, which refers to a period of accelerated economic growth resulting from a growing number of the working-age population and a relatively low ratio of young and elderly dependents, is declining in China. China's demographic dividend is quantity-oriented rather than quality-oriented (Zhang M. 2012). The declining demographic dividend was one of the main reasons for China having a 7.4 percent of GDP growth in 2014, which failed to meet the official target of 7.5 percent in 2014 and was the slowest since 1990 (Liu 2015). Third, the shrinking population may lead to working people having less household savings because 'they need to support larger cohorts of elderly family members' (OECD 2015: 28). 'In cities, the emerging "4–2–1" family structure (four grandparents; two parents, neither of whom has siblings; and one child) is emblematic of the potential problem' (Feng *et al.* 2012: 2765).

Health status of older adults in China

Although Chinese people have long life expectancy, they are expected to spend the last eight years of their lives in poor health (Wang 2019). Chronic illnesses pose the greatest threat to the health of older adults in China, according to *the Survey Report on the Living Conditions of China's Urban and Rural Older Adults* (hereafter *the Survey Report on Chinese Older Adults*), which examined the health status of about 220,000 older adults aged 60 and above in 31 provinces, autonomous regions, and municipalities in 2015 (Dang 2018). *The Survey Report on Chinese Older Adults* found that about 31 percent of older adults aged 60 and above suffered from one or more chronic disease conditions, about 14 percent suffered from three or more chronic disease conditions, and about 4 percent suffered from five or more chronic disease conditions (Dang 2018: 29). The top five chronic disease conditions of older adults surveyed were osteoarthritis (43.7%), high blood pressure (36.9%), cardiovascular disease (26.0%), stomach disease (17.8%), and cataracts/glaucoma (16%) (Dang 2018: 29). A two-week prevalence rate of the diseases among older adults was about 17.5 percent, while a two-week medical consultation rate was about 79 percent (Dang 2018: 29). Financial difficulty (about 47%), self-perception of having a mild medical condition (about 39%), and mobility limitations (about 24%) were main reasons for not seeking medical consultation among older adults (Dang 2018: 29).

A study that drew data from the 1998 and 2008 waves of the Chinese Longitudinal Healthy Longevity Surveys (CLHLS) showed that both annual mortality and disability of the Chinese oldest-old (those aged 80 years old and above) were significantly reduced in the later cohorts compared with the cohorts born ten years earlier (Zeng *et al.* 2017: 1621). However, the later cohorts had poorer physical function (e.g. standing up from a chair, picking up a book from the floor, and turning-around 360°) and cognitive function than the cohorts born ten years earlier (Zeng *et al.* 2017: 1625–6). The research findings showed that while progress in effective disease treatment, healthier lifestyles, and improved standards of living might compress disability (Zeng *et al.* 2017: 1626), 'lifespan extension might expand disability of physical and cognitive functioning as more frail, elderly individuals survive with health problems' (Zeng *et al.* 2017: 1619).

Old-age disability in China

China has faced a significant increase in the number of disabled elders. A national survey conducted by China Research Centre on Ageing (CRCA) reported that there were 33 million disabled elders experiencing difficulties in performing activities of daily living (ADLs) in the nation in 2010, representing 19 percent of the total ageing population (The Research Group of China Research Centre on Ageing 2011: 11). It reported that 10.8 million of them had completely lost their ability to perform at least one ADL, representing about 6.2 percent of the total ageing population (The Research Group of China Research Centre on Ageing 2011: 11). Besides, a higher proportion of disabled elders lived in rural areas (The Research Group of China Research Centre on Ageing 2011). In 2015, the number of fully or partially disabled elders had reached 40.63 million in the nation (China News Service 2016a). It is expected that the number of disabled elders will increase to 42 million by 2020, 61.68 million by 2030, and 97.50 million by 2050, according to CNCA (China News Service 2016b). The fast-growing number of disabled elders will increase long-term care (LTC) expenditures in the next few decades. Additionally, the prevalence of disability increases substantially with age. The proportion of disability among elders aged 60 was only 1.1 percent, elders aged 70 was 2.7 percent, elders aged 80 was 8.8 percent, and elders aged 90 was 24. 3 percent (Chen 2018: 153). This has raised concerns over the provision of proper care to oldest-old disabled elders in the nation.

According to *the Survey Report on Chinese Older Adults*, there were regional differences in old-age disability in the nation. Northeast China had the highest rate of old-age disability (6.3%), which was followed by western China (4.8%), central China (4%), and eastern China (3.5%) (Chen 2018: 154–5). It showed that 'different socio-economic factors cause the spatially uneven distribution of the number of disabled elderly people' (Liu and Sun 2015: 358). The northeast region, which is the traditional industrial base, has heavy metal pollution that causes permanent intellectual and developmental disabilities (Hu *et al.* 2014). Poor environmental conditions have caused the relatively high proportion of disabled elders (Liu and Sun 2015: 358). Additionally, the absence of physical exercise due to having long and cold winter is another cause for the relatively high proportion of disabled elders in the northern region (Liu and Sun 2015: 358). Eastern China has a higher level of economic development and a higher standard of living (Liu and Sun 2015: 359). It has abundant medical resources and gives elders better access to healthcare (Chen 2018). Hence, there is lower proportion of disabled elders in the eastern region.

Besides, there were urban–rural differences in old-age disability in the region. Rural areas had the higher rate of old-age disability. '[T]he gap in prevalence of disability between rural and urban areas increased from 1987 to 2006, particularly in the early-retirement years (60–75)' (Peng *et al.* 2010: e12129). In 2015, the proportion of disabled elders in rural areas was 4.3 percent, while it was 4.0 percent in urban areas (Chen 2018: 143). An empirical study found that rural people faced an increased risk of disability due to 'the harder life, poorer working standards, as well as limited availability of healthcare and rehabilitation services' (Peng *et al.* 2010: e12129). Besides, disabled elders in rural areas experienced greater economic difficulties than their urban counterparts. About 58.5 percent of disabled elders in rural areas experienced economic difficulties, which was

15.9 percent higher than their urban counterparts (Chen 2018: 148–9). This is because disabled elders enjoyed only very low pension benefits or had no pension benefits at all (Chen and Williamson 2010). If disabled elders in rural areas have little savings or do not receive any financial support from their children, they will face a serious economic predicament.

There is also gender difference in old-age disability. There is higher rate of disability in females. While the proportion of old-age disability in females was 4.8 percent, the proportion of old-age disability in males was only 3.5 percent (Chen 2018: 143). It is because women live longer than men, but they spend more years of their lives in poor health (World Health Organization 2015: 7). The equivalent loss of healthy years (i.e. life expectancy minus healthy life expectancy) was seven years for men and eight years for women (World Health Organization 2015: 7). For female disabled elders who become widowed, they will rely more heavily on their children or homes for the aged to take care of them (Chen 2018: 154). According to *the Survey Report on Chinese Older Adults*, rural areas had higher proportion of female disabled elders (5.1%) than urban areas (4.4%) (Chen 2018: 143).

Disabled elders face poorer physical and mental health conditions. Chronic conditions are the leading cause of disability worldwide (World Health Organization 2005). 'People with disability are more likely to develop chronic conditions, and people with chronic conditions are more likely to develop disability' (Australian Institute of Health and Welfare 2018: vi). According to *the Survey Report on Chinese Older Adults*, 97 percent of disabled elders reported that they suffered from chronic diseases (Chen 2018: 149). About 21 percent of them suffered from one chronic illness, 29.7 percent of them suffered from two chronic illnesses, and 46.2 percent of them suffered from three or more chronic illnesses (Chen 2018: 149–50). *The Survey Report on Chinese Older Adults* also found that disabled elders were especially vulnerable to loneliness. Almost 20 percent of disabled elders felt lonely all the time, which was almost 3.5 times higher than elders who could take care of themselves (Chen 2018: 151). Besides, about 25 percent of disabled elders thought that elders were a burden on their family, which was almost two times higher than elders who could take care of themselves (Chen 2018: 151). Almost 20 percent of disabled elders reported that they were 'rather unhappy' or 'very unhappy', which was almost 3.3 times higher than elders who could take care of themselves (Chen 2018: 151). The proportion of disabled elders experiencing loneliness, feeling as though they were a burden to their family, and feeling unhappy was higher in rural areas (Chen 2018: 151).

Prevalence of dementia in China

Dementia is a major cause of disability in China (Chen S. *et al*. 2013: 133). It is 'a clinical syndrome characterized by progressive cognitive decline that interferes with the ability to function independently' (Duong *et al*. 2017: 118). China has the largest number of people with dementia (PWD) in the world (Jia *et al*. 2020: 81). It has about 10 million PWD (Zhong *et al*. 2020), which accounts for 20 percent of the entire population with dementia worldwide. China has experienced a significant increase in the prevalence of dementia. From 1985 to 2018, the pooled prevalence rate of dementia in China was 4.9 percent (95% CI: 4.3–5.4), and the prevalence rate from 2015 to 2018 among them was 7.4 percent (95% CI: 5.3–9.5) (Wang Y. *et al.* 2019: 1096). The estimated number of older PWD aged 60 will increase dramatically in the next three decades (Wang Y. *et al.* 2019: 1096). It will increase from 24.25 million in 2030 to 35.98 million in 2050 (Wang Y. *et al.* 2019: 1098).

The increasing prevalence of dementia will lead to a substantial increase in the economic burden of dementia in China (Xu *et al.* 2017: 21). A study in 2009 found that the total amount of out-of-pocket (OOP) costs (direct plus indirect) associated with dementia care per person averaged US$487 per month (Mould-Quevedo *et al.* 2013: 668). Direct costs included money spent on doctor visits, medication, and hospital visits, while indirect costs were money spent on hiring housekeepers (Mould-Quevedo *et al.* 2013: 668). This amount of OOP cost exceeded 'the reported per capita disposable income of urban dwellers (US$210) as well as the per capita net income of rural dwellers (US$63) in China' (Mould-Quevedo *et al.* 2013: 668). An estimate of the total costs of dementia in China for 2030 represents about 10 percent of the forecasted US$1,110 billion global cost in 2030 (Xu *et al.* 2017: 21). How to prevent and manage dementia effectively will be a priority for public health (Frankish and Horton 2017).

In recent years, studies have shown that there are age, gender, urban–rural, and regional differences in the prevalence of dementia in China. The prevalence of dementia and its subgroups including Alzheimer's disease (AD) and Vascular Dementia (VAD) increased progressively with increasing age in both males and females (Zhu *et al.* 2019: 578). Besides, the prevalence of dementia differs by sex. A systematic review and meta-regression analysis of 51 surveys showed that from 1985 to 2015, '[t]he prevalence of AD was significantly higher in females (3.24, 95% CI: 3.08–3.41%) than in males (1.58, 95% CI: 1.46–1.70%)' (Zhu *et al.* 2019: 578). Similarly, a systematic analysis of 75 studies from 1990 to 2010 showed that the prevalence of dementia controlled for age was higher for females than for males (Chan *et al.* 2013: 2021). Prevalence ratio of females to males was 1.65 (Chan *et al.* 2013: 2020). The same patterns hold for AD (Chan *et al.* 2013: 2021). Gender difference in the prevalence of dementia can be attributed to the influence of longevity (i.e. females live longer than males), biological differences (e.g. hormonal differences, differences in brain structure and function), and gendered social roles and opportunities (e.g. educational opportunities, occupational complexity) (Andrew and Tierney 2018: 2–5).

There is also urban–rural difference in the prevalence of dementia in China. A 2012 study found that there was higher prevalence rate of dementia cases in rural elders in Anhui, while there were higher prevalence rates of dementia cases and subcases in the rural elders in Shanghai, Shanxi, Guangdong, and Heilongjiang provinces (Chen *et al.* 2012: 695). Another study showed that there was a higher prevalence of AD between 2007 and 2017 in rural than urban areas (95% CI: 4.27–4.78 vs 3.89–4.09) (Li *et al.* 2018: 1618). The prevalence was 452 per 10,000 for rural people and 399 per 10,000 for urban people (Li *et al.* 2018:

1618). The difference can be attributed to low health literacy of rural people and their limited access to healthcare (Maestre 2012: 513).

As regards regional differences, a 2018 study showed that northern China had a higher prevalence rate of dementia (5.5%) than central China (5.2%) and south China (4.8%) (Wu *et al.* 2018: 716). Another study showed that north China, northeast China, and northwest China 'showed higher prevalence rates of VAD (p= 0.0006/0.0009/0.0046), which was not observed in dementia or AD' (Zhu *et al.* 2019). The higher prevalence rate of VAD in the northern area of China could be attributed to severe air pollution that injured brain structures and cognition (Zhu *et al.* 2019). Meanwhile, a study showed that the age-standardized mortality from AD and other forms of dementia in eastern China was higher than those in the west and middle regions (Bo *et al.* 2019). Associated chronic disease risk factors (e.g. poorer sleep hygiene and unhealthy eating habits) caused by the accelerated urbanization process explained why residents of eastern China were more susceptible to dementia (Bo *et al.* 2019).

Conclusion

To conclude, China's population has been ageing rapidly over the past two decades. Chinese people live longer, but many of them suffer from poor health, disability, and dementia. This increases the level of dependency among older people and calls for policy actions to finance and deliver LTC services more effectively so that the care and support needs of elderly persons can be met. The next chapter will examine the development of LTC services in China.

Acknowledgement

Part of the content comes from Luk, S. C. Y. (2017) *Financing Healthcare in China: Towards Universal Health Insurance.* London: Routledge, pp. 11–19. Reproduced with permission of The Licensor through PLSclear.

References

Albert, E. (2021) *China's Population Is Peaking.* Online. Available HTTP: https://thediplomat.com/2021/05/chinas-population-is-peaking/ (accessed 9 July 2021).

Andrew, M. K. and Tierney, M. C. (2018) 'The Puzzle of Sex, Gender and Alzheimer's Disease: Why Are Women More Often Affected Than Men?' *Women's Health*, 14: 1–8.

Anhui Ageing Commission Office (2008) *An Analysis of the Current Situation of Population Ageing* (Chinese version). Online. Available HTTP: www.ahllb.cn/DocHtml/2/2008/8/8/11765725135.html (accessed 16 August 2015).

Australian Institute of Health and Welfare (2018) *Chronic Conditions and Disability 2015.* Online. Available HTTP: www.aihw.gov.au/getmedia/7b4b9ed6-a41f-4974-a76b-d23cfc248784/aihw-cdk-8.pdf.aspx?inline=true (accessed 29 September 2019).

BBC News (2018) *China Birth Rate: Mothers, Your Country Needs You!* 25 December. Online. Available HTTP: www.bbc.com/news/world-asia-china-46558562 (accessed 20 July 2019).

Bo, Z., Wan, Y., Meng, S. S., Lin, T., Kuang, W., Jiang, L. and Qiu, P. (2019) 'The Temporal Trend and Distribution Characteristics in Mortality of Alzheimer's Disease and Other Forms of Dementia in China: Based on the National Mortality Surveillance System (NMS) from 2009 to 2015', *PLOS ONE*, 14 (1): e0210621.

Cai, F., Giles, J., O'Keefe, P. and Wang, D. (2012) *The Elderly and Old Age Support in Rural China: Challenges and Prospects*. Online. Available HTTP: https://openknowledge.worldbank.org/handle/10986/2249 (accessed 12 August 2015).

Chan, K. Y., Wang, W., Wu, J. J., Liu, L., Theodoratou, E., Car, J., Middleton, L., Russ, T. C., Deary, I. J., Campbell, H., Wang, W. and Rudan, I. (2013) 'Epidemiology of Alzheimer's Disease and Other Forms of Dementia in China, 1990–2010: A Systematic Review and Analysis', *Lancet*, 381: 2016–23.

Chen, C. and Williamson, J. B. (2010) 'China's New Rural Pension Scheme: Can It Be Improved?', *International Journal of Sociology and Social Policy*, 30 (5/6): 239–50.

Chen, K. and Chan, A. (2011) 'The Ageing Population of China and a Review of Gerontechnology', *Gerontechnology*, 10 (2): 63–71.

Chen, R., Ma, Y., Wilson, K., Hu, Z., Sallah, D., Wang, J., Fan, L., Chen, R. and Copeland, J. R. (2012) 'A Multicentre Community-Based Study of Dementia Cases and Subcases in Older People in China: The GMS-AGECAT Prevalence and Socio-Economic Correlates', *International Journal of Geriatric Psychiatry*, 27 (7): 692–702.

Chen, S., Boyle, L. L., Conwell, Y., Chiu, H., Li, L. and Xiao, S. (2013) 'Dementia Care in Rural China', *Mental Health in Family Medicine*, 10 (3): 133–41.

Chen, T. (2018) 'An Analysis on Demand of Urban and Rural Disabled Elders for Long-Term Care', in J. Dang, Y. Wei and N. Liu (eds.) *Survey Report on the Living Conditions of China's Urban and Rural Older Adults 2018* (Chinese version). Beijing: Social Sciences Academic Press (China), pp. 138–67.

Chi, D. (2018a) 'China's Elderly Population to Peak at Half a Billion in 2050', *GBTIMES*, 20 July. Online. Available HTTP: https://gbtimes.com/chinas-elderly-population-to-peak-at-half-a-billion-in-2050 (accessed 20 July 2019).

Chi, D. (2018b) 'China's Elderly Population Continues to Rise, with 241 Million Now 60 or Over', *GBTIMES*, 27 February. Online. Available HTTP: https://gbtimes.com/chinas-elderly-population-continues-to-rise (accessed 20 July 2019).

China Daily (2019a) 'China's Senior Population May Surge from 2025', *China Daily*, 9 February. Online. Available HTTP: www.chinadaily.com.cn/a/201902/09/WS5c5e3f3ea3106c65c34e8732.html (accessed 20 July 2019).

China Daily (2019b) 'Life Expectancy of Chinese Increases by 42 Years in Nearly 70 Years', *China Daily*, 23 May. Online. Available HTTP: www.chinadaily.com.cn/a/201905/23/WS5ce65408a3104842260bd68e.html (accessed 20 July 2019).

China Economic Herald (2012) *China's Total Fertility Rate Was Only 1.18 in 2010* (Chinese version). 10 July. Online. Available HTTP: www.ceh.com.cn/ceh/jryw/2012/7/10/121921.shtml (accessed 14 August 2015).

Chinese Academy of Social Sciences, Indian National Science Academy, Indonesian Academy of Sciences, National Research Council of the U.S. National Academies and Science Council of Japan (2011) *Preparing for the Challenges of Population Aging in Asia: Strengthening the Scientific Basis of Policy Development*. Online. Available HTTP: www.ncbi.nlm.nih.gov/books/NBK53399/pdf/Bookshelf_NBK53399.pdf (accessed 6 February 2016).

China News Service (2016a) 'Survey Showed That the Number of Fully or Partially Disabled Elderly Had Reached 40.63 Million in China', (Chinese version), *China News Service*, 9 October. Online. Available HTTP: www.chinanews.com/gn/2016/10-09/8025644.shtml (accessed 28 September 2019).

China News Service (2016b) 'The Number of Disabled Elderly Will Reach 42 Million by 2020', (Chinese version), *China News Service*, 27 October. Online. Available HTTP: www.chinanews.com/gn/2016/10-27/8044647.shtml (accessed 28 September 2019).

Dang, J. (2018) 'The Living Conditions of the Urban and Rural Elderly in China', in J. Dang, Y. Wei and N. Liu (eds.) *Survey Report on the Living Conditions of China's Urban and Rural Older Persons 2018* (Chinese version). Beijing: Social Sciences Academic Press (China), pp. 1–54.

Duan, D., Dong, Y., Zhang, H., Zhao, Y., Diao, Y., Cui, Y., Wang, J., Chai, Q. and Liu, Z. (2017) 'Empty-Nest-Related Psychological Distress Is Associated with Progression of Brain White Matter Lesions and Cognitive Impairment in the Elderly', *Scientific Reports*, 7: 43816.

Duong, S., Patel, T. and Chang, F. (2017) 'Dementia: What Pharmacists Need to Know', *Canadian Pharmacists Journal*, 150 (2): 118–29.

Feng, Z., Liu, C., Guan, X. and Mor, V. (2012) 'China's Rapidly Aging Population Creates Policy Challenges in Shaping a Viable Long-Term Care System', *Health Affairs*, 31 (12): 2764–73.

Frankish, H. and Horton, R. (2017) 'Prevention and Management of Dementia: A Priority for Public Health', *The Lancet*, 390 (10113): 2614–5.

Gao, M., Li, Y., Zhang, S., Gu, L., Zhang, J., Li, Z., Zhang, W. and Tian, D. (2017) 'Does an Empty Nest Affect Elders' Health? Empirical Evidence from China', *International Journal of Environmental Research and Public Health*, 14: 463.

Gao, Y., Wei, Y., Shen, Y., Tang, Y. and Yang, J. (2014) 'China's Empty Nest Elderly Need Better Care', *Journal of the American Geriatrics Society*, 62 (9): 1821–2.

Gietel-Basten, S. (2017) 'Why China's Two-Child Policy Is Failing the Reality Test', *South China Morning Post*, 4 February. Online. Available HTTP: www.scmp.com/comment/insight-opinion/article/2067770/why-chinas-two-child-policy-failing-reality-test (accessed 20 July 2019).

Hu, H., Jin, Q. and Kavan, P. (2014) 'A Study of Heavy Metal Pollution in China: Current Status, Pollution-Control Policies and Countermeasures', *Sustainability*, 6: 5820–38.

Hu, Z. and Peng, X. (2015) 'Household Changes in Contemporary China: An Analysis Based on the Four Recent Censuses', *The Journal of Chinese Sociology*, 2: 9.

Jia, L., Quan, M., Fu, Y., Zhao, T., Li, Y., Wei, C., Tang, Y., Qin, Q., Wang, F., Qiao, Y., Shi, S., Wang, Y., Du, Y., Zhang, J., Zhang, J., Luo, B., Qu, Q., Zhou, C., Gauthier, S. and Jia, J. (2020) 'Dementia in China: Epidemiology, Clinical Management, and Research Advances', *The Lancet Neurology*, 19 (1): 81–92.

Johnston, L. (2012) *Getting Old After Getting Rich: Comparing China with Japan*. Online. Available HTTP: www.eastasiaforum.org/2012/12/22/getting-old-after-getting-rich-comparing-china-with-japan/ (accessed 12 August 2015).

Leng, S. (2019) 'China's Birth Rate Falls Again, with 2018 Producing the Fewest Babies Since 1961, Official Data Shows', *South China Morning Post*, 21 January. Online. Available HTTP: www.scmp.com/economy/china-economy/article/2182963/chinas-birth-rate-falls-again-2018-producing-fewest-babies (accessed 20 July 2019).

Li, K., Wei, S., Liu, Z., Hu, L., Lin, J., Tan, S., Mai, Y., Peng, W., Mai, H., Hou, Q. and Tu, G. (2018) 'The Prevalence of Alzheimer's Disease in China: A Systematic Review and Meta-Analysis', *Iranian Journal of Public Health*, 47 (11): 1615–26.

Liu, B. (2015) *The Working-Age Population Has Decreased for Three Consecutive Years in China and Demographic Dividend Is Declining* (Chinese version). Online. Available HTTP: http://news.qq.com/a/20150122/001709.htm (accessed 12 August 2015).

Liu, J. (2014) 'Ageing, Migration and Familial Support in Rural China', *Geoforum*, 51: 305–12.

Liu, L. and Guo, Q. (2008) 'Life Satisfaction in a Sample of Empty-Nest Elderly: A Survey in the Rural Area of a Mountainous County in China', *Quality of Life Research: An International Journal of Quality of Life Aspects of Treatment, Care, and Rehabilitation*, 17: 823–30.

Liu, S. (1997) 'Some Thoughts about Population Ageing in Different Regions of China', (Chinese version), *Population Journal*, 3: 33–40.

Liu, T. and Sun, L. (2015) 'An Apocalyptic Vision of Ageing in China: Old Age Care for the Largest Elderly Population in the World', *Zeitschrift für Gerontologie und Geriatrie*, 48 (4): 354–64.

Lu, H. (2017) *The Growth of Empty-Nest Elderly People Is Becoming an Issue in China*. Online. Available HTTP: https://social.shorthand.com/RileyLu66/ny3Epbw3d3/the-growth-of-empty-nest-elderly-people-is-becoming-an-issue-in-china (accessed 21 July 2019).

Luk, S. C. Y. (2017) *Financing Healthcare in China: Towards Universal Health Insurance*. London: Routledge.

Luk, S. C. Y. and Preston, P. (2016) *The Logic of Chinese Politics: Cores, Peripheries and Peaceful Rising*. Cheltenham, UK: Edward Elgar Publishing Ltd.

Maestre, G. E. (2012) 'Assessing Dementia in Resource-Poor Regions', *Current Neurology and Neuroscience Reports*, 12: 511–9.

Mould-Quevedo, J. F., Tang, B., Harary, E., Kurzman, R., Pan, S., Yang, J. and Qiao, J. (2013) 'The Burden of Caring for Dementia Patients: Caregiver Reports from a Cross-Sectional Hospital-Based Study in China', *Expert Review of Pharmacoeconomics & Outcomes Research*, 13 (5): 663–73.

National Bureau of Statistics of China (2013) *China Statistical Yearbook 2013*, Beijing: China Statistics Press.

National Bureau of Statistics of China (2016a) *China Statistical Yearbook 2016* (Chinese version). Online. Available HTTP: www.stats.gov.cn/tjsj/ndsj/2016/indexch.htm (accessed 21 July 2019).

National Bureau of Statistics of China (2016b) *Statistical Reports on 2015 National Economic and Social Development* (Chinese version). Online. Available HTTP: www.stats.gov.cn/tjsj/zxfb/201602/t20160229_1323991.html (accessed 21 July 2019).

National Bureau of Statistics of China (2018) *China Statistical Yearbook 2018* (Chinese version). Online. Available HTTP: www.stats.gov.cn/tjsj/ndsj/2018/indexch.htm (accessed 21 July 2019).

National Bureau of Statistics of China (2019) *Statistical Reports on 2018 National Economic and Social Development* (Chinese version). Online. Available HTTP: www.stats.gov.cn/tjsj/zxfb/201902/t20190228_1651265.html (accessed 21 July 2019).

National Health Commission of the People's Republic of China (2019) *Statistical Communiqué of the People's Republic of China on the 2018 Hygiene and Health Development* (Chinese version). Online. Available HTTP: www.nhc.gov.cn/guihuaxxs/

s10748/201905/9b8d52727cf346049de8acce25ffcbd0.shtml (accessed 22 July 2019).

OECD (2015) *OECD Economic Surveys: China 2015*. Online. Available HTTP: www. oecd.org/eco/surveys/China-2015-overview.pdf (accessed 12 August 2015).

Peng, X., Song, S., Sullivan, S., Qiu, J. and Wang, W. (2010) 'Ageing, the Urban-Rural Gap and Disability Trends: 19 Years of Experience in Chin: 1987 to 2006', *PLOS ONE*, 5 (8): e12129.

Phillips, T. (2015) 'China Ends One-Child Policy after 35 Years', *The Guardian*, 29 October. Online. Available HTTP: <www.theguardian.com/world/2015/oct/29/china-abandons-one-child-policy> (accessed 20 July 2019).

Population Census Office and Department of Population and Employment Statistics (2012a) *Tabulation on the 2010 Population Census of the People's Republic of China (Book I)* (Chinese version). Beijing: China Statistics Press.

Population Census Office and Department of Population and Employment Statistics (2012b) *Tabulation on the 2010 Population Census of the People's Republic of China (Book III)* (Chinese version). Beijing: China Statistics Press.

The Research Group of China Research Centre on Ageing (2011) 'Current Situation of Old-Age Disability among Urban and Rural Elders in China', (Chinese version), *Disability Research*, 2: 11–6.

Scharping, T. (2003) *Birth Control in China, 1949–2000: Population Policy and Demographic Development*, London; New York: Routledge.

South China Morning Post (2015) 'China's Workforce Shrinks by Nearly 4 Million Amid Greying Population', *South China Morning Post*, 20 January. Online. Available HTTP: www.scmp.com/news/china/article/1683778/chinas-workforce-shrinks-nearly-4-million-amid-greying-population (accessed 12 August 2015).

Southern Metropolis Daily (2015) 'Floating Population Will Reach 300 Million within Five Years, the Average Age of Floating Population of Floating Population Continues to Increase', (Chinese version), *Southern Metropolis Daily*, 12 November. Online. Available HTTP: http://gd.sina.com.cn/finance/industry/2015-11-12/cj-ifxknutf1715330.shtml (accessed 6 February 2016).

Tulchinsky, T. and Varavikova, E. (2014) *The New Public Health: An Introduction for the 21st Century*, San Diego, CA; London: Academic Press.

United Nations (2013) *World Population Ageing 2013*. Online. Available HTTP: www.un.org/en/development/desa/population/publications/pdf/ageing/WorldPopulationAgeing2013.pdf (accessed 7 August 2015).

Wang, F. (2017) 'Scholar: China Will Become a Super-Aged Society by 2040 and the Trend Will Be Irreversible', (Chinese version), *Phoenix New Media*, 17 April. Online. Available HTTP: http://finance.ifeng.com/a/20170417/15303347_0.shtml (accessed 20 July 2019).

Wang, G., Hu, M., Xiao, S. and Zhou, L. (2017) 'Loneliness and Depression among Rural Empty-Nest Elderly Adults in Liuyang, China: A Cross-Sectional Study', *BMJ Open*, 7: e016091.

Wang, T. T. (2012) 'The Scale of Aging Population in China Is Larger Than That of Ageing Population in Europe', (Chinese version). *The Mirror*, 7 April. Online. Available HTTP: http://finance.ifeng.com/news/macro/20120407/5886522.shtml (accessed 20 July 2019).

Wang, X. (2019) 'Disability Rate among Elderly Sparks Efforts', *China Daily*, 30 July. Online. Available HTTP: www.chinadaily.com.cn/a/201907/30/WS5d3f97a5a310d83056401abb.html (accessed 28 September 2019).

Wang, X. H. (2018) *The Proportion of Empty Nester Elderly Households Will Reach 90 Percent* (Chinese version). Online. Available HTTP: https://baijiahao.baidu.com/s?id=1619440967500302408&wfr=spider&for=pc (accessed 9 July 2021).

Wang, Y., Jia, R., Liang, J., Li, J., Qian, S., Li, J. and Xu, Y. (2019) Dementia in China (2015–2050) 'Estimated Using the 1% Population Sampling Survey in 2015', *Geriatric & Gerontology International*, 19: 1096–1100.

White, T. (2006) *China's Longest Campaign: Birth Planning in the People's Republic, 1949–2005*, Ithaca, NY: Cornell University Press.

The World Bank (2015) *GDP per Capita (Current US$)*. Online. Available HTTP: http://data.worldbank.org/indicator/NY.GDP.PCAP.CD (accessed 12 August 2015).

The World Bank Group (2019) *Fertility Rate, Total (Births Per Woman)*. Online. Available HTTP: https://data.worldbank.org/indicator/SP.DYN.TFRT.IN?locations=CN-US-IN&name_desc=true (accessed 20 July 2019).

World Health Organization (2005) *Chronic Diseases and Their Common Risk Factors*. Online. Available HTTP: www.who.int/chp/chronic_disease_report/media/Factsheet1.pdf (accessed 11 July 2021).

World Health Organization (2013) *China-WHO Country Cooperation Strategy 2013–2015: Bridging the Past towards a New Era of Collaboration*. Online. Available HTTP: www.who.int/countryfocus/cooperation_strategy/ccs_chn_en.pdf (accessed 16 August 2015).

World Health Organization (2014) *World Health Statistics 2014*. Online. Available HTTP: http://apps.who.int/iris/bitstream/10665/112738/1/9789240692671_eng.pdf (accessed 17 August 2015).

World Health Organization (2015) *China Country Assessment Report on Ageing and Health*. Online. Available HTTP: https://apps.who.int/iris/bitstream/handle/10665/194271/9789241509312_eng.pdf;jsessionid=E8CB59F0055FC449D43BF3AC32557FBD?sequence=1 (accessed 20 July 2019).

Wu, Y., Ali, G., Guerchet, M., Prina, A. M., Chan, K. Y., Prince, M. and Brayne, C. (2018) 'Prevalence of Dementia in Mainland China, Hong Kong and Taiwan: An Updated Systematic Review and Meta-Analysis', *International Journal of Epidemiology*, 47 (3): 709–19.

Xin, Z. and Leng, S. (2019) 'China Birth Numbers Expected to Fall to Lowest Level Since 2000, Creating New Economic and Social Challenges', *South China Morning Post*, 2 January. Online. Available HTTP: www.scmp.com/economy/china-economy/article/2180339/china-birth-rate-expected-fall-lowest-level-2000-creating-new (accessed 20 July 2019).

Xinhuanet (2018) 'China's Population Aged 60 years and over Hit 241 Million, Accounting for More than 17.3 Percent of the Total Population', (Chinese version). 27 February. Online. Available HTTP: www.xinhuanet.com/health/2018-02/27/c_1122457257.htm (accessed 20 July 2019).

Xinhua News (2004) 'From 35 Years to 72 Years: Life Expectancy in China Becomes Higher and Higher', (Chinese version), *Xinhua News*, 28 September. Online. Available HTTP: http://news.xinhuanet.com/newscenter/2004-09/28/content_2032154.htm (accessed 17 August 2015).

Xu, J., Wang, J., Wimo, A., Fratiglionid, L. and Qiud, C. (2017) 'The Economic Burden of Dementia in China, 1990–2030: Implications for Health Policy', *Bulletin of the World Health Organization*, 95: 18–26.

Yan, H. (2006) *China's One-Child Policy in Need of Change*, Singapore: East Asian Institute, National University of Singapore.

Zeng, Y., Feng, Q., Hesketh, T., Christensen, K. and Vaupel, J. W. (2017) 'Survival, Disabilities in Activities of Daily Living, and Physical and Cognitive Functioning among the Oldest-Old in China: A Cohort Study', *The Lancet*, 389: 1619–29.

Zhang, C., Hou, L., Zheng, X., Zhu, R., Zhao, H., Lu, J., Cheng, J., Yang, X. Y. and Yang, T. (2019) 'Risk Factors of Mental Disorders among Empty and Non-Empty Nesters in Shanxi, China: A Cross-Sectional Study', *Health and Quality of Life Outcome*, 17: 18.

Zhang, M. (2012) *The Impact of Declining Demographic Dividend and Socio-economic Transformation*. Online. Available HTTP: www.chinausfocus.com/political-social-development/the-impact-of-declining-demographic-dividend-and-socioeconomic-transformation/ (accessed 12 August 2015).

Zhang, W. (2012) *Ageing China: Changes and Challenges*. Online. Available HTTP: www.bbc.com/news/world-asia-china-19572056 (accessed 7 August 2015).

Zhang, X. and Zhang, D. (2012) 'China's Average Life Expectancy Increase by Five Years of Age in Twenty Years', (Chinese version), *Remin Daily News* (Overseas edition), 8 August. Online. Available HTTP: http://paper.people.com.cn/rmrbhwb/html/2012-08/08/content_1093795.htm?div=-1 (accessed 17 August 2015).

Zhao, X. (2016) 'Authorities Working on Plan to Delay Retirements', *China Daily*, 23 July. Online. Available HTTP: www.chinadaily.com.cn/china/2016-07/23/content_26192140.htm (accessed 21 July 2019).

Zhong, Q., Xia, K. and Lu, Y. (2020) 'China Focus: Fighting Alzheimer's Disease in China', *Xinhuanet*, 21 September. Online. Available HTTP: www.xinhuanet.com/english/2020-09/21/c_139385194.htm (accessed 11 July 2021).

Zhou, C., Ji, C., Chu, J., Medina, A., Li, C., Jiang, S., Zheng, W., Liu, J. and Rozelle, S. (2015) 'Non-Use of Health Care Service among Empty-Nest Elderly in Shandong, China: A Cross-Sectional Study', *BMC Health Services Research*, 15: 294.

Zhu, Y., Liu, H., Lu, X., Zhang, B., Weng, W., Yang, J., Zhang, J. and Dong, M. (2019) 'Prevalence of Dementia in the People's Republic of China from 1985 to 2015: A Systematic Review and Meta-Regression Analysis', *BMC Public Health*, 19: 578.

3 Long-term care, dementia care, and end-of-life care in China

Introduction

'China has the largest and most rapidly ageing population in the world – dramatically increasing its need for long-term care (LTC) services' (United Nations Economic and Social Commission for Asia and the Pacific 2015: 5). The government has established a national support system for the care of older adults consisting of three tiers: home care, community-based care, and institutional care (Feng *et al.* 2012; United Nations Economic and Social Commission for Asia and the Pacific 2015). But major challenges facing the national support system for the care of older adults include insufficient LTC service capacity, urban–rural disparities, slow development of integrated medical and elderly care services, enormous variations in service provision, service standards, and service quality due to the lack of regulatory oversight and the underdevelopment of both dementia service system and end-of-life (EoL) care. This chapter examines the living arrangement of older adults, China's LTC policies, care and support for disabled older adults, dementia care, and the development of EoL care in LTC settings.

Living arrangements of older adults

Living arrangements affect family caregiving for older adults. According to *the Survey Report on the Living Conditions of China's Urban and Rural Older Adults* (hereafter *the Survey Report on Chinese Older Adults*), over 50 percent of older adults surveyed lived alone or lived with only their spouse (Liu 2018: 79). Among them, about 13 percent lived alone while about 38 percent lived with their spouse (Liu 2018: 79). About 42 percent of older adults surveyed still lived with their children, a decrease of 19 percent when compared to that in 2000 (Liu 2018: 80). Moreover, about 7 percent of older adults surveyed lived with other people, such as older parents, siblings, grandchildren, and nannies (Liu 2018: 80).

In recent years, both rural and urban areas have experienced a drastic decrease in co-residence between older adults and their children. In 2015, the percentage of rural older adults living with children was 40.6 percent, a decrease of 23 percent when compared to that in 2000 (Liu 2018: 80). But the percentage of rural older adults living alone, living with spouse, and living with other people

DOI: 10.4324/9780429057199-3

increased by about 7 percent, 12 percent, and 4 percent respectively (Liu 2018: 80). Similarly, the percentage of urban older adults living with children was 42.8 percent, a decrease of 15.4 percent when compared to that in 2000 (Liu 2018: 80). But the percentage of urban older adults living alone, living with spouse, and living with other people increased by about 5.4 percent, 8.2 percent, and 1.9 percent respectively (Liu 2018: 80).

At present, filial piety (*xiao*) that commands the young in the family to respect, obey, and serve his/her parents and other ageing members related to the family remains a strongly held value in China (Kwan 2000; Li *et al.* 2012). Many ageing parents still 'hold on to the traditional norm that care by adult children is the best arrangement' (Li *et al.* 2012: 621). However, a decrease in co-residence between ageing parents and adult children does not mean that ageing parents lack care completely. In China, there is a fraction of older adults choosing to live alone or with their spouse because they are healthy and financially independent to take care of themselves. They prefer to live apart from their children to 'reduce the likelihood of intergenerational conflicts' (Li *et al.* 2012: 620). Additionally, a decrease in co-residence between ageing parents and adult children is accompanied by having adult children to live nearby (e.g. within the same community or neighbourhood) to maintain frequent contact and provide care needs of their parents while maintaining the independence or privacy of both ageing parents and their adult children (Lei *et al.* 2015: 208). The nationally representative 2011–2012 China Health and Retirement Longitudinal Study (CHARLS) showed that most of the older adults who lived alone had access to assistance from their children (Lei *et al.* 2015: 198).

Nevertheless, older adults whose children are away for better job opportunities in other cities or provinces can rely on only their spouse, siblings, or nannies to provide care for them. Although there is an increasing trend of mutual care between spouses or older adults relying on their spouse for primary caregiving, the spouse who is limited by his/her own ageing is not a reliable source of care in the long run (Li *et al.* 2012: 619). Siblings are also not a reliable source of care for older adults in the long run because they are limited by their own ageing or illness. Paid nannies allow older adults to remain in their own homes while receiving care. But the supply of nannies and the financial ability of older adults or their adult children to pay nannies will affect the provision of care for older adults. Shocking incidents of older adults being violently abused by nannies in recent years have made family members reluctant to turn to helpers/nannies for elder care (Feng 2018; Jiang 2017; Liao Shen Evening News 2018).

Development of LTC services in China

Stage 1: a residual approach (1949 to the mid-1980s)

In China, LTC services are developed in different stages. From 1949 to the mid-1980s, the government adopted a residual approach shaped by the Confucian concept of filial piety to provide LTC services (Zhang 2013). Care for older family members 'has traditionally been provided at home by spouses, children, in-laws (particularly daughters-in-law) and extended family members' (Xu and Chow 2011: 375). The role of the government was limited to provide residential care and basic daily needs (e.g. meals) through state social welfare institutions for the urban older adults classified as 'three no's' – no family support, no source of income, and no ability to work (Shum *et al.* 2015; Wong and Leung 2012; Zhang 2013). The government also provided 'three no's' older adults in rural areas with the 'five guarantees' – namely food, clothing, housing, medical care, and burial after death (Wu *et al.* 2009: 473). These rural older adults lived in state-funded 'homes of respect for older persons' (*jing lao yuan*) (Dai 2016: 16). LTC services under the residual approach had restrictive coverage and limited service provisions due to insufficient state funding (Mok and Liu 1999: 145). Older adults who received institutional care were stigmatized (Zhan *et al.* 2006: 88). 'Few families could imagine placing a loved one in an institution to be cared for by strangers' (Feng *et al.* 2012: 2767). The state provision of care for 'three no's' older adults in urban and rural areas almost stopped during the Cultural Revolution (1966–1976) (Dai 2019).

Stage 2: socialization of social welfare (the mid-1980s to the 1990s)

From the mid-1980s to the 1990s, the government 'implemented reforms to decentralize the operation and financing of state welfare institutions' (Feng *et al.* 2012: 2767). It became 'responsible for planning, formulating guidance and supervising care providers rather than directing care provision to older persons' (United Nations Economic and Social Commission for Asia and the Pacific 2015: 16). It endorsed welfare pluralism. In 1986, the Ministry of Civil Affairs (MCA) proposed the policy of 'socialization of social welfare' (*shehuifuli shehuihua*) as a new orientation to develop and reform social welfare through the use of diversified service providers and funding sources (Wong and Leung 2012: 573–4; Dai 2019). Social welfare was 'considered not the sole responsibility of the government, but a duty of every member, every organization, and every sector of the community' (Mok and Liu 1999: 145).

In the aspect of LTC services, the goals of socialization included (1) establishing a pluralistic service system which comprised residential homes and community services for older adults and a variety of providers from the public, private, and collective sectors; (2) funding LTC services through government allocation, public donation, and payments by service users; and (3) allowing state social welfare institutions to admit older adults who could pay service charges while the responsibility for providing care to 'three no's' older adults rested primarily with local governments (Shum *et al.* 2015; Wong and Leung 2012: 573–5). In other words, the government under the socialization policy no longer took sole responsibility for the provision of institutional care services for older adults. The wider society (i.e. enterprises, collectives, social groups) was expected by the government to assume more responsibilities in providing institutional care for older adults and private and non-government resources would be used to develop institutional care services for older adults (Ding 2011: 137–9). Institutional care service agencies no longer just served the 'three no's' older adults but also older adults who could afford to pay the fees (Wong and Leung 2012). Socializing the provision of institutional care for older adults was necessary as a result of weakened family support caused by 'the economic and social transformation, shrinkage in family size, and decrease in potential caregivers' (Ding 2011: 138). The policy was thus to meet the increasing demand for care services for older adults and ease the burden of family caregivers (Ding 2011: 139).

In October 1998, the government enacted *Provisional Regulations on the Registration and Management of Civil, Non-Enterprise Institutions*, which officially protected the lawful rights and interests of non-governmental, non-commercial enterprises (The Congressional-Executive Commission on China, n.d.). This facilitated the establishment of homes for the aged by non-governmental organizations (NGOs) (*minbian feiqiye*) (Qu 2015). In December 1999, the MCA released *the Provisional Measures for the Management of Social Welfare Institutions*, which provided 'broad outlines of the application and registration process including required procedures, qualifications and documentation of supporting materials in order to open an elder care facility' (Feng *et al.* 2014: 424).

Stage 3: setting the standards for elder care facilities and old-age care workers (the early 2000s)

In 2001, *the Basic Standards of Social Welfare Institutions for the Elderly* was issued by the MCA to regulate the operations of types of elder care facilities such as homes for the aged, hostels for older adults (i.e. senior apartments), nursing homes, and elderly service centres (Feng *et al.* 2014). It 'set out general rules for meals, personal care, rehabilitation, and psychosocial services' (Glinskaya and Feng 2018: 22). It also set out 'general requirements with regard to facility permit and naming rules, personnel and human resources, organizational management and documentation systems' (Feng *et al.* 2014: 428). 'However, detailed criteria differentiating residents by levels of care are lacking' (Feng *et al.* 2012: 2769).

In 2002, the Ministry of Labor and Social Security (MLSS) issued *the National Occupational Standards for Elder Care Workers*, which set out the basic educational and training requirements for persons who provided daily living assistance or nursing care for older adults. It classified elder care workers into four ranks according to work experience, training, and skills level: entry (equivalent to National Occupational Qualification Grade V), intermediate (National Occupational Qualification Grade IV), advanced (National Occupational Qualification Grade III), and technician (National Occupational Qualification Grade II) (Ministry of Civil Affairs 2009). The basic educational requirement for this occupation was junior secondary school graduation. A minimum of 180 hours of training at a full-time vocational school was required for becoming an entry-level worker. Additional training hours of 150 was required for promotion to intermediate level, 120 for promotion to advanced level, and 90 for promotion to technician level (Ministry of Civil Affairs 2009). A certificate at each level would be awarded to those who passed two separate exams (Ministry of Civil Affairs 2009). Since *the National*

Occupational Standards for Elder Care Workers clearly defined the occupational category of elder care workers, the recruitment and training of elder care workers had received a higher priority (Wong and Leung 2012: 575). 'However, the number of workers who have actually met these basic requirements is widely believed to be very small' (Feng *et al.* 2012: 2769).

Stage 4: establishing a three-tiered model (2006–2014)

In February 2006, *Opinions on Accelerating the Development of the Elderly Services Industry* was jointly issued by 10 ministries and commissions, including Office of the National Commission on Ageing, the MCA, and the MLSS. It suggested that the provision of elderly care services should be based on a three-tiered model, with home care as the foundation, community services as the support, and institutional care for the aged as the supplement (Office of the National Commission on Ageing *et al.* 2006). Besides, it suggested that local governments encourage NGOs to establish hostels for older adults and nursing homes that provided residential, educational, entertainment, and fitness training services for older adults (Office of the National Commission on Ageing *et al.* 2006). It also suggested that local governments encourage NGOs to develop and provide a variety of home care services for older adults, which included activities of daily living (ADLs) care, housekeeping, counselling, rehabilitation, and emergency services (Office of the National Commission on Ageing *et al.* 2006).

In January 2008, *Opinions on Comprehensively Promotion the Work of Home Care Services* was jointly issued by 10 ministries and commissions. It ordered to establish the home-based elderly care service network with various forms and extensive coverage in urban communities nationwide and establish integrated elderly welfare services centres that provided residential care, community care, and home care in 80 percent of rural villages (Office of the National Commission on Ageing *et al.* 2008). It suggested that home care service teams that consisted of professional old-age care workers and volunteers should be built (Office of the National Commission on Ageing *et al.* 2008). Tax incentives could be used to encourage organizations to develop home care services (Office of the National Commission on Ageing *et al.* 2008).

In September 2011, the State Council issued *the 12th Five-year Development Plan of Undertakings on Ageing*, which comprehensively covered 11 aspects related to older adults (e.g. social security, healthcare) and called for the development of medium- and long-term plans to cope with population ageing (The State Council 2011a). It established targets for the development of aged care services by 2015, which included:

(1) establishing a three-tiered elderly care system, with home care as the foundation, community services as the support, and institutional care for the aged as the supplement;
(2) improving the service network of home care and community care, and having 30 beds per 1,000 older adults nationwide;

(3) fully implementing technical standards for construction for older adults in both urban and rural areas and establishing standards for elderly care facilities in new communities;

(4) upgrading barrier-free facilities; and

(5) increasing facilities for culture, education, sports and fitness for older adults.

(The State Council 2011a)

In December 2011, the State Council issued *the Development Plan for the Elderly Service System (2011–2015)*, which clearly presented the objective, scope, and functions of the three-tiered elderly care system. *The Development Plan* stated that the three-tiered elderly care system consisting of home care, community care, and institutional care services focused on meeting the actual needs of older adults and gave priority to the protection of older adults who lived alone, had no caregivers, had low income, or were disabled (The State Council 2011b). It explained the scope and functions of each tier as follows:

(1) Home care services covered ADLs care, housekeeping services, family visits, medical care, rehabilitation care, and psychological counselling (The State Council 2011b). Local governments could explore the possibility of providing special subsidies to help disabled older adults receive home care and deploy the necessary rehabilitation equipment so that their quality of life and self-care ability could be improved (The State Council 2011b).

(2) Community care services played an important role in supporting home care services for older adults. It provided day care, short-term care, and catering services for older adults whose families had temporary difficulties in or were incapable of taking care of them (The State Council 2011b).

(3) Institutional care services covered ADLs care, rehabilitation care, and emergency assistance. They were mainly provided by rehabilitation institutions and other elderly institutions for the partially or fully disabled older adults. Rehabilitation institutions were encouraged to establish internal medical departments to meet the healthcare needs of older adults (The State Council 2011b).

The Development Plan sought to develop 'home-based care as the "basis", community-based services as "backing", and institutional care as "support"' (Feng *et al.* 2012: 2767). It ordered the establishment of a basically sound home care and community care service network by 2015 and established the following targets:

(1) Increase the number of beds for daily care and institutional care by about 3.4 million and upgrade 30 per cent of current beds;

(2) Provide home modifications to create a barrier-free living environment for older adults;

(3) Establish elderly day care centres, nursing homes, senior activity centres and elderly mutual assistance service centres so that day care services could basically cover all urban communities and more than half of rural communities;

(4) At least one rehabilitation or elderly institution should be established in county-level cities to provide care for the partially and fully disabled older adults;
(5) A number of training facilities for older adults should be established at the provincial and national levels;
(6) Professional nursing care equipment, auxiliary equipment and special vehicles for elderly care services should be developed; and
(7) Modern technology should be used to provide efficient and convenient services for older adults.

(The State Council 2011b)

In September 2013, the State Council issued *Several Opinions on Accelerating the Development of Elderly Service Industry* (hereafter *Several Opinions*), which proposed major goals and tasks to develop the three-tiered elderly care system in both urban and rural areas by 2020. *Several Opinions* established the following targets:

(1) ADLs care, medical care, psychological counselling and emergency assistance would be available to all home-based older adults;
(2) Qualified day care centres and senior activity centres would be available in all urban communities;
(3) Facilities or sites that provided integrated services for older adults should be available to over 90 percent of counties and towns and over 60 percent of rural communities;
(4) 35–40 beds per 1,000 elderly population should be provided nationwide.

(The State Council 2013)

Regarding major tasks, *Several Opinions* ordered local governments to strengthen the development of community services and facilities in new towns and districts, old town and districts, and existing communities (The State Council 2013). A senior home care service network that could satisfy various needs of older adults should be strengthened by bringing in social organizations, housekeeping companies, and property management companies to provide diversified elderly services such as day care and catering services (The State Council 2013). Innovative home care service model such as an online home care service platform could be developed to provide different types of services for older adults, including housekeeping appointment, health consultation, service payment, and emergency call (The State Council 2013). The development of integrated medical and elderly care services should be promoted. Qualified elderly care institutions should be supported by the Department of Health Management to set up healthcare divisions (The State Council 2013). Telehealth pilots could be introduced in elderly care institutions (The State Council 2013).

Stage 5: integrating medical and elderly care services (2015–the present)

Integrating medical and elderly care services refers to 'the organic combination of medical and elderly care resources that draw together daily care and rehabilitation' (Deloitte China 2018: 6). Since most of the older adults 'suffer from symptoms requiring repeated treatments such as chronic diseases' (Deloitte China 2018: 6), it is extremely inconvenient for them to go back and forth to medical institutions and elderly care institutions (Deloitte China 2018: 6). Medical institutions established in the senior care institutions ensure that older adults obtain immediate medical diagnosis and treatment with qualified services when needed (Deloitte China 2018: 12). In November 2015, the State Council set up the following targets in *Guiding Opinions on Promoting the Integration of Medical and Elderly Care Services* (hereafter *Guiding Opinions*):

(1) A policy framework for integrating medical and elderly care services, standards, and management system should be initially set up by 2017 (The State Council 2015);
(2) To increase elders' access to healthcare, by 2017, over 80 percent of medical institutions should offer fast channels of registration and medical consultation for older adults while over 50 percent of elderly care institutions should provide various medical services for older adults (The State Council 2015);
(3) By 2020, an integrated medical and elderly care service network with shared resources should be established to cover both urban and rural areas (The State Council 2015). All medical institutions should offer fast channels of registration and medical consultation for older adults while all elderly care institutions should provide various medical services for older adults to meet the basic healthcare needs of older adults (The State Council 2015).

Guiding Opinions encouraged the establishment of a cooperation mechanism between medical institutions and elderly care institutions based on the principle of mutual benefit (The State Council 2015). It also encouraged the use of private capitals to integrate medical and elderly care institutions (The State Council 2015).

In June 2016, 50 cities (e.g. Beijing, Shanghai) were designated to be the first batch of national pilot units for integrated medical and elderly care services (Office of the National Health and Family Planning Commission and Ministry of Civil Affairs 2016a). In September 2016, 40 cities were designated to be the second batch of national pilot units for integrated medical and elderly care services (Office of the National Health and Family Planning Commission and Ministry of Civil Affairs 2016b). As of July 2017, 'there were 5,814 institutions providing integrated medical and elderly care services in China' (Deloitte China 2018: 6). This accounted for only 4 percent of the total number of elderly care institutions (Deloitte China 2018: 6). In October 2019, the government decided to accelerate the development of integrated medical and elderly care services by simplifying the approval and registration procedures to establish institutions which provide integrated medical and elderly care services, providing preferential policy treatments such as tax exemptions, tax reduction, capital support, and reduced utility (i.e. electricity, water, and gas) rates for institutions which provide integrated medical and elderly care services and supporting commercial insurance companies to develop insurance for integrated medical and elderly care services (National Health Commission of the People's Republic of China *et al.* 2019).

Stage 6: piloting the long-term care insurance system (2016–the present)

The rapid growth of ageing population has raised concerns about future levels of expenditure on LTC and how this care should be funded (Comas-Herrera *et al.* 2011: 10). The cost of LTC 'is closely related to the health status of elderly people and care patterns, including home care and institutional care' (Li and Otani 2017: 482). It 'can be high and thereby place a significant burden on users, especially those living on low-income or with high levels of dependency' (OECD 2011: 214). In response, some local governments starting from the 2000s began to look for new models to finance LTC. For example, Shanghai used its health insurance schemes to reimburse nursing care at designated nursing homes, while Nanjing used a means-tested model to finance institutional LTC for the poor elderly (Yang *et al.* 2016: 1392). In 2012, Qingdao, a coastal city in eastern Shandong province, introduced the country's first urban long-term care insurance (LTCI) scheme (United Nations Economic and Social Commission for Asia and Pacific 2015: 14). Such a scheme aimed to provide financial support for older adults who required continuing care, either in an institutional or in a residential location due to suffering from a moderate or severe level of impairment (Lu *et al.* 2017: 183; United Nations Economic and Social Commission for Asia and Pacific 2015: 14). The scheme was funded by money transferred from the urban medical insurance system and from the public welfare fund (United Nations Economic and Social Commission for Asia and Pacific 2015: 14). It covered three types of services provided at prices (per unit) set by LTCI: home care, nursing home care, and intensive care (24-hour a day) at designated Grade II or Grade III hospitals (Lu *et al.* 2017: 184). By June 2014, about 3.7 million people had participated in the urban LTCI scheme, and RMB450 million in direct benefits were paid to 250,000 participants in Qingdao (United Nations Economic and Social Commission for Asia and Pacific 2015: 15).

Based on the successful experience of Qingdao, the Ministry of Human Resources and Social Security (MOHRSS) in June 2016 issued *the Guiding Opinions on Piloting the Long-Term Care Insurance System*, which signified the official initiation of LTCI in China (Wang *et al.* 2018). A total of 15 cities were selected as the pilot sites to implement LTCI (Ministry of Human Resources and Social Security of the People's Republic of China 2016). Chapter 4 will examine the LTCI reform in 15 pilot cities in detail.

Challenges in developing and providing LTC services in China

The provision of accessible and affordable LTC services to older adults has already become an urgent issue to be addressed by the government (Wong and Leung 2012: 571). Nevertheless, LTC services for older adults are marked by insufficient LTC service capacity, urban–rural disparities, the slow development of integrated medical and elderly care services, and enormous variations in service provision, service standards, and service quality. According to *Civil Affairs Development Statistics Bulletin 2018*, there were 29,000 registered elderly care institutions with 3.79 million beds at the end of 2018 (Ministry of Civil Affairs 2019: 4). 'Although the number of institutions has increased rapidly, the service capacity cannot meet the growing need' (United Nations Economic and Social Commission for Asia and the Pacific 2015: 13). Home and community-based services that are promoted by the government and preferred by most older adults 'remain spotty across most cities and towns in China and are virtually nonexistent in rural areas' (Feng *et al.* 2012: 2770). The development of home and community-based services in rural areas 'faces many practical challenges because of the physical environment and the lack of resources and infrastructure' (Feng *et al.* 2012: 2768). Services provided within a rural community 'are generally limited to helping carry water, calling for a doctor, administering medicines and helping with farm work' (United Nations Economic and Social Commission for Asia and the Pacific 2015: 24), which could hardly meet the needs of older adults. Nevertheless, 'cost-effective solutions for community and home-based care that enable older persons to stay at home for as long as possible are urgently needed' (United Nations Economic and Social Commission for Asia and the Pacific 2015: 17). Community-based care services can provide older adults with supplemental care and other needed supports that family members who live and work in distant cities cannot provide (Xu and Chow 2011: 377). They have 'great potential to develop further in quantity and content' (United Nations Economic and Social Commission for Asia and the Pacific 2015: 24).

The development of integrated medical and elderly care services is slow (Deloitte China 2018: 7) because of two main reasons. First, there is the problem of multiple regulators. 'Medical care and elderly care industries are relatively separated and follow two different sets of regulatory systems' (Deloitte China 2018: 7). The entry and regulation of integrated medical care and elderly care industries are under the charge of both civil affairs department and health and family planning department (Deloitte China 2018: 7), while 'matters involving expense reimbursement is under the charge of the human resources and social security departments' (Deloitte China 2018: 7). 'The overlapping functions of competent authorities and unclear responsibilities lead to troubles for the practice of integrating medical and elderly care services' (Deloitte China 2018: 7). Second, most of the registered elderly care institutions lack medical facilities and medical professionals. In China, less than 60 percent of elderly care institutions contained medical consulting rooms while less than 20 percent of them contained rehabilitation rooms (Zhang 2011). Besides, over 60 percent of elderly care institutions in rural areas in western China lacked medical professionals, while over 50 percent of them had no doctors (Zhang 2011). Also, less than 30 percent of nursing assistants received the professional and systematic training needed to be qualified for providing daily assistance or nursing care for older adults (Zhang 2011). There was high turnover among elder care workers due to low wages, difficult working conditions, no clear promotion path, and limited recognition of care work in society (United Nations Economic and Social Commission for Asia and the Pacific 2015: 19–20). While about 93 percent of non-governmental elderly care institutions could provide professional LTC services, less than 40 percent of public elderly care institutions could do so (Zhang 2011) because of 'inadequate funding and limited capacity of services and management' (United Nations Economic and Social Commission for Asia and the Pacific 2015: 6). Most of the elderly care institutions that could provide professional LTC services were found in urban areas.

A survey conducted by Insurance Association of China in 2016 found that most of the ageing respondents thought that the current elderly care system failed to meet their needs. About 40 percent of the 34,790 ageing respondents aged 60 and above thought that home care services could meet their needs (Insurance Association of China 2016). But only 29 percent of ageing respondents thought that nursing homes could meet their needs, while 12 percent of elderly respondents thought that community care institutions could meet their needs (Insurance Association of China 2016). There are enormous variations in service provision, service standards, and service quality (Zhang 2011) due to little regulatory oversight (Feng *et al.* 2012: 2770). Such variations seriously affect equity of access to LTC services, timeliness of LTC service delivery, as well as the sustainability of LTC services (Zhang 2011). There is serious inequality of access to LTC services in rural areas. The government should establish uniform standards for LTC service provision and quality management systems (United Nations Economic and Social Commission for Asia and the Pacific 2015: 9).

Care and support for disabled older adults

At present, 'China is currently facing severe challenges in caring for disabled older adults' (Li and Dai 2019: 127). Family members are still primarily responsible for the care of disabled older adults in the nation (Liu and Sun 2015: 359). Spouse, son, daughter-in-law, and daughter were primary caregivers of fully disabled elders in both urban and rural areas (Zhang 2011). According to *the Survey Report on Chinese Older Adults*, 95 percent of disabled older adults in rural areas relied on their children or spouse to take care of them, which was almost 6 percent higher than their urban counterparts (Chen 2018: 159). Besides, the proportion of daughter-in-law taking care of disabled older adults was higher in rural areas (13.3%) than in urban areas (9.4%) (Chen 2018: 159). Nevertheless, taking care of disabled older adults in the family has a different meaning for spousal caregivers and adult child caregivers (Li and Dai 2019: 127). While spousal caregivers treat caring for a disabled spouse as a marriage commitment (Li and Dai 2019: 137), adult child caregivers, especially those who are married, tend to treat caring for a disabled parent as extra work and are more likely to experience a conflict between the demands of work and of family (Li and Dai 2019: 129). A recent study suggests that designing caregiver interventions in China should take into account the different needs of spouse and adult child caregivers (Li and Dai 2019: 137). For example, spousal caregivers may gain most from respite care (Li and Dai 2019), which provides a temporary relief or rest from their prolonging caregiving responsibilities. Meanwhile, 'adult child caregivers may gain the most from family-focused interventions targeted at strengthening relationships with the care recipient' (Li and Dai 2019: 138). Such interventions help 'deal with diverging expectations or open disagreement between family members as to how to provide care and how to appreciate caregiving efforts' (Pinquart and Sörensen 2011: 9).

China has the problem of uneven spatial distribution of social resources for LTC (Liu and Sun 2015). Only urban communities in the rich eastern coastal provinces are able to provide better professional and social services for disabled older adults (Liu and Sun 2015: 359). Moreover, in the central and western regions, 'many communities can provide only marginal subsidies and rudimentary relief for families with elderly people' (Liu and Sun 2015: 359). The use of LTC services by disabled older adults also varies in urban and rural areas (Li *et al.* 2013). For example, a study found that in Zhejiang province, use of formal care by the urban and high-income disabled older adults was significantly higher than in the rural and low-income disabled elders (Li *et al.* 2013). About 37 percent of disabled older adults in urban areas received formal care while the percentage in rural areas was only about 6 percent (Li *et al.* 2013). The study also found that on average, time spent on formal care was estimated at 612 hours per month for urban residents and 533 hours per month for rural residents (Li *et al.* 2013). Recognizing that there is a lack of access to LTC by rural disabled residents, some local governments in recent years have provided more home care services through assistance offered by volunteers. Since 2017, local governments in Guizhou, Shaanxi, and Yunnan provinces have launched a 'caring rural left-behind older adults' programme (Chu and Zhao 2019). Every selected volunteer who has completed three professional training courses is tasked to oversee at least 30 households and regularly visit them three times a month (Chu and Zhao 2019). During the visits, volunteers provide lonely or disabled older adults with home care services such as bathing, doing housework, and cooking meals (Chu and Zhao 2019). They also chat with rural older adults and help them solve their problems (Chu and Zhao 2019). In 2018, more than 4.7 million yuan was raised by the programme through the online charity platform Tencent Charity to be used as the salaries of volunteers, gifts for older adults, and funds for holding activities (Chu and Zhao 2019). So far, a total of 53 local volunteers have provided home care to 2,652 left-behind older adults in 19 towns (Chu and Zhao 2019).

One of the most pressing problems facing the nation is that there is an obvious imbalance between the huge numbers of disabled older adults who need care beyond what the family can provide and the scarceness of personnel who are qualified to provide the necessary level of professional care to disabled older adults (Liu and Sun 2015: 360). Having only 300,000 nursing assistants is barely enough to meet the needs of more than 30 million disabled older adults in the nation (Liu and Sun 2015: 360). Another problem is that almost half of the elderly care institutions do not accept disabled older adults (Zhang 2011). Some of them would expel older residents when the latter become disabled (Zhang 2011). One possible explanation is that most of the homes for the aged lack professionally licensed staff and assistive devices or facilities to provide appropriate care for disabled older adults. Under this circumstance, disabled older adults and their family members become very helpless because there is no better alternative to provide professional and proper care for disabled older adults.

Dementia care in China

Underdiagnosis and undertreatment of dementia

China has the largest number of people with dementia (PWD) in the world (Jia *et al.* 2020: 81). However, the level of undetected dementia cases is very high in the country due to a lack of understanding and knowledge of dementia among PWD, caregivers, and doctors. A study found that about 93 percent of PWD aged 60 and above went undetected in the country (Chen R. *et al.* 2013: 204). This level of undetected dementia was significantly associated with low education level, low occupational class, and living in rural areas (Chen R. *et al.* 2013: 204) and was 33 percent higher than had been seen in the studies undertaken in high-income countries (Chen R. *et al.* 2013: 207).

Family caregivers can be 'a spouse, son, daughter, and sometimes friends' (Zhang M. *et al.* 2018: 428). Unfortunately, having inadequate knowledge of dementia and mistaking dementia symptoms for normal ageing prevent caregivers from delivering optimal care to PWD (Chen *et al.* 2017). Under most circumstances, family caregivers treat older PWD like children and discipline their behaviours without taking them to seek professional assistance (Hsiao *et al.* 2016: 353). A study found that about 63 percent of 1,387 caregivers of PWD in China reported that 'they had a limited understanding of dementia' (Tang *et al.* 2013: 121). Among caregivers of people who were diagnosed with dementia at the time of screening, only about 43 percent reported taking PWD to the doctor immediately after the first signs or symptoms (Tang *et al.* 2013: 121). The latency period between the appearance of dementia symptoms and seeing a neurologist was 6–12 months (13.7%), 1–2 years (17.4%), 2–3 years (12.6%), and more than 3 years (22.9%) (Tang *et al.* 2013: 121). Unawareness of symptom severity (40.9%), unawareness of signs/symptoms of dementia (36.9%), belief that the symptoms were part of the ageing process (30.5%), and being in denial of dementia (24.4%) were the most common reasons for caregivers not taking PWD to the doctor immediately (Tang *et al.* 2013: 121).

Stigmatization also prevents PWD and their caregivers from seeking proper assistance. 'The term for dementia in Chinese is "*laonian chidai*", which literally means "stupid, demented elderly"' (Chen *et al.* 2017: 7). It is considered an insulting language (Zou *et al.* 2017: 1850) and 'causes an individual to be classified by others in an undesirable, rejected stereotype' (Alzheimer's Disease International 2012: 5). The stigma can bring shame, guilt, a loss of status, and respect to PWD and their caregivers (Xie *et al.* 2016: 318). Some family caregivers who are confronted with threatening behaviour from PWD would lock PWD at home to avoid embarrassment in front of neighbours (Hsiao *et al.* 2016: 354). Shame and stigmatization lead to 'the avoidance of help-seeking behaviors therefore, delaying the diagnosis and the utilization of health and social services' (Kim *et al.* 2019: 100351).

In China, there is the shortage of trained dementia specialists (Jia *et al.* 2020: 85). Doctors 'do not receive formal training or education specific to dementia care as part of their regular curricula in medical school' (Hsiao *et al.* 2016: 343).

They also 'receive very limited on-the-job training for dementia care' (Xu *et al.* 2018: 930). Hence, many of them lack competency and confidence in diagnosing dementia, performing drug or non-drug intervention on PWD, and providing practical counselling about ways to manage caregiver stress or resources that benefit caregivers. In cities, the diagnosis of dementia is made by dementia specialists or neurologists. Dementia specialists are doctors who have 'clinical practice experience treating cognitive disorders over the past 5 years, [and] more than 1 year of learning experience in the dementia centre' (Jia *et al.* 2020: 86). They usually work at memory clinics at tertiary hospitals affiliated with a medical school or university (Jia *et al.* 2020). They make a diagnosis by standard procedures (Jia *et al.* 2020: 85). Afterwards, they initiate 'follow-up on pharmacological and non-pharmacological interventions, including cognitive training and psychosocial intervention' (Wang H. *et al.* 2019: 020321). Neurologists without specialised training in dementia usually work at non-academic tertiary hospitals (Jia *et al.* 2020: 85). They make a diagnosis 'by standard procedures and personal experience' (Jia *et al.* 2020: 85). In county hospitals, however, the diagnosis of dementia is typically made by 'internists with little experience regarding dementia, resulting in high proportions of incorrect and missed diagnoses' (Jia *et al.* 2020: 85).

A study which examined mental health providers' knowledge, attitude, and clinical practices for PWD in Beijing found that mental health providers in both city and town settings indicated a strong desire for training needs due to insufficient knowledge about ways to perform early diagnosis and treatment of dementia (Hsiao *et al.* 2016: 355). They also expressed a strong desire for the government to develop specialist care and referral systems for PWD (Hsiao *et al.* 2016: 353). Another study which examined the training needs of dementia care from the perspective of mental health providers found that there was a significant need to train doctors and nurses in hospital and community-based settings, with the training focusing on clinical knowledge of dementia such as pathogenesis and clinical symptoms of different stages of dementia and approaches for preventing dementia deterioration (Xu *et al.* 2018: 932–4). Moreover, it found that there is a significant need to equip mental health providers with various clinical practice skills, including 'diagnostic skills to differentiate dementia from other diseases, provision of stage-based treatment' (Xu *et al.* 2018: 934), 'caregiving skills to coach informal caregivers for home care' (Xu *et al.* 2018: 934), counselling skills to help caregivers cope with stress, and communication skills to effectively explain diagnosis and treatment of dementia with PWD and their caregivers (Xu *et al.* 2018: 934–5).

Caregiver burden

'Dementia is a progressive neurological disorder that causes a high degree of dependency' (Risco *et al.* 2015: 980). Due to physical, cognitive, and behavioural impairments, PWD need supervision and assistance in their daily living (Åkerborg *et al.* 2016: 1449). In China, over 90 percent of PWD are cared for by family members because of the prevalence of traditional family values and the

underdevelopment of aged care institutions (Yang *et al.* 2019: 414). The Confucian notion of filial piety obligates 'adult children to provide direct care alone and
consider seeking external help as an abnegation of obligation' (Zhang L. *et al.*
2018: 166). Care duties may be split among children (Yang 2019). For example,
a study found that an older PWD lived with 'each of his three sons for 10 days
before rotating, an arrangement that allowed his caregivers to continue working
part time' (Yang 2019). 'People with mild and moderate dementia usually stay at
home' (Wang H. *et al.* 2019: 020321). Often, older people in advanced stages
of dementia 'are transferred from being cared for at home to long-term care in
a nursing home' (Eska *et al.* 2013: 427) when caregivers realized that they can
no longer take care of PWD on their own. The institutionalized care of PWD is
associated with substantial spending on professional LTC services (Schwarzkopf
et al. 2013) and 'is generally considered as a last resort, especially when this possibility is contemplated by spouses' (López *et al.* 2012: 84).

However, dementia service system is underdeveloped in China (Chen *et al.*
2017). There are limited home- and community-based dementia-specific services (Chen *et al.* 2017). Most of the employees in LTC institutions 'are rural
migratory workers, who lack the training needed to manage the behavioural and
psychological symptoms of dementia' (Wu *et al.* 2016: 167). 'Therefore, capacity
building is the primary challenge for improving care quality for PWD' (Wang
et al. 2019: 020321). For example, in a typical elder care home in the urban
districts of Nanjing, 55 percent of direct-care staff were rural migratory workers,
and this proportion was notably higher in non-government and newer elder care
homes (Feng *et al.* 2011: 741). Clinical staff such as professional nurses or physicians were employed in fewer than one-third of all elder care homes in the urban
districts of Nanjing (Feng *et al.* 2011: 741). Due to the lack of well-trained staff
and resources to cope with the needs of PWD, many LTC institutions simply
refuse to admit any PWD (Chen *et al.* 2017; Wu *et al.* 2016). A study in Chengdu
found that five out of the 10 LTC institutions rejected people with advanced
dementia (Wu *et al.* 2016: 167). In Lanxi county, the government-owned rural
LTC institution also refused to admit any older PWD (Wu *et al.* 2016: 169).
Although some LTC institutions admit PWD, they fail to provide any rehabilita-
tive or psychological support for PWD (Wu *et al.* 2016: 169). Meanwhile, the
wait list for public nursing homes that admit PWD is excessively long (David
2018). Under these circumstances, many caregivers have no other choice but
continue to take care of PWD at home.

The nervous and mental symptoms and behaviour disorders of PWD can be
challenging for family caregivers (Zhang M. *et al.* 2018: 431), which can lead to
significant burden and strain. Caregiver burden can be classified into objective
burden and subjective burden (Xiao *et al.* 2014). Objective burden refers to 'time
spent on care, tasks performed and financial problems faced by the caregiver'
(Xiao *et al.* 2014: 6), while 'subjective burden refers to the caregivers' perceived
impact of the objective burden on them' (Xiao *et al.* 2014: 6). A comparative
study that examined the burden experienced by family caregivers of PWD in
China and Australia showed that Chinese caregivers experienced a higher level

of objective burden than their Australian counterparts because of having sig-nificantly longer hours per day on care activities, performing more complex care tasks, the financial burden associated with medical treatments for care recipients with more chronic diseases, and the undeveloped dementia services (Xiao *et al.* 2014). But Chinese family caregivers experienced a lower level of subjective bur-den than their Australian counterparts because of Chinese 'caregivers' acceptance of cultural norms influenced by collectivism and filial piety' (Xiao *et al.* 2014).

In 2018, a study that examined the burden and strain of 212 family caregiv-ers of PWD in China found that 58.5 percent of respondents reported a level of moderate burden (Zhang M. *et al.* 2018: 430), while 65.1 percent of respon-dents reported a high level of strain, with the low income group being more likely to have high levels of burden and strain (Zhang M. *et al.* 2018: 430). Besides, it found that younger caregivers such as children of PWD experienced higher strain because of having difficulties in balancing various social roles (i.e. caregiver, spouse, parent) and having no spare time to do their own things (Zhang M. *et al.* 2018: 431). It also found that 'caregivers who provided care for longer than one year suffered from severe burden and high strain' (Zhang M. *et al.* 2018: 431). Hence, there is a need for family caregivers to 'learn skills or techniques of man-aging stress at multiple levels to avoid burnout' (Xu *et al.* 2018: 936). Besides, there is a need to provide appropriate support and services to reduce the burden and strain of family caregivers of PWD (Zhang M. *et al.* 2018: 431–2). Commu-nity aged care, rehabilitation services, respite care, and affordable treatment for dementia were the most mentioned expectations for government-funded demen-tia care by Chinese caregivers (Xiao *et al.* 2014).

Support for caregivers

'One of the most important forms of aid and support for caregivers is the support group' (Cuijpers *et al.* 1996: 575). Support group which is a form of respite for family caregivers have proved to be effective in reducing the burden on family caregivers of PWD (Gräßel *et al.* 2010: 219). It provides a safe and comfort-able environment for caregivers to exchange personal experiences (Cuijpers *et al.* 1996: 577), share emotions and anxieties (Küçükgüçlü *et al.* 2018: 152), and 'receive advice on how to handle problematic situations they encounter' (Cui-jpers *et al.* 1996: 577). It helps decrease caregivers' burden and stress levels, alleviate depression, prevent feelings of social isolation (Küçükgüçlü *et al.* 2018: 152) while 'increasing their coping skills, well-being, and quality of life' (Küçük-güçlü *et al.* 2018: 152). It also provides 'an opportunity to establish new social contacts and even make friends' (Diehl *et al.* 2003: 158).

In China, the first caregiver support group of dementia was established by Peking University Sixth Hospital in 2000 (Wang H. *et al.* 2019). The activities of the care-giver support group include professionals giving mini-lectures on the essentials of dementia and caregiving skills, cognitive training, relaxation training, group psy-chological intervention, and recreational activities (Wang H. *et al.* 2019). Care-giver support groups have now been established in more than 10 cities, including

Beijing, Changsha, Hangzhou, Shanghai, Taiyuan, Tianjin, Wenzhou, and Xi'an (Alzheimer's Disease International 2017: 13; Wang H. *et al.* 2019).

However, time constraints and other concerns may prevent caregivers of PWD from joining caregiver support groups (Zhang S. Y. *et al.* 2019). A quasi-experimental study conducted in Shanghai showed that caregivers of PWD participating in the group sessions of a caregiving self-management support programme reported 'better health-related quality of life, improved responses to behavioral disturbances, and efficacy in the management of stress than those who received telephone instructions' (Zhang S. Y. *et al.* 2019: 147). However, time constraints caused by jobs, heavy caregiver burden, inability to travel long distances, or a preference for privacy in discussions about their PWD's conditions were reasons for caregivers to choose telephone sessions (Zhang S. Y. *et al.* 2019: 156).

In recent years, the internet, mobile applications, and other digital devices have provided alternative platforms for caregivers to get useful information about dementia and caregiving skills. Web-based interventions have the potential to provide education, training, and support for family caregivers (Zhao *et al.* 2019; Zhang L. *et al.* 2018). A study found that the prototype of a web-based self-directed learning (SDL) system developed for Chinese family caregivers of PWD was able to improve caregivers' knowledge and caregiving skills, improve their caregiving self-efficacy and effectiveness in providing care while reducing their perceived burden and stress (Zhang L. *et al.* 2018: 165–70).

Nowadays, some caregivers choose to receive support from online forums, instant-message groups, and microblogging groups (Liu 2013). For example, a WeChat Group was set up by a hospital in Changsha, Hunan province, to facilitate communication and offer support and encouragement to the growing number of caregivers dealing with the trauma and day-to-day difficulties of looking after PWD due to low cost, better convenience, and round-the-clock availability for the use of WeChat Group (Schmitt and Xi 2018). Moreover, an official account called Yellow Wristband was jointly launched by Eisai China and the China Population Welfare Foundation on WeChat to provide registered users with updated articles on dementia, 'videos on the symptoms of dementia and know-how on caregiving' ('Remember I Love You' 2019), 'information about simple diagnostic tools and a list of the outpatient centers for dementia across China' ('Remember I Love You' 2019).

Meanwhile, some non-profit social organizations in China provide community support for PWD and their caregivers. Jinmei Care, which was established by several family members of PWD in 2012, is a Shanghai-based social organization providing various services for PWD and their caregivers, 'including dementia risk screening, consultations, non-medical interventions, and organizing family support groups' (Sixth Tone 2019). It also helps the district government of Changning 'create the city's first official guidelines for creating a dementia-friendly community' (Sixth Tone 2019). In Guangzhou, Hengfu Social Work Service Association helps PWD and their caregivers through visiting their homes, case follow-up, delaying progression of dementia, and popularizing dementia-related knowledge in the community ('Seek social support for people with dementia' 2018). It also helps caregivers reduce their stress and cope with aggressive or angry behaviours of PWD ('Seek social support for people with dementia' 2018).

Development of EoL care in LTC settings in China

Nursing homes 'have increasingly become the final residence for a growing cohort of individuals living with a variety of chronic life-limiting conditions' (Thompson *et al.* 2018: 49). Since the mid-2000s, the central government has been encouraging nursing homes and other LTC facilities to develop and support EoL care, which aims to maintain the quality of life and comfort of older adults, who are imminently dying, and their families, through management of pain and physical, emotional, social, and spiritual support (Mistry *et al.* 2015; National Cancer Institute n.d.). In 2006, supporting the development of LTC and EoL care became one of the important aspects of developing the elderly services industry (People's Daily Overseas Edition 2017). Subsequently, the provision of EoL care by LTC facilities or the establishment of EoL care institutes has been emphasized in different government documents, including *Guiding Opinions on Promoting the Integration of Medical and Elderly Care Services (2015), the 13th Five-year Plan on Civil Affairs Development (2016), the 13th Five-year Plan on Hygiene and Health (2016),* and *the 13th Five-year Plan on Healthy Ageing (2017)* (National Health Commission of the People's Republic of China 2017; People's Daily Overseas Edition 2017).

In 2017, National Health and Family Planning Commission (NHFPC) of the People's Republic of China issued *Basic Standard and Management Specification of End-of-life Care Centres (Trial),* which was an operational manual on how to set up EoL care centres (e.g. architecture and design, the number of EoL care beds, minimum staffing requirements, basic equipment) as well as how to manage EoL centres (e.g. centre management, quality management, disease control and safety management) (National Health and Family Planning Commission of the People's Republic of China 2017a). In the same year, NHFPC issued *End-of-life Care Practice Guideline (Trial),* which covered the general principles and different ways to provide comfort and care to dying patients (National Health and Family Planning Commission of the People's Republic of China 2017b).

In October 2017, a pilot EoL care programme was first launched in five cities, including Haidian District in Beijing, Putuo District in Shanghai, Changchun city in Jilin province, Luoyang city in Henan province, and Deyang city in Sichuan province (National Health Commission of the People's Republic of China 2017). The pilot programme resulted in the establishment of a three-tiered EoL care system at city level, district level, and street level (Xinhuanet 2019). The number of EoL care institutes increased from 35 to 61, while the number of EoL care beds increased from 412 to 957 (Xinhuanet 2019). In 2018, a total number of 283,000 patients received EoL care in China (Xinhuanet 2019). In May 2019, the government launched the second pilot EoL care programme in 71 cities so that more patients could benefit from EoL care (Xinhuanet 2019). It also called for more research on EoL care, talent acquisition, and improvement in mechanisms which support EoL care (China Daily 2019c).

EoL care is still underdeveloped in the nation and is facing many challenges, including Confucian filial piety values, the death taboo, social stigma, affordability, lack of national strategies and designated funding support for developing EoL care, limited EoL care facilities, the shortage of EoL care professionals at all levels, and no certification programme for EoL care nurses (Lu *et al.* 2018; Yang 2017). Over the past few years, hospitals and NGOs have been introducing some measures to increase public awareness and acceptance of EoL care and increase medical professionals' knowledge and skills of EoL care. For example, NGOs such as the Chinese Association for Life Care promote EoL care through training courses, activities, websites, journals, and so on (Lu *et al.* 2018: 30). Some hospitals introduced the pain education programme to educate cancer patients about ways to take the pain relief medication accurately (Lu *et al.* 2018: 29). Some hospitals educate caregivers about ways to talk about dying and death, provide support for dying family members, deal with emotions, as well as the importance of respecting patients' right to know the truth (Lu *et al.* 2018: 29–30). Besides, EoL care has become a part of continuing education courses available for both doctors and nurses to increase their clinical competencies to provide quality EoL care (Lu *et al.* 2018: 28). For example, courses offered by the Chinese Nurses Association include 'nursing care at the end of life, pain and other symptoms management, communication, ethical issues, spiritual care, and grief and bereavement' (Lu *et al.* 2018: 29). Live courses using audio–video teleconferencing were offered by the Oncology Nursing Committee to over 3,000 nurses in remote provinces (Lu *et al.* 2018: 29). However, the development of EoL care cannot solely rely on the efforts of hospitals and NGOs. It is important for the government to provide more policy support for developing EoL care.

From the patients' perspective, there are five key elements of quality EoL care: 'receiving adequate pain and symptom management, avoiding inappropriate prolongation of dying, achieving a sense of control, relieving burden, and strengthening relationships with loved ones' (Singer *et al.* 1999: 163). From the service providers' perspective, there are six key elements of quality EoL care: 'responding to resident needs, creating a homelike environment, support for families, providing quality care procedures, recognizing death as a significant event, and having sufficient institutional resources' (Brazil *et al.* 2004: 85). The government needs to formulate and implement EoL policies that take into account the views of patients and service providers on quality EoL care so that the culture and experience of dying can be transformed and patients can die in a humane and dignified manner.

Conclusion

To conclude, the growing demand for LTC due to rapidly ageing population has driven the government to establish a three-tiered elder care system consisting of home care, community-based care services, and institutional care. Nevertheless, home care and community-based care services are still underdeveloped. To facilitate the development of LTC, the government needs to improve medical facilities and medical professionals in registered elderly care institutions, increase the number of trained elder care workers, provide better status and treatment for elder care workers, improve older adults' access to LTC services, improve the quality of LTC services through legislation, and develop quality dementia care and EoL care in LTC facilities.

References

Åkerborg, Ö., Lang, A., Wimo, A., Sköldunger, A., Fratiglioni, L., Gaudig, M. and Rosenlund, M. (2016) 'Cost of Dementia and Its Correlation with Dependence', *Journal of Aging and Health*, 28 (8): 1448–64.

Alzheimer's Disease International (2012) *World Alzheimer Report 2012: Overcoming the Stigma of Dementia*. Online. Available HTTP: http://alz.org.sg/wp-content/uploads/2017/04/Report-World-Alzheimer-Report-2012.pdf (accessed 12 March 2020).

Alzheimer's Disease International (2017) *Dementia Friendly Communities: Global Development* (2nd edition). Online. Available HTTP: http://alzheimerheraklion.gr/wp-content/uploads/2017/09/DFC-Global-Developments-2017-Email.pdf (accessed 20 March 2020).

Brazil, K., McAiney, C., Caron-O'Brien, M., Kelley, M. L., O'Krafka, P. and Sturdy-Smith, C. (2004) 'Quality End-of-Life Care in Long-Term Care Facilities: Service Providers' Perspective', *Journal of Palliative Care*, 20 (2): 85–92.

Chen, R., Hu, Z., Chen, R., Ma, Y., Zhang, D. and Wilson, K. (2013) 'Determinants for Undetected Dementia and Late-Life Depression', *The British Journal of Psychiatry*, 203: 203–8.

Chen, T. (2018) 'An Analysis on Demand of Urban and Rural Disabled Elders for Long-Term Care', in J. Dang, Y. Wei and N. Liu (eds.) *Survey Report on the Living Conditions of China's Urban and Rural Older Persons 2018* (Chinese version). Beijing: Social Sciences Academic Press (China), pp. 138–67.

Chen, Z., Yang, X., Song, Y., Song, B., Zhang, Y., Liu, J., Wang, Q. and Yu, J. (2017) 'Challenges of Dementia Care in China', *Geriatrics*, 2: 7.

China Daily (2019c) 'China to Promote End-of-Life Care Services', *China Daily*, 11 June. Online. Available HTTP: http://govt.chinadaily.com.cn/a/201906/11/WS5cff0c0e498e079e6802289e.html (accessed 2 October 2019).

Chu, Y. and Zhao, P. (2019) 'China Focus: Home-Based Elderly Care Deepens in Rural China', *Xinhuanet*, 9 February. Online. Available HTTP: www.xinhuanet.com/english/2019-02/09/c_137809319.htm (accessed 4 October 2020).

Comas-Herrera, A., Malley, J., Wittenberg, R., Hu, B. and Jagger, C. (2011) 'Disability, Dementia and the Future Costs of Long-Term Care', *Eurohealth*, 17 (2–3): 10–12.

The Congressional-Executive Commission on China (n.d.) *Provisional Regulations on the Registration and Management of Civil, Non-Enterprise Institutions*. Online. Available HTTP: www.cecc.gov/resources/legal-provisions/temporary-regulations-on-the-registration-and-management-of-non-1#body-chinese (accessed 29 July 2019).

Cuijpers, P., Hosman, C. M. H. and Munnichs, J. M. A. (1996) 'Change Mechanisms of Support Groups for Caregivers of Dementia Patients', *International Psychogeriatrics*, 8 (4): 575–87.

Dai, J. H. (2016) *Planning and Design of Medical-Nursing Combined Residential Facilities for the Aged in Urban Community* (Chinese version). Beijing: China Architecture & Building Press.

Dai, W. (2019) 'V-shaped Responsibility of China's Social Welfare for the Elderly: Based on Analyzing Historical Evolution and Future Sustainability', *Sustainability*, 11: 2385.

David, M. (2018) *Tech Gadgets: The Poster Child of the Chinese Market for Alzheimer's*. Online. Available HTTP: https://daxueconsulting.com/tech-gadgets-for-chinese-market-for-alzheimers/ (accessed 21 March 2020).

Deloitte China (2018) *Trends in Integrated Elderly Care and Medical Services in China*. Online. Available HTTP: www2.deloitte.com/content/dam/Deloitte/cn/Documents/life-sciences-health-care/deloitte-cn-lshc-the-last-mile-of-senior-care-en-181024.pdf (accessed 8 December 2020).

Diehl, J., Mayer, T., Förstl, H. and Kurz, A. (2003) 'A Support Group for Caregivers of Patients with Frontotemporal Dementia', *Dementia*, 2 (2): 151–61.

Ding, H. (2011) 'China's "Socializing Social Welfare" Policy: A Study on Service Quality in Society-Run Homes for the Aged in Beijing', *China Journal of Social Work*, 4 (2): 137–51.

Eska, K., Graessel, E., Donath, C., Schwarzkopf, L., Lauterberg, J. and Holle, R. (2013) 'Predictors of Institutionalization of Dementia Patients in Mild and Moderate Stages: A 4-Year Prospective Analysis', *Dementia and Geriatric Cognitive Disorder Extra*, 3: 426–45.

Feng, Q. (2018) *A 79-Year-Old Elder Is Abused by the Nanny: Why Is the Nanny So Cruel?* (Chinese version). Online. Available HTTP: http://dy.163.com/v2/article/detail/E43TP7D00521A9C4.html (accessed 26 July 2019).

Feng, Z., Guan, X., Feng, X., Liu, C., Zhan, H. J. and Mor, V. (2014) 'Long-Term Care in China: Reining in Market Forces through Regulatory Oversight', in V. Mor, T. Leone and A. Maresso (eds.) *Regulating Long-Term Care Quality: An International Comparison*, Cambridge, England; New York: Cambridge University Press, pp. 409–43.

Feng, Z., Liu, C., Guan, X. and Mor, V. (2012) 'China's Rapidly Aging Population Creates Policy Challenges in Shaping a Viable Long-Term Care System', *Health Affairs*, 31 (12): 2764–73.

Feng, Z., Zhan, H. J., Feng, X., Liu, C., Sun, M. and Mor, V. (2011) 'An Industry in the Making: The Emergence of Institutional Elder Care in Urban China', *Journal of the American Geriatrics Society*, 59: 738–44.

Glinskaya, E. and Feng, Z. (2018) 'Overview', in E. Glinskaya and Z. Feng (eds.) *Options for Aged Care in China: Building an Efficient and Sustainable Aged Care System*, Washington, DC: World Bank, pp. 1–78.

Gräßel, E., Trilling, A., Donath, C. and Luttenberger, K. (2010) 'Support Groups for Dementia Caregivers: Predictors for Utilisation and Expected Quality from a Family Caregiver's Point of View: A Questionnaire Survey Part I', *BMC Health Services Research*, 10: 219.

Hsiao, H., Liu, Z., Xu, L., Huang, Y. and Chi, I. (2016) 'Knowledge, Attitudes, and Clinical Practices for Patients with Dementia Among Mental Health Providers in China: City and Town Differences', *Gerontology & Geriatrics Education*, 37 (4): 342–58.

Insurance Association of China (2016) *The 2016 Survey on Long-Term Care in China* (Chinese version). Online. Available HTTP: www.199it.com/archives/565396.html (accessed 1 October 2019).

Jia, L., Quan, M., Fu, Y., Zhao, T., Li, Y., Wei, C., Tang, Y., Qin, Q., Wang, F., Qiao, Y., Shi, S., Wang, Y., Du, Y., Zhang, J., Zhang, J., Luo, B., Qu, Q., Zhou, C., Gauthier,

S. and Jia, J. (2020) 'Dementia in China: Epidemiology, Clinical Management, and Research Advances', *The Lancet Neurology*, 19 (1): 81–92.

Jiang, G. (2017) 'A Nanny in Hunan Is Arrested for Abusing an Elderly', (Chinese version). *The Paper*, 11 November. Online. Available HTTP: www.thepaper.cn/ newsDetail_forward_1853364> (accessed 26 July 2019).

Kim, S., Werner, P., Richardson, A. and Anstey, K. J. (2019) 'Dementia Stigma Reduction (DESeRvE): Study Protocol for a Randomized Controlled Trial of an Online Intervention Program to Reduce Dementiarelated Public Stigma', *Contemporary Clinical Trials Communications*, 14: 100351.

Küçükgüçlü, Ö., Söylemez, B. A., Yener, G. and Işık, A. T. (2018) 'The Effects of Support Groups on Dementia Caregivers: A Mixed Method Study', *Geriatric Nursing*, 39 (2): 151–6.

Kwan, K. K. (2000) 'Counseling Chinese Peoples: Perspectives of Filial Piety', *Asian Journal of Counselling*, 7 (1): 23–41.

Lei, X., Strauss, J., Tian, M. and Zhao, Y. (2015) 'Living Arrangements of the Elderly in China: Evidence from the CHARLS National Baseline', *China Economic Journal*, 8 (3): 191–214.

Li, F. and Otani, J. (2017) 'Financing Elderly People's Long-Term Care Needs: Evidence from China', *The International Journal of Health Planning and Management*, 33 (2): 479–88.

Li, L. W., Long, Y., Essex, E. L., Sui, Y. and Gao, L. (2012) 'Elderly Chinese and Their Family Caregivers' Perceptions of Good Care: A Qualitative Study in Shandong, China', *Journal of Gerontological Social Work*, 55 (7): 609–25.

Li, M. and Dai, H. (2019) 'Determining the Primary Caregiver for Disabled Older Adults in Mainland China: Spouse Priority and Living Arrangements', *Journal of Family Therapy*, 41: 126–41.

Li, M., Zhang, Y., Zhang, Z., Zhang, Y., Zhou, L. and Chen, K. (2013) 'Rural-Urban Differences in the Long-Term Care of the Disabled Elderly in China', *PLOS ONE*, 8 (11): e79955.

Liao Shen Evening News (2018) *A 86-Year-Old Elder Is Beaten by a Nanny for Eight Times within Half a Month* (Chinese version). 13 August. Online. Available HTTP: www.ln.chinanews.com/news/2018/0813/168971.html (accessed 26 July 2019).

Liu, N. (2018) 'The Basic Situation of China's Urban and Rural Elderly and Their Relationship with Family Members', in J. Dang, Y. Wei and N. Liu (eds.) *Survey Report on the Living Conditions of China's Urban and Rural Older Persons 2018* (Chinese version). Beijing: Social Sciences Academic Press (China), pp. 55–108.

Liu, T. and Sun, L. (2015) 'An Apocalyptic Vision of Ageing in China: Old Age Care for the Largest Elderly Population in the World', *Zeitschrift für Gerontologie und Geriatrie*, 48 (4): 354–64.

Liu, Z. (2013) 'Caregivers of Dementia Patients Seek Support Groups', *China Daily*, 16 October. Online. Available HTTP: www.chinadaily.com.cn/life/2013-10/16/ content_17035617.htm (accessed 20 March 2020).

López, J., Losada, A., Romero-Moreno, R., Márquez-González, M. and Martínez-Martín, P. (2012) 'Factors Associated with Dementia Caregivers' Preference for Institutional Care', *Neurología*, 27 (2): 83–9.

Lu, B., Mi, H., Zhu, Y. and Piggott, J. (2017) 'A Sustainable Long-Term Health Care System for Aging China: A Case Study of Regional Practice', *Health Systems & Reform*, 3 (3): 182–90.

Lu, Y., Gu, Y. and Yu, W. (2018) 'Hospice and Palliative Care in China: Development and Challenges', *Asia-Pacific Journal of Oncology Nursing*, 5 (1): 26–32.

Ministry of Civil Affairs (2009) *The National Occupational Standards for Elder Care Workers* (Chinese version). Online. Available HTTP: http://jnjd.mca.gov.cn/ article/zyjd/ylhly/201003/20100300063434.shtml (accessed 29 July 2019).

Ministry of Civil Affairs (2019) *Civil Affairs Development Statistics Bulletin 2018* (Chinese version). Online. Available HTTP: http://images3.mca.gov.cn/www2017/ file/201908/1565920301578.pdf (accessed 1 October 2019).

Ministry of Human Resources and Social Security of the People's Republic of China (2016) *The Guiding Opinions on Piloting the Long-Term Care Insurance System* (Chinese version). Online. Available HTTP: http://www.mohrss.gov.cn/ SYrlzyhshbzb/shehuibaozhang/zcwj/yiliao/201607/t20160705_242951.html (accessed 28 November 2020).

Mistry, B., Bainbridge, D., Bryant, D., Toyofuku, S. T. and Seow, H. (2015) 'What Matters Most for End-of-Life Care? Perspectives from Community-Based Palliative Care Providers and Administrators', *BMJ Open*, 5: e007492.

Mok, B. and Liu, J. (1999) 'In the Service of Market Socialism: The Quest for a Welfare Model in China', *The Journal of Sociology & Social Welfare*, 26 (3): 137–50.

National Cancer Institute (n.d.) *NCI Dictionary of Cancer Terms: End-of-Life Care*. Online. Available HTTP: www.cancer.gov/publications/dictionaries/cancer-terms/ def/end-of-life-care (accessed 1 October 2019).

National Health and Family Planning Commission of the People's Republic of China (2017a) *Basic Standard and Management Specification of End-of-Life Care Centres (Trial)* (Chinese version). Online. Available HTTP: www.st120.cn/ NewsDetail/89/523.html?fol=News (accessed 2 October 2019).

National Health and Family Planning Commission of the People's Republic of China (2017b) *End-of-Life Care Practice Guideline (Trial)* (Chinese version). Online. Available HTTP: www.nhc.gov.cn/yzygj/s3593/201702/83797c0261a94781b1 58dbd76666b717.shtml (accessed 2 October 2019).

National Health Commission of the People's Republic of China (2017) *Responses to No. 8189 Suggestions in the Fifth Session of the Twelfth National People's Congress* (Chinese version). Online. Available HTTP: www.nhc.gov.cn/wjw/jiany/201801/ 3a9b4b91909845f9acc68ef4d1d86976.shtml (accessed 1 October 2019).

National Health Commission of the People's Republic of China, Ministry of Civil Affairs, National Development and Reform Commission, Ministry of Education, Ministry of Finance, Ministry of Human Resources and Social Security, Ministry of National Resources, Ministry of Housing and Urban-rural Development, State Administration for Market Regulation, National Healthcare Security Administration, National Administration of Traditional Chinese Medicine and China National Committee on Ageing (2019) *Opinions on Further Accelerating the Development of Integrated Medical and Elderly Care Services* (Chinese version). Online. Available HTTP: www.gov. cn/xinwen/2019-10/26/content_5445271.htm (accessed 8 December 2020).

OECD (2011) *Help Wanted? Providing and Paying for Long-Term Care*. Online. Available HTTP: https://read.oecd-ilibrary.org/social-issues-migration-health/ help-wanted_9789264097759-en#page1 (accessed 12 December 2020).

Office of the National Commission on Ageing, National Development and Reform Commission, Ministry of Education, Ministry of Civil Affairs, Ministry of Labor and Social Security, Ministry of Finance, Ministry of Housing and Urban-Rural Development, Ministry of Health, Population and Family Planning Commission and State Administration of Taxation (2006) *Opinions on Accelerating the Development of the*

Elderly Services Industry (Chinese version). Online. Available HTTP: www.yanglaocn. com/shtml/20151125/144845381161167.html (accessed 30 July 2019).

Office of the National Commission on Ageing, National Development and Reform Commission, Ministry of Education, Ministry of Civil Affairs, Ministry of Labor and Social Security, Ministry of Finance, Ministry of Housing and Urban-rural Development, Ministry of Health, Population and Family Planning Commission and State Administration of Taxation (2008) *Opinions on Comprehensively Promotion the Work of Home Care Services* (Chinese version). Online. Available HTTP: www.gov.cn/zwgk/2008-02/25/content_899738.htm (accessed 31 July 2019).

Office of the National Health and Family Planning Commission and Ministry of Civil Affairs (2016a) *Circular on Determining the First Batch of Pilot National Units for Integrated Medical and Elderly Care Services* (Chinese version). Online. Available HTTP: www.nhc.gov.cn/rkjcyjtfzs/zcwj2/201606/51233c30598c4751a57d631 65d5e277f.shtml (accessed 8 December 2020).

Office of the National Health and Family Planning Commission and Ministry of Civil Affairs (2016b) *Circular on Determining the Second Batch of Pilot National Units for Integrated Medical and Elderly Care Services* (Chinese version). Online. Available HTTP: www.nhc.gov.cn/jtfzs/s3581/201609/46bad905688f403c8eae4ca5 6fbb7d84.shtml (accessed 8 December 2020).

People's Daily Overseas Edition (2017) 'Attention Should Be Paid to End-of-Life Care', (Chinese version), *People's Daily Overseas Edition*, 20 March. Online. Available HTTP: www.cn-healthcare.com/article/20170320/content-490738.html (accessed 2 October 2019).

Pinquart, M. and Sörensen, S. (2011) 'Spouses, Adult Children, and Children-in-Law as Caregivers of Older Adults: A Meta-Analytic Comparison', *Psychology and Aging*, 26 (1): 1–14.

Qu, Q. (2015) *The Legal Dilemma for Homes for the Aged* (Chinese version). Online. Available HTTP: www.lawyers.org.cn/info/98aa4fc5ba0f4e5b832013a63505 6cf6 (accessed 29 July 2019).

Remember I Love You: A Project to Improve Understanding of Dementia in China (2019) Online. Available HTTP: www.eisai.com/hhc/activity/063.html (accessed 20 March 2020).

Risco, E., Cabrera, E., Jolley, D., Stephan, A., Karlsson, S., Verbeek, H., Saks, K., Hupli, M., Sourdet, S. and Zabalegui, A. (2015) 'The Association between Physical Dependency and the Presence of Neuropsychiatric Symptoms, with the Admission of People with Dementia to a Long-Term Care Institution: A Prospective Observational Cohort Study', *International Journal of Nursing Studies*, 52: 980–7.

Schwarzkopf, L., Menn, P., Leidl, R., Graessel, E. and Holle, R. (2013) 'Are Community-Living and Institutionalized Dementia Patients Cared for Differently? Evidence on Service Utilization and Costs of Care from German Insurance Claims Data', *BMC Health Services Research*, 13: 2.

Shum, M. H. Y., Lou, V. W. Q., He, K. Z. J., Chen, C. C. H. and Wang, J. (2015) 'The "Leap Forward" in Nursing Home Development in Urban China: Future Policy Directions', *JAMDA*, 16: 784–89.

Singer, P. A., Martin, D. K. and Kelner, M. (1999) 'Quality End-of-Life Care: Patients' Perspective', *JAMA*, 281 (2): 163–8.

Schmitt, L. and Xi, Z. (2018) *The Wechat Group Helping People Deal with Dementia*. Online. Available HTTP: https://news.cgtn.com/news/32636a4d79677a63335 66d54/share_p.html (accessed 20 March 2020).

Seek Social Support for People with Dementia (Chinese version) (2018) Online. Available HTTP: www.sohu.com/a/221712306_825958 (accessed 20 March 2020).

Sixth Tone (2019) *The Dementia Campaigners Getting Communities Involved in Care.* Online. Available HTTP: www.sixthtone.com/news/1004585/the-dementia-campaigners-getting-communities-involved-in-care (accessed 20 March 2020).

The State Council (2011a) *The 12th Five-Year Development Plan of Undertakings on Ageing* (Chinese version). Online. Available HTTP: www.gov.cn/zhengce/content/2011-09/23/content_6338.htm (accessed 31 July 2019).

The State Council (2011b) *The Development Plan for the Elderly Service System (2011–2015)* (Chinese version). Online. Available HTTP: www.gov.cn/zwgk/2011-12/27/content_2030503.htm (accessed 1 August 2019).

The State Council (2013) *Several Opinions on Accelerating the Development of Elderly Service Industry* (Chinese version). Online. Available HTTP: www.gov.cn/zhengce/content/2013-09/13/content_7213.htm (accessed 1 August 2019).

The State Council (2015) *Guiding Opinions on Promoting the Integration of Medical and Elderly Care Services* (Chinese version). Online. Available HTTP: www.gov.cn/zhengce/content/2015-11/20/content_10328.htm (accessed 1 August 2019).

Tang, B., Harary, E., Kurzman, R., Mould-Quevedo, J., Pan, S., Yang, J. and Qiao, J. (2013) 'Clinical Characterization and the Caregiver Burden of Dementia in China', *Value in Health Regional Issue*, 2: 118–26.

Thompson, G. N., McClement, S. E., Labun, N. and Klaasen, K. (2018) 'Developing and Testing a Nursing Home End-of-Life Care Chart Audit Tool', *BMC Palliative Care*, 17: 49.

United Nations Economic and Social Commission for Asia and the Pacific (2015) *Long-Term Care of Older Persons in China*. Online. Available HTTP: www.unescap.org/sites/default/files/SDD%20Working%20Paper%20Ageing%20Long%20Term%20Care%20China%20v1-2.pdf (accessed 5 October 2019).

Wang, H., Xie, H., Qu, Q., Chen, W., Sun, Y., Zhang, N., Liu, Y., Li, T., Chan, K. Y., Gauthier, S. and Yu, X. (2019) 'The Continuum of Care for Dementia: Needs, Resources and Practice in China', *Journal of Global Health*, 9 (2): 020321.

Wang, Q., Zhou, Y., Ding, X. and Ying, X. (2018) 'Demand for Long-Term Care Insurance in China', *International Journal of Environmental Research and Public Health*, 15: 6.

Wong, Y. C. and Leung, J. (2012) 'Long-Term Care in China: Issues and Prospects', *Journal of Gerontological Social Work*, 55 (7): 570–86.

Wu, B., Mao, Z. and Zhong, R. (2009) 'Long-Term Care Arrangements in Rural China: Review of Recent Developments', *JAMDA*, 10 (7): 472–7.

Wu, C., Gao, L., Chen, S. and Dong, H. (2016) 'Care Services for Elderly People with Dementia in Rural China: A Case Study', *Bulletin of the World Health Organization*, 94 (3): 167–73.

Xiao, L. D., Wang, J., He, G., De Bellis, A., Verbeeck, J. and Kyriazopoulos, H. (2014) 'Family Caregiver Challenges in Dementia Care in Australia and China: A Critical Perspective', *BMC Geriatrics*, 14: 6.

Xie, C., Chen, D., Jin, C., Du, L., Wang, C., Xin, H., Feng, Z., Yang, Y. and Ding, H. (2016) 'Higher Incidence of Deteriorated Mental Health in Older People Being Mistakenly Labeled as Dementia: A Two-Year Consecutive Community-Dwelling Study in Shanghai, China, *The Tohoku Journal of Experimental Medicine*, 238: 317–24.

Xinhuanet (2019) 'End-of-Life Care Services Are Developed Quickly in China: A Total Number of 283,000 Patients Received End-of-Life Care', (Chinese version),

Xinhuanet, 3 June. Online. Available HTTP: www.xinhuanet.com/politics/2019-06/03/c_1124578776.htm (accessed 2 October 2019).

Xu, L., Hsiao, H., Deng, W. and Chi, I. (2018) 'Training Needs for Dementia Care in China from the Perspectives of Mental Health Providers: Who, What, and How', *International Psychogeriatrics*, 30 (7), 929–40.

Xu, Q. and Chow, J. C. (2011) 'Exploring the Community-Based Service Delivery Model: Elderly Care in China', *International Social Work*, 54 (3): 374–87.

Yang, F. (2019) *China Mustn't Forget Its Dementia Caregivers*. Online. Available HTTP: www.sixthtone.com/news/1003622/china-mustnt-forget-its-dementia-caregivers (accessed 28 March 2020).

Yang, F., Ran, M. and Luo, W. (2019) 'Depression of Persons with Dementia and Family Caregiver Burden: Finding Positives in Caregiving as a Moderator', *Geriatrics & Gerontology International*, 19: 414–8.

Yang, W., He, A. J., Fang, L. and Mossialos, E. (2016) 'Financing Institutional Long-Term Care for the Elderly in China: A Policy Evaluation of New Models', *Health Policy and Planning*, 31: 1391–1401.

Yang, Y. (2017) *Development of End-of-Life Care in China*. Online. Available HTTP: http://cmaao.org/ (accessed 2 October 2019).

Zhan, H. J., Liu, G., Guan, X. and Bai, H. (2006) 'Recent Developments in Institutional Elder Care in China', *Journal of Aging & Social Policy*, 18 (2): 85–108.

Zhang, K. (2011) *Press Conference Transcript: Current Situation of Old-Age Disability among Urban and Rural Elders in China* (Chinese version). Online. Available HTTP: www.docin.com/p-1453165691.html (accessed 28 September 2019).

Zhang, L., Shair, J. Y., Wang, Y., Li, R. and Chen, H. (2018) 'Usability Assessment of a Web-Based Self-Directed Learning (SDL) System for Chinese Dementia Caregivers', in J. Zhou and G. Salvendy (eds.) *Human Aspects of IT for the Aged Population: Applications in Health, Assistance and Entertainment: 4th International Conference, ITAP 2018, Held as Part of HCI International 2018, Las Vegas, NV, USA, July 15–20, 2018, Proceedings, Part II*, Cham: Springer International Publishing, pp. 165–76.

Zhang, M., Chang, Y., Liu, Y. J., Gao, L. and Porock, D. (2018) 'Burden and Strain among Familial Caregivers of Patients with Dementia in China', *Issues in Mental Health Nursing*, 39 (5), 427–32.

Zhang, S. Y., Wu, F., Tang, D. L., Rong, X. S., Guo, Q. H., Fang, M., Zhao, Q. H. and Zhao, Y. H. (2019) 'Pilot Testing the Caregiver Self-Management Intervention for Caregivers of Relatives with Dementia', *Geriatric Nursing*. Available online 26 August 2019.

Zhang, W. (2012) Ageing China: Changes and Challenges. Online. Available HTTP: www.bbc.com/news/world-asia-china-19572056 (accessed 7 August 2015).

Zhang, Y. (2013) 'Meeting the Ageing Challenge: China's Social Care Policy for the Elderly', in G. Wang and Y. Zheng (eds) *China: Development and Governance*. Singapore: World Scientific.

Zhao, Y., Feng, H., Hu, M., Hu, H., Li, H., Ning, H., Chen, H., Liao, L. and Peng, L. (2019) 'Web-Based Interventions to Improve Mental Health in Home Caregivers of People with Dementia: Meta-Analysis', *Journal of Medical Internet Research*, 21 (5): e13415.

Zou, Y., Song, N., Hu, Y., Gao, Y., Zhang, Y., Zhao, Q., Guo, Q., Li, X., Li, G., Xiao, S., Chen, S., Ren, R. and Wang, G. (2017) 'Caregivers' Attitude toward Disclosure of Alzheimer's Disease Diagnosis in Urban China', *International Psychogeriatrics*, 29 (11): 1849–55.

4 Long-term care insurance reform in China

Introduction

In China, the need for establishing the long-term care (LTC) financing system is getting more acute with the rapid weakening of the traditional family support for older persons as a result of a series of social factors, including the decline in marriage rates (Shu 2017), large-scale rural–urban migration, the one-child policy, rapidly ageing population (Zhang and Goza 2006), and an increase in LTC costs (Li and Otani 2018). LTC financing systems developed in different cities starting from the 2000s include medical insurance schemes covering LTC, stand-alone long-term care insurance (LTCI) schemes, and tax-funded, means-tested, safety-net LTC schemes (Yang *et al.* 2016). Diverse developments in LTC financing systems are natural and inevitable, given the sheer size of China, and the huge variations in social conditions of different parts of the country. In June 2016, the central government issued a central directive on LTC financing (Zhang and Yu 2019). The central directive provided a framework for a more uniform development of LTC financing in China, while allowing a certain degree of discretion on the part of local governments. This chapter describes and analyses LTCI schemes of the first 15 pilot cities in details.

The Guiding Opinions on Piloting the LTCI System (2016, 2020)

In June 2016, the Ministry of Human Resources and Social Security (MOHRSS) issued the Guiding Opinions on Piloting the Long-Term Care Insurance System (hereafter the 2016 Guiding Opinions), which signified the official initiation of LTCI in China (Ministry of Human Resources and Social Security of the People's Republic of China 2016; Wang *et al.* 2018). Another Guiding Opinions document was jointly issued by National Healthcare Security Administration and Ministry of Finance in 2020, adding 14 more cities to the list of pilot cities, with the essential policy parameters remaining basically the same (National Healthcare Security Administration and Ministry of Finance 2020). The key elements of the guidelines are discussed in this section.

Participating cities: A total of 15 cities from 14 provinces or provincial-level municipalities have been selected as the first batch of pilot sites to implement

DOI: 10.4324/9780429057199-4

LTCI (Glinskaya *et al.* n.d.: 14). They are Anqing (Anhui province), Changc-hun (Jilin province), Chengde (Hebei province), Chengdu (Sichuan province), Chongqing (municipality), Jingmen (Hubei province), Guangzhou (Guangdong province), Nantong (Jiangsu province), Ningbo (Zhejiang province), Qingdao (Shandong province), Qiqihar (Heilongjiang province), Shangrao (Jiangxi province), Shanghai (municipality), Shihezi (Uygur Autonomous Region of Xinjiang), and Suzhou (Jiangsu province) (Ministry of Human Resources and Social Security of the People's Republic of China 2016). They are selected based on three common characteristics. First, they have a high percentage of disabled elderly population (Guo 2019). Second, they have relatively well-developed elder care service industry (Guo 2019). Third, they have the financial capacity to support the implementation of LTCI (Guo 2019). Municipal governments can determine the details for the implementation of LTCI based on the general guidelines provided by the 2016 Guiding Opinions (Glinskaya *et al.* n.d.: 14). In 2020, 14 more cities/districts were added to the list. They are Shijingshan District (Beijing municipality), Tianjin (Tianjin municipality), Jincheng (Shanxi province), Huhhot (Inner Mongolia Autonomous Region), Panjin (Liaoning province), Fuzhou (Fujian province), Kaifeng (Henan province), Xiangtan (Hunan province), Nanning (Guangxi Zhuang Autonomous Region), Qianxinan Buyei and Miao Autonomous Prefecture (Guizhou province), Kunming (Yunnan province), Hanzhong (Shaanxi province), Gannan Tibetan Autonomous Prefecture (Gansu province), and Urumqi (Xinjian Uighur Autonomous Region) (National Healthcare Security Administration and Ministry of Finance 2020).

Objectives : The 2016 Guiding Opinions document has two stated objectives. First, it aims to establish an insurance system in a number of cities to provide financial support to basic care in activities of daily living (ADLs) and related medical and nursing care to persons with long-term disability (Ministry of Human Resources and Social Security of the People's Republic of China 2016). Second, it aims to provide a nationwide LTCI policy framework with the experience accumulated in the pilot cities (Ministry of Human Resources and Social Security of the People's Republic of China 2016).

Insured population : Enrolment in the LTCI is tightly linked to an individual's medical insurance status (Chang *et al.* 2020). LTCI mainly covers individuals enrolled in Urban Employee Basic Medical Insurance (UEBMI), which is a compulsory medical insurance for urban employees and retirees in both the public and private sectors (Luk 2020). It allows cities to expand the coverage, based on local circumstances, and some cities have included residents enrolled in Urban Resident Basic Medical Insurance (URBMI), which covers 'non-working urban residents, including young children, primary and secondary school students, the severely disabled and the elderly' (Luk 2017: 63). Some cities have included residents enrolled in Urban and Rural Resident Basic Medical Insurance (URRBMI), which covers residents in rural areas as well. It has been said that participation in LTCI is voluntary (Feng *et al.* 2020: 1366). However, it is not clear whether there are ways for enrollees in UEBMI or URBMI or URRBMI to opt out of LTCI if they choose to do so, especially for schemes which require individuals to contribute additional amounts on the top of the regular medical insurance contributions.

Beneficiaries and benefits : Beneficiaries are confined to insured persons under UEBMI (and URBMI or URRBMI if applicable) who have been disabled in a severe manner for an extended period of time, after going through disability assessment for eligibility. Benefits include partial expense reimbursement of service expenses for ADLs care and related medical and nursing care. Each pilot city can determine the qualified beneficiaries and specific benefits covered, according to the city's and the scheme's financial status. It may gradually adjust the scope of beneficiaries and benefits.

Financing sources : LTCI is financed by funds transferred from the social pooling fund (SPF) of UEBMI. The percentage of UEBMI premium contributed by employees can be adjusted upward (Ministry of Human Resources and Social Security of the People's Republic of China 2016). The guidelines required the adherence to the rules of 'balancing revenues and expenses, with a small surplus maintained' (Glinskaya *et al.* n.d.: 12) and the 'reimbursement rates controlled at around 70 percent of allowable expenses' (Glinskaya *et al.* n.d.: 13). Substantive co-payment by users is, therefore, expected from all LTCI schemes.

Payment for services : Cities can appoint LTC providers through contracting. The Guiding Opinions requires municipal governments to supervise and audit service providers and specify protocols and standards for their contractors. It allows both the benefit package and the mode for payment for services to vary among the cities. Payment mode can be on fee-for-service basis or on a per diem basis. Reimbursement of service expenses by LTCI could be a fixed amount for the type of service or a percentage of the full service fee. There are no cash benefit payments. There are no restrictions on the amount that the provider can charge the users on top of the insurance payment (Feng *et al.* 2020: 1366).

Comparing key features of LTCI schemes in the 15 pilot cities

This section examines key features of LTCI schemes in the first 15 pilot cities based on the relevant policy documents issued by government agencies from these pilot cities (Office of the People's Government of Anqing City 2017; Ministry of Human Resources and Social Security of Chongqing City and Ministry of Finance of Chongqing City 2017; Office of the People's Government of Changchun City 2015; Office of the People's Government of Qiqihaer City 2017; Office of the People's Government of Ningbo City 2017; The People's Government of Chengde City 2016; The People's Government of Chengdu City 2017; Ministry of Human Resources and Social Security of Guangzhou City *et al.* 2017; The People's Government of Jingmen City 2016; The People's Government of Nantong City 2015; The People's Government of Qingdao City 2014; Shanghai Municipal People's Government 2016a; Office of the People's Government of Shangrao City 2016; The People's Government of Shihezi City

2017; The People's Government of Suzhou City 2017). The insured population, the financing sources, and the arrangement for contribution in the 15 pilot cities are compared in the following.

Insured population : All LTCI schemes in the 15 pilot cities cover UEBMI enrollees. LTCI schemes in Changchun and Shihezi cover URBMI enrollees also, while LTCI schemes in Qingdao, Nantong, Jingmen, Suzhou, and Shanghai cover URRBMI enrollees as well.

Financing sources : Funding for LTCI includes transfer from the SPF of one or more of the city's medical insurance schemes, individual contributions, additional employer's contribution, transfer from designated lottery fund, and government subsidies. The share from each of the sources varies from city to city. For the individual contribution part, the contribution can wholly or partly come from an individual's Medical Savings Account (MSA) under UEBMI schemes. Funds in MSAs are considered as assets of the individuals and are generally used to pay for out-of-pocket (OOP) expenses. Since URBMI and URRBMI schemes normally do not have MSAs, people enrolled in these two schemes have to make individual contributions to LTCI through OOP payment or transferring money from their pension accounts.

For transfer from the medical insurance scheme, all LTCI schemes including Shanghai receive funds from the SPF of UEBMI, while some cities also extend the practice to URBMI and URRBMI. The case of Shanghai requires further elaboration here. Article 26 of the Shanghai government document states that premium contribution from UEBMI participants, their employers, and URRBMI participants stated in Article 6 would not be carried out in the pilot phase. Instead, LTCI would be financed by fund transferred from the surplus of the SPF of the UEBMI fund (Shanghai Municipal People's Government 2016a). Hence, LTCI enrollees in Shanghai do not have to make individual contribution until further notice.

For individual contributions, most cities simply deduct an amount from an individual MSA of UEBMI, without requiring an individual to make extra payment. Some cities require additional contribution from individuals to LTCI, especially for participants covered under URBMI and URRBMI, as these schemes normally do not have an individual MSA.

Not all cities require additional employer's contribution. Some cities also do not receive government subsidies for their LTCI schemes. Some receive funding from a designated lottery fund.

Contribution arrangements : The contribution arrangements from each of the funding source to the LTCI scheme of the 15 pilot cities are quite different.

The first group, Guangzhou and Ningbo, has a single source of funding. These cities are totally dependent on transfer from the SPF of basic medical insurance (BMI) schemes.

The second group of cities, comprising Anqing, Qiqihar, Chongqing, Qingdao, and Changchun, has two funding tracks. Their LTCI schemes are financed by money transferred from the SPF of BMI schemes and additional individual contributions.

The third group, comprising Nantong, Chengde, Jingmen, Suzhou, and Shihezi, has three major sources of funds. The LTCI scheme in this group of cities, with the exception of Shihezi, relies on transfers from SPF of BMI, individual contributions, and government subsidies. For Shihezi, UEBMI enrollees are not required to make additional individual contributions. Government subsidies are provided to UEBMI and URBMI enrollees, and annual transfers from a special lottery fund are provided to Shihezi's LTCI fund.

The fourth group, comprising Shangrao, Chengdu, and Shanghai, has four major sources of funds: transfer from the SPF of BMI, additional individual contributions, government subsidies, and additional employer's contributions. In Shangrao, for employers with financial hardship, their contribution can come from government and/or the welfare lottery fund.

In terms of LTCI scheme groupings of the pilot cities, He *et al.* (2019) categorizes schemes into three major models depending on the enrollees' contribution method: (1) fixed amount contribution model – requiring enrollees to contribute a fixed sum every year as LTCI premium. Anqing, Guangzhou, Nantong, Ningbo, Qiqihaer, Shangrao, Chongqing, and Shihezi adopt this approach; (2) percentage of income contribution model – enrollees contribute a certain percentage of their previous year's average salary or the average disposable income of all residents in the city. This method is adopted by Chengde, Jingmen, and Suzhou; and (3) mixed model – different method based on type of the medical insurance scheme of the enrollee (i.e. UEBMI, or URBMI, or URRBMI) or the age of the enrollee (He *et al.* 2019). The categorization of LTCI schemes of the various pilot cities presented in Table 4.1 is based on the income source and the weighting of each source for the LTCI scheme in each of the pilot cities to shed light on the sustainability of the schemes.

These key features of the 15 pilot cities are summarized in Table 4.1.

From Table 4.1, it can be observed that the amount and/or proportion from each income source varies hugely from city to city. The transfer from UEBMI scheme ranges from 0.1 percent to 0.5 percent of payroll, RMB 20 to RMB 180 per person per year, a one-time transfer of RMB 20 million or a one-time transfer of up to 10–20 percent of the accumulated surplus of the SPF of UEBMI. Individual contributions can come from different sources, including zero to 0.1 percent of salary, 0.2 percent of the per capita disposable income of the previous year, 0.1 to 37.5 percent of money deducted from an individual MSA, or zero to RMB10 to RMB 90 per year through additional contribution or from an individual MSA. Government subsidies range from no subsidies to 0.1 percent of payroll to RMB 50 per year.

Evaluating the financial sustainability of LTCI schemes in the 15 pilot cities

Given the rather huge differences in terms of the contribution mix of the LTCI schemes, the sustainability of these schemes is obviously going to vary. The following paragraphs examine the financial sustainability of the schemes in the first

Table 4.1 Comparing LTCI schemes in 15 pilot cities

Pilot cities	Sources of funds	Contribution arrangements	Enrollees
Single funding source			
[1] Guangzhou	The social pooling fund (SPF) of basic medical insurance (BMI)	RMB 130/person/year	UEBMI* enrollees
[2] Ningbo	Accumulated surplus of the SPF of BMI	RMB 20 million transferred from the accumulated surplus of the SPF of BMI to form a start-up fund	UEBMI enrollees
Two funding sources			
[3] Anqing	Accumulated surplus of the SPF of BMI + individual contribution (paid by Critical Illness Medical Assistance of UEBMI)	RMB 30/person/year (RMB 20 from the accumulated surplus of the SPF of BMI; RMB 10 from individual contribution)	UEBMI enrollees
[4] Qiqihar	The SPF of BMI + individual contribution [from an individual medical savings account (MSA) or temporarily from the outpatient SPF prior to from out of pocket]	RMB 60/person/year (RMB 30 from the SPF of BMI; individual contribution: RMB 30 from an individual MSA or outpatient SPF)	UEBMI enrollees
[5] Qingdao	UEBMI*: accumulated surplus of the SPF of BMI + individual contribution (from an individual MSA) URRBMI*: annual transfer from medical insurance premium	UEBMI*: a one-time transfer of up to 20% of the accumulated surplus of the SPF of BMI and a monthly transfer of money from the employee BMI fund, the amount of which was equivalent to 0.5% of the employee's salary contributed to an individual MSA URRBMI*: an annual transfer of money from the URRBMI fund, the amount of which was no more than 10% of the residents' total social medical insurance premium contribution	UEBMI* and URRBMI* enrollees

(*Continued*)

Table 4.1 (Continued)

Pilot cities	Sources of funds	Contribution arrangements	Enrollees
[6] Changchun	UEBMI: A one-time transfer of up to 10% of the accumulated surplus of the SPF of BMI to establish a start-up fund; annual transfer from the SPF of BMI + individual contributions (from an individual MSA) URBMI: the SPF of BMI	UEBMI: one-time transfer of 10% of the accumulated surplus of the SPF of BMI; annual transfer of 0.3% from the SPF of BMI; and 0.2% from an individual MSA URBMI: RMB 30/person/year from the SPF of BMI	UEBMI and URBMI enrollees
[7] Chongqing	The SPF of BMI + individual contributions (from an individual MSA)	UEBMI: RMB 60/person/year from the SPF of BMI; RMB 90/person/year from an individual MSA	UEBMI enrollees
[8] Nantong	**Multiple funding sources including government subsidies** UEBMI: the SPF of BMI + individual contribution (from an individual MSA) + government subsidies URRBMI: the SPF + individual contribution + government subsidies	UEBMI: RMB 100/person/year (RMB 30 from the SPF of BMI; RMB 30 from an individual MSA; and RMB 40 from the government) URRBMI: RMB 100/person/year (RMB 30 from the SPF; RMB 30 from individual contribution; and RMB 40 from the government)	UEBMI and URRBMI enrollees
[9] Chengde	The SPF of BMI + individual contribution (from an individual MSA) + government subsidies	0.4% of salary of the previous year (0.2% from the SPF; 0.15% from an individual MSA; and 0.05% from the government)	UEBMI enrollees

[10] Jingmen	UEBMI: the SPF of BMI + individual contribution (from an individual MSA) + government subsidies URRBMI: the SPF + individual contribution + government subsidies	UEBMI: 0.4% of the per capita disposable income of the previous year (25% from the SPF; 37.5% from an individual MSA or pension accounts for those who do not have an individual MSA; and 37.5% from the government) URRBMI: 0.4% of the per capita disposable income of the previous year (25% from the SPF; 37.5% from an individual MSA or pension accounts; and 37.5% from the government)	UEBMI and URRBMI enrollees
[11] Suzhou	UEBMI: the accumulated surplus of the SPF of BMI + individual contribution + government subsidies URRBMI: the accumulated surplus of the SPF + individual contribution + government subsidies	URBMI: RMB 70 from the accumulated surplus of the SPF of BMI; individual contribution amounting to 0.2% of the per capita disposable income of the previous year; and RMB 50 from the government. URRBMI: RMB 35 from the accumulated surplus of the SPF; individual contribution amounting to 0.2% of the per capita disposable income of the previous year; and RMB 50 from the government. No individual contribution during the first phase of the pilot reform.	UEBMI and URRBMI enrollees
[12] Shihezi	UEBMI: the accumulated surplus of the SPF of BMI + government subsidies URBMI*: the accumulated surplus of the SPF + government subsidies annual transfers from a special lottery fund	UEBMI: RMB 180/person/year from the accumulated surplus of the SPF of BMI; RMB 40/person/year from the government URBMI*: RMB 24/person/year from the accumulated surplus of the SPF; RMB 40/person/year from the government; RMB 500,000 per year to the LTCI scheme from the welfare lottery fund to the LTCI fund	UEBMI and URBMI* enrollees

(Continued)

Table 4.1 (Continued)

Pilot cities	Sources of funds	Contribution arrangements	Enrollees
Multiple funding sources including employer's contribution			
[13] Shangrao	UEBMI: the SPF of BMI + individual contributions (from an individual MSA or out of pocket) + employer's contributions + government subsidies	UEBMI: RMB 100/person/year (RMB 30 from the SPF of BMI; RMB 40 from an individual MSA or OOP payment (OOP payment is required for those who have no individual MSA or whose MSA have insufficient money); RMB 30 from employers (for employers with hardship, their contribution will come from the government and/or welfare lottery fund	UEBMI enrollees
[14] Chengdu	[1] UEBMI: individual contributions (from an individual MSA) + employer's contributions + government subsidies [2] A one-time transfer of up to RMB 50 million from the accumulated surplus of the UEBMI fund to establish a start-up fund	UEBMI: individual contributions (under 40 years old: 0.1% from an individual MSA; over 40 years old: 0.2% from an individual MSA; Retirees: 0.3% from an individual MSA) The employer's contributions (0.2% from the SPF of BMI), government subsidies (0.1% of previous year's average salary)	UEBMI enrollees
[15] Shanghai	UEBMI: individual contributions + employer's contributions URRBMI: individual contributions + government subsidies	UEBMI: individual contributions (0.1% of the average monthly salary in the previous year; Retirees: no contributions); employer's contributions (1% of their employees' average monthly salary in the previous year) URRBMI: individual contributions (15% of the total premium, with the rest of the premium being shared by the municipal and district finance in 1:1 ratio) No premium contribution from UEBMI participants, employers and URRBMI participants during the pilot phase	UEBMI and URRBMI enrollees

* *Notes*: In some recent government documents, UEBMI is also referred to as Employee Social Medical Insurance in Guangzhou, and Social Medical Insurance for Employee (SMIE) in Qingdao. URRBMI is referred to as Resident Basic Medical Insurance in Shihezi. URRBMI is referred to as Social Medical Insurance for Resident (SMIR) in Qingdao.

Sources:

(1) Guangzhou: Ministry of Human Resources and Social Security of Guangzhou City, Ministry of Finance of Guangzhou City, Ministry of Civil Affairs of Guangzhou City, and Health and Family Planning Commission of Guangzhou City (2017) *Piloting Long-term Care Insurance in Guangzhou* (Chinese version). Online. Available HTTP: www.gz.gov.cn/gfxwj/sbmgfxwj/gzsylbzj/content/post_5488593.html (accessed 27 June 2021).

(2) Ningbo: Office of the People's Government of Ningbo City (2017) *Notification on Issuing Rules for Implementing a Pilot Program on Long-term Care Insurance in Ningbo* (Chinese version). Online. Available HTTP: www.cnki.com.cn/Article/CJFDTotal-NBZB2017S1026.htm (accessed 27 June 2021).

(3) Anqing: Office of the People's Government of Anqing City (2017) *Notification on Issuing Rules for Implementing Long-term Care Insurance of Urban Employees in Anqing City (Pilot)* (Chinese version). Online. Available HTTP: http://aqxxgk.anqing.gov.cn/show.php?id=505293 (accessed 27 June 2021).

(4) Qiqihaer: Office of the People's Government of Qiqihaer City (2017) *Notification on Issuing Rules for Implementing Long-term Care Insurance in Qiqihaer (Pilot)* (Chinese version). Online. Available HTTP: www.qqhr.gov.cn/News_showNews.action?messagekey=141239 (accessed 27 June 2021).

(5) Qingdao: The People' s Government of Qingdao City (2014) *Measures of Qingdao Municipality for the Social Medical Insurance* (Chinese version) Online. Available HTTP: www.huangdao.gov.cn/n10/upload/1910171415226605104/19101714152262370.pdf (accessed 27 June 2021).

(6) Changchun: Office of the People's Government of Changchun City (2015) *Opinions on Establishing a Medical Care Insurance System for Disabled People* (Chinese version). Online. Available HTTP: www.changchun.gov.cn/zw_33994/zfwj/sfbwj_108294/201612/20161210_2026705.html (accessed 27 June 2021).

(7) Chongqing: Ministry of Human Resources and Social Security of Chongqing City and Ministry of Finance of Chongqing City (2017) *Notification on Issuing Opinions on Piloting Long-term Care Insurance System in Chongqing* (Chinese version). Online. Available HTTP: http://rlsbj.cq.gov.cn/zwxx_182/tzgg/201712/r20171222_6719581.html (accessed 27 June 2021).

(8) Nantong: The People's Government of Nantong City (2015) *Notification on Issuing Opinions on Establishing A Basic Care Insurance System (Pilot)* (Chinese version). Online. Available HTTP: www.nantong.gov.cn/ntsrmzf/2015ndswq/content/51793459-2b25-4563-ade9-27326b4fab089.html (accessed 27 June 2021).

(9) Chengde: The People's Government of Chengde city (2016) *Opinions on Establishing A Long-term Care Insurance System for Urban Employees (Pilot)* (Chinese version). Online. Available HTTP: www.chengde.gov.cn/art/2016/11/30/art_9943_305632.html (accessed 27 June 2021).

(10) Jingmen: The People's Government of Jingmen City (2016) *Notification on Piloting Long-term Care Insurance in Jingmen* (Chinese version). Online. Available HTTP: www.jingmen.gov.cn/art/2016/11/22/art_6606_3872.html (accessed 27 June 2021).

(11) Suzhou: The People's Government of Suzhou City (2017) *Notification on Issuing Opinions on Implementing a Pilot Program on Long-term Care Insurance* (Chinese version) http://hrss.suzhou.gov.cn/jsszhrss/zxfgk/201706/a561f05283ae42c99d1a79121843bb6a.shtml (accessed 27 June 2021).

(Continued)

Table 4.1 (Continued)

(12) Shihezi: The People's Government of Shihezi City (2017) *Notification on Issuing Rules for Implementing Long-term Care Insurance in Shihezi (Pilot)* (Chinese version). Online. Available HTTP: www.shz.gov.cn/zwdt/tzgg/15466.htm (accessed 27 June 2021).

(13) Shangrao: Office of the People's Government of Shangrao City (2016) *Notification on Issuing Implementation Plans on Long-term Care Insurance in Shangrao (Pilot)* (Chinese version). Online. Available HTTP: www.zgsr.gov.cn/doc/2017/09/01/272130.shtml (accessed 27 June 2021).

(14) Chengdu: The People's Government of Chengdu City (2017) *Notification on Implementing a Pilot Program on Long-term Care Insurance System in Chengdu* (Chinese version). Online. Available HTTP: http://gk.chengdu.gov.cn/govInfoPub/detail.action?id=88855&tn=6 (accessed 27 June 2021).

(15) Shanghai: Shanghai Municipal People's Government (2016a) *Pilot Measures for Long-term Care Insurance in Shanghai* (Chinese version). Available HTTP: http://law.esnai.com/view/179508/ (accessed 12 April 2021).

15 pilot cities based on their existing financial arrangements and the guidelines as prescribed in the 2016 Guiding Opinions. The central government policy guidelines specify the following: (1) the LTCI scheme should strive for a balanced budget with modest amount of surplus; (2) it should provide protection to the severely disabled group, at least initially, covering basic LTC services for ADLs; (3) overall, the reimbursement by LTCI should be within 70 percent of total LTC expenditure (i.e. co-payment by users should constitute 30% of the expenses overall) (Ministry of Human Resources and Social Security of the People's Republic of China 2016). Given these parameters, the range of individual contributions and government subsidies are calculated in the following based on the results from a study by Hu and Li (2017).

Hu and Li (2017), using the national data, estimated the cost of providing LTC from 2014 to 2050 to different groups of disabled persons: (1) the severely disabled; (2) the severely plus the moderately disabled; (3) the severely plus the moderately plus the mildly disabled. A range of cost figures was presented – the lower limit is computed based on the quantity of services demanded given the various co-payment assumptions under LTCI; the upper limit is the estimated cost for providing the quantity of services based solely on need. It then examines different combinations of individual contribution rates, government subsidy rates, and reimbursement rates required to meet the expenses. The amount of individual contribution is expressed as a percentage of disposable income. The amount of government subsidies is expressed in terms of percentage of total government revenue. The results show that, as required by the 2016 Guiding Opinions, to cover the severely disabled group, with a reimbursement rate of 70 percent, and to achieve a balanced budget, the share between an individual and the government should be 5:5, and that individual contributions should be within the range of 0.09 percent to 0.26 percent of personal disposable income, while government subsidy should be within the range of 0.13 percent to 0.37 percent of government revenue (Hu and Li 2017: 125). The adequacy and sustainability of the schemes of the various pilot cities are assessed using these parameters. Table 4.2 presents the summary results showing: (1) the total amount of funds from the different contributory sources available to finance LTC (2) and the range of required expenditure (lower limit based on the assumption of 30 percent co-payment; upper limit based on need) that is required to cover the cost of the LTC services given the estimated size of the severely disabled population in the cities. Cities with funds from various contributory sources that are within the range of required expenditure suggest that their LTCI schemes have adequate resources to cover LTC services within the parameters laid down by the central government. Cities with funds below the lower limit suggest that their scheme is not likely to be sustainable. Cities with funds above the upper limit can consider lowering the contribution from their enrollees.

The results show that most of the schemes in pilot cities can meet the LTC expenses of their severely disabled persons (within the range defined by Hu and Li 2017). Details are as follows:

Results show that Guangzhou in the first group of cities that has a single source of funding, relying solely on transfer from the SPF of BMI schemes, has adequate

Table 4.2 Total financing available vs total funding requirements in 15 pilot cities

Name of city	Total funding available for LTC from various contributory sources (10,000 RMB)	Total funding required to meet the cost of providing LTC to the severely disabled group. Lower limit based on 30% co-payment; upper limit based on need (10,000 RMB)
Guangzhou	UEBMI:82,787	UEBMI:66,190~189,634
Ningbo	UEBMI:2,000	UEBMI:34,715~99,570
Anqing	UEBMI:1,309	UEBMI:5,423~15,480
Qiqihar	UEBMI:4,506	UEBMI:7,363~21,026
Qingdao	UEBMI:299,709	UEBMI:28,743~82,283
	URRBMI:34,844	URRBMI:33,580~96,257
Changchun	UEBMI:287,788	UEBMI:14,535~41,560
	URBMI:7,377	URBMI:16,894~48,377
Chongqing	UEBMI:90,714	UEBMI:68,140~194,625
Nantong	UEBMI:18,792	UEBMI:22,406~64,054
	URRBMI:9,090	URRBMI:18,979~54,154
Chengde	UEBMI:5,772	UEBMI:4,926~14,063
Jingmen	UEBMI:3,347	UEBMI:5,278~15,053
	URRBMI:4,421	URRBMI:5,521~15,758
Suzhou	UEBMI:76,211	UEBMI:53,169~152,655
	URRBMI:23,531	URRBMI:35,648~102,038
Shihezi	UEBMI:3,814	UEBMI:1,314~3,767
	URBMI:368	URBMI:1,119~3,204
Shangrao	UEBMI:6,250	UEBMI:8,082~23,072
Chengdu	UEBMI:191,382	UEBMI:53,405~152,930
Shanghai	UEBMI:851,284	UEBMI:161,725~463,362
	URRBMI:157,759	URRBMI:106,467~303,728

Note: The data are calculated by the authors.

funding. Ningbo in the same group, however, appears to be way short probably due to the fact that in the Ningbo official document there is no explicit mention of annual transfer of funds to the LTC scheme.

The majority of the cities from the second group that has two funding tracks – transfer from the SPF of BMI schemes and additional individual contributions – has adequate funding for their UEBMI enrollees. Qingdao has adequate funding for both UEBMI and URRBMI enrollees. Changchun has adequate funding for its UEBMI enrollees but not adequate for enrollees in its URBMI. Chongqing has adequate funding for UEBMI enrollees. Both Anqing and Qiqihar have inadequate funding.

The third group, comprising Nantong, Chengde, Jingmen, Suzhou, and Shihezi, has three major sources of funds: transfer from the SPF of BMI, individual contributions, and government subsidies. Chengde, Shihezi, and Suzhou have adequate funding for UEBMI enrollees. Nantong and Jingmen do not have adequate funding for both UEBMI and URRBMI enrollees. Suzhou does not have adequate funding for its URRBMI enrollees. Shihezi does not have adequate funding for its URBMI enrollees.

The fourth group, comprising Shangrao, Chengdu, and Shanghai, has multiple sources of funds: transfer from the SPF of BMI, additional individual contributions, government subsidies, and additional employer's contributions. All except Shangrao have adequate funding.

Discussions

This section assesses the LTC financing system developed so far in the first 15 pilot cities in terms of their sustainability, adequacy, and equity. It seeks to identify models that are likely to be sustainable and are more equitable in providing adequate protection to the elderly population. The shortcomings of some of the arrangements in some pilot cities are also discussed.

Questionable sustainability: overly dependent on the social pooling fund of the medical insurance scheme

The earlier presented estimates show that many of the schemes in pilot cities cannot meet the LTC expenses of their severely disabled persons (within the range defined by Hu and Li 2017). All of these LTCI schemes rely, to varying degrees, on the transfer from the SPF of the medical insurance scheme as an important contributory source. Table 4.1 shows that Guangzhou's and Ningbo's LTCI schemes rely solely on the transfer from the SPF of the medical insurance scheme. For Anqin and Qiqihar, the transfer from the SPF constitutes more than 50 percent of their LTCI schemes' income. For the other cities, the share is not insignificant, even though it may be below 50 percent.

'The problems of ageing population and early retirement present challenges to the financial sustainability of the BMI fund, which are especially serious in the UEBMI' (Luk 2017: 77). Some cities and provinces (e.g. Jixi city and Mudanjiang city in Heilongjiang province) in China have already experienced a deficit in the BMI fund due to rising medical costs, an increase in the reimbursement ratio, and an increase in the number of UEBMI participants (Luk 2017: 84–5). Some cities are in the danger of having deficits (Zhao 2018). At present, medical schemes that are in relatively good financial health are confined to cities in the eastern provinces such as Guangdong, Jiangsu, Zhejiang, and Shandong (Wang 2016). Nationwide, it has been estimated that the total deficit of the SPF of the basic medical insurance in China will exceed RMB 700 billion by 2024 (Fang 2014). Contributions to medical insurance schemes come mainly from payroll of the working population. But LTC services are mostly for the retired. With a shrinking working population and a growing number of retirees requiring LTC services, it is obvious that over reliance on contributions to the medical insurance scheme to fund LTC services is not likely to be viable in the longer term. Having multiple sources of contributions – individual contributions, employers' contributions, government subsidies, transfer from lottery – independent of the medical insurance scheme is important. This is also the experience of Germany, Japan, and the Republic of Korea (ROK) (Li and Zhang 2018: 74). Table 4.2 suggests that LTCI schemes that are in good financial health are found in major metropolitan centres, such as Guangzhou, Shanghai, Qingdao, and Chengdu. Most of the smaller cities are experiencing some financial difficulties, especially for their URBMI enrollees.

Equity issues need to be addressed: contribution arrangement and protecting the less well-off

Among the 15 pilot cities, Anqing, Guangzhou, Nantong, Qiqihar, Shangrao, Chongqing, and Shihezi require enrollees to contribute a fixed sum every year as LTCI premium. Fixed sum contribution is less equitable than contribution based on a percentage of enrollees' income, as under the fixed sum contribution system, low-income persons contribute the same amount as high-income persons. There are also cities like Jingmen, for example, which require individuals to contribute a percent of the city's per capita disposable income of the previous year as premium. Such contributory method is basically the same as the fixed sum contribution method from an equity perspective (Jing 2015; Xia *et al.* 2018).

Some cities, such as Chengdu, for example, has the contribution rate vary according to UEBMI enrollees' age: 0.1 percent of income for employees under 40 years old, 0.2 percent for employees over 40 years old, and 0.3 percent for retirees. This is regressive, as retirees' income is mostly confined to their pensions and is generally less than that of the working population. They are, however, required to contribute a higher percentage of their income towards the LTCI premium than the younger, working enrollees. This might cause hardship for some retirees, especially those requiring LTC services given that there is substantial co-payment involved on top of annual premium payment.

Many cities also provide LTCI only to UEBMI enrollees, who are in general better off than those under URBMI or URRBMI. The less well-off older adults without insurance protection are likely to suffer great hardship if and when they become disabled. With only five out of 15 pilot cities (i.e. Qingdao, Nantong, Jingmen, Suzhou, and Shanghai) providing LTCI to urban and rural residents not covered by UEBMI, universal insurance coverage for LTC services for the entire country is still a rather long way away. Of the seven cities providing LTCI to residents under URBMI/URRBMI, five of them rely on transfer from the SPF of the medical insurance scheme. Most of these medical schemes provide minimum protection to their enrollees, with OOP payment constituting a significant percentage of payment for medical expenses. Transferring funds from the SPF of these medical schemes will cause further hardship to many of the enrollees when receiving medical care.

Conclusion

The issuance of the 2016 and 2020 Guiding Opinions on LTCI signals the intention of the central government to establish a more formal system of LTC financing for the country. The two batches of pilot cities, covering almost every region of the country [of the 31 provinces/direct-administered municipalities/ autonomous regions in the country, only four provinces/autonomous regions (i.e. Hainan, Qinghai, Tibet Autonomous Region, and Ningxia Hui Autonomous Region) do not have a pilot city in them], indicate a high level of readiness of the country to launch LTCI on a national level. Given the speed of population ageing and the changed social circumstances associated with the weakening of family support for older adults, this central government initiative is necessary and timely. The approach of providing broad directions while allowing local governments to vary according to local circumstances is practical and sensible.

This chapter examines the recent development of LTCI in the pilot cities. All of the LTCI schemes in the pilot cities are extensions of the existing medical insurance schemes – UEBMI, URBMI, and URRBMI. The income for the LTCI schemes is dependent, some more so than others, on the contributions from the SPF of the public medical insurance schemes. Such a feature facilitates a more rapid development of LTCI, as those public medical schemes are now ubiquitous throughout the country. However, all of these medical schemes are pay-as-you-go schemes, which are highly dependent on contributions from the working population. The reliance of the newly established LTCI schemes on the transfer of funds from the SPF of their associated medical insurance schemes is unhealthy in the longer term. Problems are likely to surface quickly for cities where the SPF does not have much surplus and where LTCI schemes that rely solely or heavily on transfer from the SPF of the medical insurance scheme. There are urban–rural differences as well as regional differences in terms of income, which constitute the base for contributions to the SPF of the medical insurance scheme. Cities that are about to develop LTCI should seriously consider having multiple sources of contribution, independent of the medical insurance scheme. Future central government guidelines should try to promote a more diverse funding arrangement for LTCI.

The lack of explicit guidelines from the central government to include populations outside the formal employment sector is problematic. It is true that most UEBMI schemes are better established and in stronger financial position than URBMI or URRBI schemes to manage such a new initiative. But older adults not covered by UEBMI are likely to have lower income and are more vulnerable. It would be desirable for future central government guidelines to mandate the inclusion of populations outside UEBMI and not leave it to the discretion of local governments to expand coverage if and when they see fit.

The current criteria confine beneficiaries to those who are severely disabled. Persons who are assessed as moderately or mildly disabled cannot benefit even if they or their family would face serious hardship. It would be desirable to mandate local governments to provide some form of means-tested protection outside of the LTCI scheme for the aforementioned groups. Chapters 5, 6, and 7 provide more detailed analyses on the performance of the LTC system in three pilot cities: Qingdao, Nantong, and Shanghai.

References

Chang, S., Yang, W. and Deguchi, H. (2020) 'Care Providers, Access to Care, and the Long-Term Care Nursing Insurance in China: An Agent-Based Simulation', *Social Science & Medicine*, 244: 112667.

Fang, P. Q. (2014) *Green Book of Health Reform and Development* (Chinese version). Beijing: People's Publishing House.

Feng, Z., Glinskaya, E., Chen, H., Gong, S., Qiu, Y., Xu, J. and Yip, W. (2020) 'Long-Term Care System for Older Adults in China: Policy Landscape, Challenges and Future Prospects', *Lancet*, 396: 1362–72.

Glinskaya, E., Feng, Z., Huang, Y. and Wang, D. (n.d.) *Options for Financing Elderly Care in China: Summary Paper*. Online. Available HTTP: http://documents1.world-bank.org/curated/en/263911563561465823/pdf/Options-for-Financing-Elderly-Care-in-China-Summary-Paper.pdf (accessed 28 November 2020).

Guo, J. H. (2019) *Long-Term Care Insurance Pilot Scheme Has Already Been Launched for Three Years: Is It Possible to Bring Positive Social and Economic Effects and Become the Sixth Insurance in China?* (Chinese version). Online. Available HTTP: www.yicai.com/news/100252720.html (accessed 28 November 2020).

He, S. Y., Dai, R. M., Wang, Y., Jiang, M., Bai, G. and Luo, L. (2019) 'Comparative Research of the Financing Scheme for Long-Term Care Insurance in Pilot Areas in China', (Chinese version), *China Health Resources*, 22 (1): 28–34.

Hu, H. W. and Li, Y. Y. (2017) 'Study on the Optimal Design of Financing and Compensation Level about Chinese Elderly Long-Term Care Social Insurance: On the Construction of Framework of Elderly Long-Term Care Social Insurance', (Chinese version), *Journal of Hebei University (Philosophy and Social Science)*, 42 (5): 117–28.

Jing, T. (2015) *The Theory and Practice of Long-Term Care Insurance System* (Chinese version). Beijing: University of International Business and Economics Press.

Li, C. Y. and Zhang, H. P. (2018). 'A Comparison on Financing Mechanism of Long-Term Care Insurance System among Developed Countries and Some Enlightenments', (Chinese version), *Truth Seeking*, 3: 69–78.

Li, F. and Otani, J. (2018) 'Financing Elderly People's Long-Term Care Needs: Evidence from China', *Health Planning and Management*, 33 (2): 479–88.

Luk, S. C. Y. (2017) *Financing Healthcare in China: Towards Universal Health Insurance*, London: Routledge.

Luk, S. C. Y. (2020) *Ageing, Long-Term Care Insurance and Healthcare Finance in Asia*, Abingdon, Oxon; New York, NY: Routledge.

Ministry of Human Resources and Social Security of Chongqing City and Ministry of Finance of Chongqing City (2017) *Notification on Issuing Opinions on Piloting Long-Term Care Insurance System in Chongqing* (Chinese version). Online. Available HTTP: http://rlsbj.cq.gov.cn/zwxx_182/tzgg/201712/t20171222_6719581.html (accessed 27 June 2021).

Ministry of Human Resources and Social Security of Guangzhou City, Ministry of Finance of Guangzhou City, Ministry of Civil Affairs of Guangzhou City and Health and Family Planning Commission of Guangzhou City (2017) *Piloting Long-Term Care Insurance in Guangzhou* (Chinese version). Online. Available HTTP: www.gz.gov.cn/gfxwj/sbmgfxwj/gzsylbzj/content/post_5488593.html (accessed 27 June 2021).

Ministry of Human Resources and Social Security of the People's Republic of China (2016) *The Guiding Opinions on Piloting the Long-Term Care Insurance System*

(Chinese version). Online. Available HTTP: www.mohrss.gov.cn/SYrlzyhshbzb/shehuibaozhang/zcwj/yiliao/201607/t20160705_242951.html (accessed 27 June 2021).

National Healthcare Security Administration and Ministry of Finance (2020) *The Guiding Opinions on the Extension of the Long-Term Care Insurance System in Pilot Cities* (Chinese version). Online. Available HTTP: www.nhsa.gov.cn/art/2020/9/16/art_37_3586.html\ (accessed 27 June 2021).

Office of the People's Government of Anqing City (2017) *Notification on Issuing Rules for Implementing Long-Term Care Insurance of Urban Employees in Anqing City (Pilot)* (Chinese version). Online. Available HTTP: http://aqxxgk.anqing.gov.cn/show.php?id=505293 (accessed 27 June 2021).

Office of the People's Government of Changchun City (2015) *Opinions on Establishing a Medical Care Insurance System for Disabled People* (Chinese version). Online. Available HTTP: www.changchun.gov.cn/zw_33994/zfwj/sfbwj_108294/201612/t20161210_2026705.html (accessed 27 June 2021).

Office of the People's Government of Ningbo City (2017) *Notification on Issuing Rules for Implementing a Pilot Program on Long-Term Care Insurance in Ningbo* (Chinese version). Online. Available HTTP: www.cnki.com.cn/Article/CJFDTotal-NBZB2017S1026.htm (accessed 27 June 2021).

Office of the People's Government of Qiqihaer City (2017) *Notification on Issuing Rules for Implementing Long-Term Care Insurance in Qiqihaer (Pilot)* (Chinese version). Online. Available HTTP: www.qqhr.gov.cn/News_showNews.action?messagekey=141239 (accessed 27 June 2021).

Office of the People's Government of Shangrao City (2016) *Notification on Issuing Implementation Plans on Long-Term Care Insurance in Shangrao (Pilot)* (Chinese version). Online. Available HTTP: www.zgsr.gov.cn/doc/2017/09/01/272130.shtml (accessed 27 June 2021).

The People's Government of Chengde City (2016) *Opinions on Establishing a Long-Term Care Insurance System for Urban Employees (Pilot)* (Chinese version). Online. Available HTTP: www.chengde.gov.cn/art/2016/11/30/art_9943_305632.html (accessed 27 June 2021).

The People's Government of Chengdu City (2017) *Notification on Implementing a Pilot Program on Long-Term Care Insurance System in Chengdu* (Chinese version). Online. Available HTTP: http://gk.chengdu.gov.cn/govInfoPub/detail.action?id=88855&tn=6 (accessed 27 June 2021).

The People's Government of Jingmen City (2016) *Notification on Piloting Long-Term Care Insurance in Jingmen* (Chinese version). Online. Available HTTP: www.jingmen.gov.cn/art/2016/11/22/art_6606_3872.html (accessed 27 June 2021).

The People's Government of Nantong City (2015) *Notification on Issuing Opinions on Establishing a Basic Care Insurance System (Pilot)* (Chinese version). Online. Available HTTP: www.nantong.gov.cn/ntsrmzf/2015ndswq/content/51793459-2b25-4563-ade9-2732b4fab089.html (accessed 27 June 2021).

The People's Government of Qingdao City (2014) *Measures of Qingdao Municipality for the Social Medical Insurance* (Chinese version). Online. Available HTTP: www.huangdao.gov.cn/n10/upload/191017141522605104/191017141522622370.pdf (accessed 27 June 2021).

The People's Government of Shihezi City (2017) *Notification on Issuing Rules for Implementing Long-Term Care Insurance in Shihezi (Pilot)* (Chinese version).

Online. Available HTTP: www.shz.gov.cn/zwdt/tzgg/15466.htm (accessed 27 June 2021).

The People's Government of Suzhou City (2017) *Notification on Issuing Opinions on Implementing a Pilot Program on Long-Term Care Insurance* (Chinese version) http://hrss.suzhou.gov.cn/jsszhrss/zxfgk/201706/a561f05283ae42c99d1a 7921f843bb6a.shtml (accessed 27 June 2021).

Shanghai Municipal People's Government (2016a) *Pilot Measures for Long-Term Care Insurance in Shanghai* (Chinese version). Online. Available HTTP: http:// law.esnai.com/view/179508/ (accessed 12 April 2021).

Shu, X. (2017) *China: Education and Family Bonds.* Online. Available HTTP: http:// worldpolicy.org/2017/10/16/china-education-and-family-bonds/ (accessed 27 June 2021).

Wang, H. R. (2016) 'The Pilot Long-Term Care Insurance Is Implemented: Does the Funding Come from the Pension Fund or the Medical Insurance Fund?', (Chinese version), *China Economic Weekly*, 37: 54.

Wang, Q., Zhou, Y., Ding, X. and Ying, X. (2018) 'Demand for Long-Term Care Insurance in China', *International Journal of Environmental Research and Public Health*, 15: 6.

Xia, Y. R., Chang, F., Lu, Y. and Pei, J. (2018) 'International Experience and China's Practice of Long-Term Nursing Insurance Financing Mechanism', (Chinese version), *Health Economics Research*, 12: 69–71, 75.

Yang, W., He, A. J., Fang, L. and Mossialos, E. (2016). 'Financing Institutional Long-Term Care for the Elderly in China: A Policy Evaluation of New Models', *Health Policy and Planning*, 31(10): 1391–1401.

Zhang, Y. and Goza, F. W. (2006) 'Who Will Care for the Elderly in China? A Review of the Problems Caused by China's One-Child Policy and Their Potential Solutions', *Journal of Aging Studies*, 20: 151–64.

Zhang, Y. and Yu, X. (2019) 'Evaluation of Long-Term Care Insurance Policy in Chinese Pilot Cities', *International Journal of Environmental Research and Public Health*, 16: 3826.

Zhao, C. (2018) *Medical Insurance Fund Will Change from Surplus to Deficit in the Coming 10 Years* (Chinese version). Online. Available HTTP: https://www.sohu. com/a/277386928_561670 (accessed 10 September 2021).

5 The long-term care model in Qingdao

Introduction

Qingdao takes the lead in implementing long-term care insurance (LTCI) to provide different types of long-term care (LTC) services for people with moderate and severe disability and people with dementia (PWD) (*shi zhi ren yuan*). This chapter examines the development of LTCI in Qingdao and designated LTC providers in the city. It also evaluates the outcomes of LTCI in terms of five criteria: utilization of medical resources, cost, equity, quality of care, and sustainability. It finds that the implementation of LTCI helps address the problem of social hospitalization and enhances efficient allocation and utilization of medical resources. Besides, the implementation of LTCI can greatly reduce the financial costs borne by care recipients and their family members. The '4+3' LTC service approach can meet different needs of care recipients. Nevertheless, urban employees enjoy better coverage and reimbursement rate than residents. Care recipients in urban areas have better access to LTC facilities and services than their rural counterparts. There is room for improvement in quality of care and the financial sustainability of LTCI in the long run.

Background

Qingdao is a coastal city in eastern Shandong province with a population of about 9.5 million (Qingdao Municipal Statistics Bureau and National Bureau of Statistics Survey Office in Qingdao 2020). 'It is often ranked among the top ten most competitive cities in China' (Zhang 2015: 273). It was designated as one of the 15 'key economic centres' in China in 1981 (Eng 2005: 129) and one of the first 14 'coastal open cities' (COCs) in 1984 to implement a wide range of preferential policies to promote foreign trade and investment (Chung 1999: 931). It attained the central economic city (CEC) status in 1987, which enabled the city to enjoy a provincial-level status in making economic policy decisions (Chung 1999: 932). It 'has recorded high economic growth rates since 1990' (Zhang and Rasiah 2013: 593). Its Gross Domestic Product (GDP) drastically increased from about renminbi (RMB) 18 billion in 1990 to about RMB 119.1 billion in 2000 and about RMB 574.9 billion in 2010 (Qingdao Municipal Statistics

DOI: 10.4324/9780429057199-5

Bureau and National Bureau of Statistics Survey Office in Qingdao 2018: 52–3). In 2019, the city's GDP reached more than RMB 1.1 trillion (Qingdao Municipal Statistics Bureau 2019). Tertiary industry has been the prime contributor to Qingdao's GDP since 2012 (Qingdao Municipal Statistics Bureau and National Bureau of Statistics Survey Office in Qingdao 2018). The main industries of Qingdao include electronics, machinery, metallurgy, automobiles, textiles and garments, and food and beverage processing (Charoenporn 2012: 201).

Qingdao has been experiencing faster population ageing than the rest of its counterparts in China. It became an ageing society in 1987, with persons aged 65 and above making up more than 7 percent of its total population (Ju *et al*. 2011). It was seven years ahead of Shandong province and 12 years ahead of China in becoming an ageing society (Ju *et al*. 2011). In Qingdao, the percentage of persons aged 65 and above increased from 7.21 percent in 1990 to 9.35 percent in 2000 and over 13 percent in 2010 (Ju *et al*. 2011). By the end of 2012, the number of people aged 60 and above reached 18.03 percent of the total population in the city, which was 3.7 percent higher than the national average (Qingdao Morning Post 2013). The number of persons aged 65 and above reached over 1.31 million at the end of 2017, which accounted for about 14.1 percent of the total population (Lou 2018). This indicated that Qingdao had become an aged society. In 2023, for the first time in Qingdao, persons aged 65 years and above are expected to outnumber persons aged between 0 and 14 years (Qingdao News 2010). Persons aged 60 years or above in Qingdao are expected to reach 32.34 percent in 2030, 35.05 percent in 2035, and 37.45 percent in 2050 (Lu *et al*. 2009: 58). By the end of 2012, there were about 260,000 fully disabled and partially disabled persons in Qingdao (Qingdao Evening News 2013). In October 2019, over 300,000 people aged above 80 in Qingdao were in need of LTC (Liu and Liu 2019). Rapid population ageing poses a challenge to the provision of an adequate and affordable LTC in the city.

Development of LTCI

The pilot LTCI scheme (2012)

In July 2012, Qingdao became the first place in China to implement a pilot LTCI scheme. The pilot LTCI scheme aimed to provide financial support for those who required continuing medical care at home, hospitals, elderly care institutions or institutions for the disabled due to old age, illnesses, and disability (The Qingdao Municipal People's Government 2012). Enrolment in this pilot scheme is tightly linked to an individual's social medical insurance status (Chang *et al*. 2020). Eligible participants in this pilot scheme must be those enrolled in the Urban Employee Basic Medical Insurance (UEBMI) or the Urban Resident Basic Medical Insurance (URBMI) (The Qingdao Municipal People's Government 2012).

The pilot scheme was funded by multiple resources. One part of the financing was transferred from an individual medical savings account (MSA) of the UEBMI and the social pooling fund (SPF) of both the UEBMI and the URBMI (The Qingdao Municipal People's Government 2012). Another part of the financing was transferred from the Public Welfare Fund, with an annual value of RMB 20 million (The Qingdao Municipal People's Government 2012). At the start of the pilot scheme, a total of RMB 100 million was transferred from the Public Welfare Fund as start-up fund to support the operation of the pilot scheme (The Qingdao Municipal People's Government 2012). The LTCI fund under this pilot scheme would be raised and used according to the principle of 'balancing revenues and expenses, with a small surplus maintained' (The Qingdao Municipal People's Government 2012).

The pilot scheme covered three types of services provided at prices (per unit) set by LTCI: home care, nursing home care, and intensive care at designated Grade II or Grade III hospitals (Lu *et al.* 2017: 184). Home care provided medical and nursing care for the chronically ill, homebound, bedridden LTCI participants or those with mobility issue at home on a weekly basis (Qingdao Morning Post 2014). Nursing home care focused on the provision of continual medical and nursing care as well as end-of-life (EoL) care for the terminally ill by institutions that integrate medical and elderly care services (National Health Commission of the People's Republic of China 2015; People's Daily 2016). Intensive care provided 24-hour medical care and activities of daily living (ADLs) care for critically ill patients (e.g. patient with a gastrostomy tube, a urinary catheter, or a tracheostomy tube; those with degenerative joint and bone disease; those with nervous system diseases) (Dazhong Web 2016; National Health Commission of the People's Republic of China 2015; People's Daily 2016). For those eligible for home care or receiving care at designated nursing homes, the unit price was RMB 60 per day per head (The Qingdao Municipal People's Government 2012; Lu *et al.* 2017: 184). For those eligible for receiving care at designated Grade II and Grade III hospitals, the unit price was RMB 170 and RMB 200 per bed respectively (The Qingdao Municipal People's Government 2012; Lu *et al.* 2017: 184). The prices of these LTCI beds per day in Grade II and Grade III were about 2.9 times and 5.4 times lower than the prices of normal beds in Grade II and Grade III hospitals (Lu *et al.* 2017). The pilot scheme would cover 96 percent of the expenses for participants eligible for home care or receiving care at designated nursing homes while covering 90 percent of the expenses for participants receiving care at designated Grade II or Grade III hospitals (The Qingdao Municipal People's Government 2012). Table 5.1 summarizes the main points of the pilot LTCI scheme in 2012.

LTCI in Qingdao (2015)

In January 2015, Qingdao implemented social medical insurance. This helped realize the integration of urban and rural medical insurance, making it possible for rural residents to enrol in the LTCI scheme (Li 2018: 139). The government issued *Social Health Insurance Measures in Qingdao* (Qingdao Municipal Order No. 235) (hereafter *the Order*), which changed the funding structure of LTCI to

Table 5.1 The pilot LTCI scheme (2012)

Description	To provide financial support for those who required continuing medical care at home, hospitals, elderly care institutions or institutions for the disabled due to old age, illnesses, and disability		
Targeted population	[a] Urban Employee Basic Medical Insurance (UEBMI) participants [b] Urban Resident Basic Medical Insurance (URBMI) participants		
Sources of finance	[1] Money transferred from an individual MSA of the UEBMI [2] Money from the SPF of both the UEBMI and the URBMI [3] Money transferred from the Public Welfare Fund, with an annual value of RMB 20 million		
Types of services			
Home care	Aim: provide medical and nursing care for the chronically ill, homebound, bedridden LTCI participants or those with mobility issue at home on a weekly basis		
Nursing home care	Aim: provide continual medical and nursing care as well as EoL care for the terminally ill by institutions that integrate medical and elderly care services		
Intensive care	Aim: provide 24-hour medical care and daily living care for critically ill patients		
Service charges	Home care: RMB 60 per day per head	Nursing home care: RMB 60 per day per head	Intensive care: [a] Designated Grade II hospitals: RMB 170 per day per head [b] Designated Grade III hospitals: RMB 200 per day per head
Reimbursement rate	Home care: 96%	Nursing home care: 96%	Intensive care: 90%

Source: The Qingdao Municipal People's Government (2012) *Notification of Opinions on the Establishment of Long-term Care Medical Insurance System (Trial)* (Chinese version). Online. Available HTTP: http://qd.bendibao.com/live/2014821/43379.shtm (accessed 11 January 2021). National Health Commission of the People's Republic of China (2015) *Qingdao Explores Long-term Care System and Actively Promotes the Integration of Medical and Elderly Care Services* (Chinese version). Online. Available HTTP: www.nhc.gov.cn/wjw/dfxw/201504/ba34fcb2ecc84e6488b18dcd24db8477.shtml (accessed 16 January 2021).

rely solely on the social medical insurance system (Lu *et al.* 2017). According to *the Order*, social medical insurance consisted of basic medical insurance, catastrophic illness insurance, and financial assistance for catastrophic illnesses. Urban employees were required to enrol in Social Medical Insurance for Employee (SMIE), while urban and rural residents were required to enrol in Social Medical Insurance for Resident (SMIR). SMIE is similar to UEBMI, while SMIR is similar to URRBMI. SMIE fund consisted of an individual MSA and the SPF, while SMIR had only the SPF. Both SMIE and SMIR participants automatically enrolled in LTCI. Article 34 of *the Order* stated that the LTCI system consisted of two funds: the LTCI fund for employees and the LTCI fund for residents (Office of the Qingdao Municipal People's Government 2014). *The Order* stipulated that the LTCI fund for employees was financed through two ways: a one-time transfer of up to 20 percent of the accumulated surplus in the employee basic medical insurance fund and a monthly transfer of money from the employee basic medical insurance fund, the amount of which was equivalent to 0.5 percent of the employee's salary contributed to an individual MSA (Office of the Qingdao Municipal People's Government 2014). For the LTCI fund for residents, there would be an annual transfer of money from the SMIR fund, the amount of which was no more than 10 percent of the residents' total social medical insurance premium contribution (Office of the Qingdao Municipal People's Government 2014).

In 2015, the government further expanded LTCI service provision (Lu *et al.* 2017). In addition to home care, nursing home care, and intensive care at hospitals, community-based mobile clinic (*she qu xun hu*) was introduced to allow the disabled and the bed-bound to receive medical care in the comfort of their own homes. A healthcare team consisting of family physicians, community nurses, public health staff, and medical technicians visited the disabled and the bed-bound patients' homes (Dazhong Daily 2019). Services included vital sign measurement, rehabilitation training, counselling, preventive care for pressure ulcer, changing different tubes for patients, and providing patients with instructions on how to take medications, self-monitor blood pressure and blood glucose, and adjust diet (Dazhong Daily 2019). Home care was charged at RMB 50 per day per head (National Health Commission of the People's Republic of China 2015). Nursing home care which integrated medical and elderly care services was charged at RMB 65 per day per head, while intensive care (24-hour a day) at designated Grade II or Grade III hospitals was charged at RMB 170 per day per head (National Health Commission of the People's Republic of China 2015). Care provided by community-based mobile clinic was charged at RMB 1,600 per year for SMIE participants and urban residents (also known as the 'first-tier' residents in the document, including adult residents, young children, and university students), and RMB 800 per year for rural adult residents (also known as the 'second-tier' residents in the document) (National Health Commission of the People's Republic of China 2015). Urban and rural residents would receive care provided by community-based mobile clinic at least twice a week and once a week respectively (National Health Commission of the People's Republic of China 2015). The

LTCI reimbursement rate was 90 percent for SMIE participants, 80 percent for urban residents, and 40 percent for rural residents (National Health Commission of the People's Republic of China 2015). Table 5.2 summarizes the main points of *Social Health Insurance Measures in Qingdao.*

Table 5.2 Social medical insurance measures in Qingdao (2015)

Description	To provide medical and nursing care for partially and fully disabled people			
Targeted population	[a] Social Medical Insurance for Employee (SMIE) participants (i.e. urban employees) [b] Social Medical Insurance for Resident (SMIR) participants (i.e. urban and rural residents)			
Sources of finance	[a] Social Medical Insurance for Employee (SMIE) participants [i] a one-time transfer of up to 20% of the accumulated surplus in the employee basic medical insurance fund [ii] a monthly transfer of money from the employee basic medical insurance fund, the amount of which was equivalent to 0.5% of the employee's salary contributed to an individual MSA [b] Social Medical Insurance for Resident (SMIR) participants an annual transfer of money from the SMIR fund, the amount of which was no more than 10% of the residents' total social medical insurance premium contribution			
Types of services	Home care	Nursing home care	Intensive care at hospitals	Community-based mobile clinic
Service charges	RMB 50 per day per head (home care)	RMB 65 per day per head (nursing home are)	170 per day per head (intensive care at hospitals)	[a] RMB 1,600 per year for SMIE participants [b] RMB 1,600 per year for urban residents [c] RMB 800 per year for rural residents (community-based mobile clinic)
Reimbursement ratio	[a] 90% for SMIE participants [b] 80% for 'first-tier' residents (i.e. urban residents) [c] 40% for 'second-tier' residents (i.e. rural residents)			

Source: National Health Commission of the People's Republic of China (2015) *Qingdao Explores Long-term Care System and Actively Promotes the Integration of Medical and Elderly Care Services* (Chinese version). Online. Available HTTP: www.nhc.gov.cn/wjw/dfxw/201504/ba34fcb2ecc84e6488b18dcd24db8477.shtml (accessed 16 January 2021).

LTCI in Qingdao (2018)

In February 2018, the government issued *Interim Measures for Long-term Care in Qingdao* (hereafter *the 2018 Interim Measures*), which extended the coverage of LTCI to PWD. *The 2018 Interim Measures* stated that the aim of LTCI was to provide financial protection for the totally disabled and people with advanced dementia who received ADLs care and medical care and for the partially disabled and people in the mild or mid-stage dementia who received rehabilitation training and guidance to delay the onset of dementia (The Qingdao Municipal People's Government 2018). Both SMIE and SMIR participants automatically enrolled in LTCI. The LTCI fund for employees was financed by multiple sources, including (1) a monthly transfer of the amount of money equivalent to 0.5 percent of the employee's salary from the SPF of the employee basic medical insurance fund; (2) a monthly transfer of the amount of money equivalent to 0.2 percent of the employee's salary from the individual MSA of the employee basic medical insurance; (3) government subsidies of RMB 30 per person per year; (4) a one-time transfer of up to 20 percent of the accumulated surplus in the employee basic medical insurance fund; and (5) social donations (The Qingdao Municipal People's Government 2018). But the LTCI fund for residents remained the same. Meanwhile, two new funds were established. One was called an Employee and Resident Long-term Care Insurance Adjustment Fund (*zhi gong ju min hu li bao xian tiao ji jin*), which aimed at counteracting financial risks and serving as reserve fund (Liu *et al.* 2019). The Adjustment Fund, with an annual value of RMB 60 million, would be financed by an annual transfer of up to 5 percent of money from the LTCI fund for employees and the LTCI fund for residents respectively (Liu *et al.* 2019; The Qingdao Municipal People's Government 2018). Another fund was a Protection Fund to support activities that prevented disability and prevented or delayed the onset of dementia (The Qingdao Municipal People's Government 2018). The Protection Fund would be financed by an annual transfer of up to 1 percent of money from the LTCI fund for employees and the LTCI fund for residents respectively as well as social donations (The Qingdao Municipal People's Government 2018).

A '4+3' service approach was introduced to meet the specific needs of different groups of people (Qingdao Municipal Bureau of Human Resources and Social Security 2019; Liu *et al.* 2019). Four types of services were provided for the disabled, including home care, nursing home care, intensive care at hospitals, and community-based mobile clinic (*she qu xun hu*) (The Qingdao Municipal People's Government 2018). Home care was upgraded to provide 60 types of services which could be divided into four categories: 25 types of basic nursing care services (e.g. sputum suction), 17 types of daily living support and personal care (e.g. bathing), 15 types of rehabilitation and training services (e.g. swallow strength training exercise), and three types of medication management services (Qingdao Municipal Bureau of Human Resources and Social Security 2019). Meanwhile, three types of services were provided for PWD through designated hospitals or nursing homes with dementia special care units. They were day respite care, short-term respite care of up to 60 days per year, and LTC (The Qingdao Municipal People's Government 2018).

Older adults' eligibility for receiving specific type of LTC services depended on their level of disability. A preliminary LTC needs assessment must be conducted to determine the level of disability of a participant. Assessment content included ADLs, mental status, social involvement, sensory and communication (Qingdao Municipal Bureau of Human Resources and Social Security *et al.* 2018a) (See Table 5.3).

Besides, a secondary assessment that involved video recording the applicant was required to show his/her physical functionality (Yang *et al.* 2021: 160–1). The level of disability was defined on six levels which followed the national standard established by the Ministry of Civil Affairs (MCA) (Qingdao Municipal Bureau of Human Resources and Social Security *et al.* 2018a). The MCA made reference to the elderly ability assessment tool adopted in the United States (US), the United Kingdom (UK), Australia, Japan, Hong Kong and Taiwan (Ministry of Civil Affairs 2013). Level zero represented no disability; level one represented mild disability; levels two and three represented moderate disability; levels four and five represented severe disability (Qingdao Municipal Bureau of Human Resources and Social Security *et al.* 2018a; Qingdao Municipal Bureau of Human Resources and Social Security 2019). The participant would receive an assessment result notification that required his/her signature (Qingdao Municipal Bureau of Human Resources and Social Security *et al.* 2018a). On average, the assessment result was valid for six months and the longest validity period should not exceed 12 months (Qingdao Municipal Bureau of Human Resources and Social Security *et al.* 2018a). A needs assessment would be carried out for the participant again once the validity period expired (Qingdao Municipal Bureau of Human Resources and Social Security *et al.* 2018a). The participant was considered to be eligible for LTC benefits if he or she was in disability level three and above (Qingdao Municipal Bureau of Human Resources and Social Security 2019). He/she could receive longer hours of services if his/her disability level was higher. For example, home care recipients in disability levels three, four and five would obtain three hours, five hours, and seven hours respectively of services every week (Qingdao Municipal Bureau of Human Resources and Social Security 2019). For community-based mobile clinic service, eligible recipients in disability levels three, four, and five would obtain three hours, five hours, and seven hours respectively of services every week (Qingdao Municipal Bureau of Human Resources and Social Security 2019).

To ensure clinically accurate and precise diagnosis of dementia, those who want to obtain access to dementia care services covered by LTC must go to the designated dementia diagnosis centres to get a dementia diagnosis. At present, there are six designated dementia diagnosis centres in Qingdao. They are the Affiliated Hospital of Qingdao University, Qingdao Municipal Hospital (Group), Qilu Hospital of Shandong University (Qingdao), Qingdao Municipal Mental Health Centre, Qingdao Cheng Yang People's Hospital, and Qingdao West Coast New Area Central Hospital ('A List of Dementia Diagnosis Centres' 2017). In the

Table 5.3 LTC needs assessment in Qingdao

Dimensions	Components	Marks	Total marks
ADLs	[1] Eating	10	100
	[2] Bathing	5	
	[3] Face washing/teeth brushing/ combing hair/shaving	5	
	[4] Putting on and taking off clothes/shoes; wearing socks and taking socks off; tying shoelaces; zipping up the clothes/pants	10	
	[5] Faecal incontinence (Yes/No)	10	
	[6] Urinary incontinence (Yes/No)	10	
	[7] Toileting	10	
	[8] Getting up from lying on a bed and sitting on a chair	15	
	[9] Walking on level ground	15	
	[10] Walking up and down the stairs	10	
Mental status	[1a] Name three unrelated objects (i.e. apple, watch, national flag) and ask the older adult to memorize them	2	6
	[1b] Clock-drawing test		
	[1c] Ask the older adult to recall the three objects previously mentioned		
	[2] Aggressive behaviours	2	
	[a] verbal: screaming, making threats, or scolding at people		
	[b] physical: biting, hitting, grabbing, kicking, pushing, or throwing things		
	[3] Symptoms of depression	2	
Sensory and communication	[1] The level of consciousness	3	14
	[2] Visual acuity	4	
	[3] Hearing	4	
	[4] Communication	3	
Social involvement	[1] Self-care ability	4	20
	[2] Ability to do work that requires physical strength or brainpower	4	
	[3] Orientation to time and space	4	
	[4] Ability to recognize people they know	4	
	[5] Social engagement	4	

Source: Qingdao Municipal Bureau of Human Resources and Social Security, Qingdao Municipal Health and Family Planning Commission and Qingdao Civil Affairs Bureau (2018a) *Notification on Implementation Measures of Qingdao Long-term Care Needs Assessment* (Chinese version). Available HTTP: www.qingdao.gov.cn/n172/n24624151/n24626255/n24626269/n24626283/180316194933717664.html (accessed 22 January 2021).

designated dementia diagnosis centres, the Mini-Mental State Exam (MMSE) and the Montreal Cognitive Assessment (MoCA) test would be carried out to detect cognitive impairment of a person. Besides, the Hachinski Ischemic Score (HIS) would be used to differentiate major types of dementia. The Hamilton Depression Rating Scale (HAMD) and an ADLs assessment would also be used to assess depression symptoms and determine a person's functional status. Once the person is diagnosed as a PWD by the designated dementia diagnosis centre, his/her family members can bring the LTCI benefit application form together with the original identification document, social insurance card, and medical record of the PWD to any designated hospital or nursing home with dementia special care units (Qingdao Municipal Bureau of Human Resources and Social Security 2016). After receiving the application, the designated hospital or nursing home would determine if the applicant is eligible for dementia care services. It will submit the documents of eligible applicants to the Social Insurance Agency via an online system (Qingdao Municipal Bureau of Human Resources and Social Security 2016). It will be notified of the Social Insurance Agency's approval decision within 10 working days (Qingdao Municipal Bureau of Human Resources and Social Security 2016). PWD with successful LTCI benefit application can obtain access to dementia care services at designated hospitals or nursing homes with dementia special care units.

Different types of LTC services were charged differently. Home care was charged at RMB 50 per day per head. Nursing home care was charged at RMB 65 per day per head. The unit price for intensive care at designated Grade II and Grade III hospitals was RMB 180 and RMB 210 per day per head respectively, while the unit price for patients with tracheostomy to receive intensive care at designed hospitals would be RMB 300 per day per head (Qingdao Municipal Bureau of Human Resources and Social Security 2019). Care provided by community-based mobile clinic was charged at RMB 2,500 per year for SMIE participants, RMB 2,200 for the 'first-tier' residents, and RMB 1,500 per year for the 'second-tier' residents (Qingdao Municipal Bureau of Human Resources and Social Security 2019). For dementia care, the price for day respite care was RMB 50 per day per head, while the price for short-term respite care and LTC was RMB 65 per day per head (Qingdao Municipal Bureau of Human Resources and Social Security 2019).

LTCI would cover the monthly expenses of ADLs care for eligible employees who lived in nursing homes and hospitals and employees with severe dementia (i.e. disability level five). The LTCI monthly payment limits for the expenses of ADLs care of eligible employees in disability levels three, four, and five were RMB 660 (RMB 22 per day), RMB 1,050 (RMB 35 per day), and RMB 1,500 (RMB 50 per day) respectively with co-payment at 10 percent (Qingdao Municipal Bureau of Human Resources and Social Security 2019). For eligible employees with severe dementia, the monthly payment limit for the expenses of ADL care was RMB 750 when receiving day respite care and RMB 1,500 when receiving short-term respite care and LTC (Qingdao Municipal Bureau of Human Resources and Social Security 2019). The LTCI reimbursement rate was 90 percent for SMIE participants, 80 percent for 'first-tier' residents, and 70 percent for 'second-tier' residents (The Qingdao Municipal People's Government 2018). Table 5.4 summarizes the important contents of the *2018 Interim Measures.*

Table 5.4 LTCI in Qingdao (2018)

Description	To provide financial protection for [a] the totally disabled and people with advanced dementia who received basic care of daily living and medical care [b] the partially disabled and people in the mild or mid-stage dementia who received rehabilitation training and guidance to delay the onset of dementia
Targeted population	[a] Social Medical Insurance for Employee (SMIE) participants (i.e. urban employees) [b] Social Medical Insurance for Resident (SMIR) participants (i.e. urban and rural residents)

Sources of finance	SMIE participants	SMIR participants
	(1) a monthly transfer of the amount of money equivalent to 0.5% of the employee's salary from the SPF of the employee basic medical insurance fund; (2) a monthly transfer of the amount of money equivalent to 0.2% of the employee's salary from the individual MSA of the employee basic medical insurance; (3) government subsidies of RMB 30 per person per year; (4) a one-time transfer of up to 20% of the accumulated surplus in the employee basic medical insurance fund; and (5) social donations	An annual transfer of money from the residents' social medical insurance fund, the amount of which was no more than 10% of the residents' total social medical insurance premium contribution

Eligibility	Older adults or PWD who are in disability level three and above

	Types of long-term care services
[1] Home care	Service content: [a] 25 types of basic nursing care services [b] 17 types of daily living support and personal care [c] 15 types of rehabilitation and training services [d] 3 types of medication management services Frequency of services: [a] People in disability level three: 3 hours per week [b] People in disability level four: 5 hours per week [c] People in disability level five: 7 hours per week Service charges: RMB 50 per day per head
[2] Nursing home care	Service content: [a] continual medical and nursing care [b] EoL care for the terminally ill Service charges: RMB 65 per day per head

(Continued)

Table 5.4 (Continued)

	The LTCI monthly payment limit for the expenses of ADL care: [a] Eligible employees in disability level three: RMB 660 (RMB 22 per day) [b] Eligible employees in disability level four: RMB 1,050 (RMB 35 per day) [c] Eligible employees in disability level five: RMB 1,500 (RMB 50 per day) with co-payment at 10%
[3] Intensive care at hospitals	Service content: 24-hour medical care and daily living care for critically ill patients Service charges: [a] Designated Grade II hospitals: RMB 180 per day per head [b] Designated Grade III hospitals: RMB 210 per day per head [c] Patients with tracheostomy: RMB 300 per day per head
[4] Community-based mobile clinic	Service content: Allow the disabled and the bed-bound to receive medical care in the comfort of their own homes Frequency of services: [a] People in disability level three: 3 hours per week [b] People in disability level four: 5 hours per week [c] People in disability level five: 7 hours per week Service charges: [a] SMIE participants: RMB 2,500 per year [b] 'First-tier' residents: RMB 2,200 per year [c] 'Second-tier' residents: RMB 1,500 per year
[5] Day respite care for PWD	Service content: Day care Service charges: RMB 50 per day Monthly payment limit for the expenses of ADL care of employees with severe dementia (i.e. disability level five): RMB 750
[6] Short-term respite care for PWD	Service content: Respite care of up to 60 days per year Service charges: RMB 65 per day Monthly payment limit for the expenses of ADL care of employees with severe dementia (i.e. disability level five): RMB 1,500
[7] Long-term care for PWD	Service content: Full-day long-term care services Service charges: RMB 65 per day Monthly payment limit for the expenses of ADL care of employees with severe dementia (i.e. disability level five): RMB 1,500
Reimbursement ratio	SMIE participants: 90% 'First-tier' residents: 80% 'Second-tier' residents: 70%

Source: The Qingdao Municipal People's Government (2018) *Interim Measures for Long-term Care in Qingdao* (Chinese version). Online. Available HTTP: www.yanglaocn.com/shtml/20180320/1521532406114318.html (accessed 22 January 2021).
Qingdao Municipal Bureau of Human Resources and Social Security (2019) *Analysing Interim Measures for Long-term Care in Qingdao* (Chinese version). Online. Available HTTP: www.qingdao.gov.cn/n172/n24624151/n31284614/n31284615/n31284623/190910135925004617.html (accessed 22 January 2021).

In March 2020, the government issued *Long-term Care Insurance Approach in Qingdao* (Office of the Qingdao Municipal People's Government 2020). The sources of finance for the employees' and residents' LTCI fund, the reimbursement rate, types of services provided for the disabled, and PWD in the 2020 document were the same as that of *the 2018 Interim Measures.*

Designated LTC service providers in Qingdao

There are different types of designated LTC service providers in Qingdao. They include elder care institutions, institutions for the disabled, medical institutions in the community, Grade II or Grade III general hospitals, and Grade III hospitals that mainly treat cardiovascular, cerebrovascular, and geriatric diseases (Qingdao Municipal Bureau of Human Resources and Social Security *et al.* 2018b). They can be publicly or privately run. They are required to use computerized accounting systems, drug management software, and intelligent monitoring systems (Qingdao Municipal Bureau of Human Resources and Social Security *et al.* 2018b). They are also required to gradually establish professional care teams to provide ADLs care, medical care, nursing care, rehabilitation service, spiritual care, and EoL care (Qingdao Municipal Bureau of Human Resources and Social Security *et al.* 2018b). In 2016, there were about 500 designated institutions providing LTC in Qingdao (Wang 2016). About 95 percent of them were privately run, providing more than 98 percent of LTC services in the city (Wang 2016). In October 2020, there were over 770 designated institutions providing LTC in Qingdao (Qingdao Municipal Medical Insurance Bureau 2020).

The validity period for a service agreement does not exceed three years in duration (Qingdao Municipal Bureau of Human Resources and Social Security *et al.* 2018b). All the designated LTC service providers have to be assessed annually by the social insurance agency and Qingdao Municipal Bureau of Human Resources and Social Security (Qingdao Municipal Bureau of Human Resources and Social Security 2018). They are assessed based on the following criteria: (a) basic management, (b) medical care and service management, (c) insurance claim management, (d) staff management, (e) financial management and drug management, and (f) customer satisfaction (Qingdao Municipal Bureau of Human Resources and Social Security 2018). The result of the annual assessment is linked to the rating of the designated LTC service providers, the appropriation and deduction of the assessment deposit, and the renewal of the service agreement (Qingdao Municipal Bureau of Human Resources and Social Security 2018). Letter grades are assigned to LTC service providers to indicate ratings, with A being the highest grade and D being the lowest. On a 100-point system, designated LTC service providers obtaining a score of 90 and above would be assigned an A rating, receive an award, and be recommended for getting a rating of AA or AAA at the provincial level (Qingdao Municipal Bureau of Human Resources and Social Security 2018). Only a maximum of 8 percent of the designated LTC service providers in Qingdao can be assigned an A rating (Qingdao Municipal Bureau of Human Resources and Social Security 2018). Those that obtain a score of 80–89 would be assigned a B rating, a score of 60–79 would be assigned a C rating, and a score of below 60 would be assigned a D rating (Qingdao Municipal Bureau of Human Resources and Social Security 2018). Those that are assigned a D rating would have their assessment deposit deducted completely and are required to take corrective actions within one month to improve the undesirable situation (Qingdao Municipal Bureau of Human Resources and Social Security 2018). Failure to take corrective action may result in the non-renewal or termination of service contract (Qingdao Municipal Bureau of Human Resources and Social Security 2018).

In order to become a designated place with dementia special care units, hospitals or nursing homes have to pass the annual assessment carried out by the social insurance agency and Qingdao Municipal Bureau of Human Resources and Social Security (Qingdao Municipal Bureau of Human Resources and Social Security 2018). Those that obtain only a C grade or a D grade in the annual assessment are not eligible to apply for having a dementia special care unit in their places (Qingdao Municipal Medical Insurance Bureau 2019). Eligible hospitals or nursing homes can submit their applications online along with the following support documents: the photocopy of the Practice License for Medical Institution, Permit for Establishing an Elder Care Institution, Employees' Professional Training Certificate in Dementia Care, digital photos of the layout of the dementia special care unit, a briefing document which explains the dementia care team scale, key features of the care delivery model, and service charges, as well as an integrity declaration form (Qingdao Municipal Medical Insurance Bureau 2019).

The application and supporting documents would be reviewed by the social insurance agency. A site assessment would be carried out by the social insurance agency, if necessary, to determine whether the hospitals or nursing homes are suitable for having a dementia special care unit in their places (Qingdao Municipal Medical Insurance Bureau 2019). Once the application is approved, the hospitals or nursing homes become designated places with dementia special care units. A 'closed-style' management should be adopted in the dementia special care units (Qingdao Municipal Medical Insurance Bureau 2019). The dementia special care units should contain at least 20 beds and have at least two medical personnel, social workers or senior elder care workers who have received professional dementia care training (Qingdao Municipal Bureau of Human Resources and Social Security 2016). The care worker-to-resident with dementia ratio should not be less than 1:3 (Qingdao Municipal Bureau of Human Resources and Social Security 2016). Personal hygiene care, diet care, bowel care, and sleep care are provided for residents (Qingdao Municipal Bureau of Human Resources and Social Security 2016). Besides, rehabilitation programmes are provided for PWD to maintain their balance, swallowing, chewing, language, cognitive, and self-care abilities while common clinical problems in dementia care would be addressed (Qingdao Municipal Bureau of Human Resources and Social Security 2016). Personalized and humane care would be provided for PWD experiencing Behavioural and Psychological Symptoms of Dementia (BPSD) (e.g. agitation, physical aggression, psychosis, depression, wandering) (Qingdao Municipal Bureau of Human Resources and Social Security 2016). Referral assistance would be offered to PWD experiencing severe BPSD or facing deteriorating medical conditions (Qingdao Municipal Bureau of Human Resources and Social Security 2016). Psychological interventions are offered to PWD and family caregivers of PWD (Qingdao Municipal Bureau of Human Resources and Social Security 2016). Guidance on nutrition and rehabilitation as well as dementia care training is provided for family caregivers of PWD (Qingdao Municipal Bureau of Human Resources and Social Security 2016). In Qingdao, the number of designated hospitals or nursing homes dementia special care units increased from six in 2017 (Qingdao Financial Daily 2018) to about 30 in January 2021. In sum, dementia special care units are closed, safe, free, and comfortable places providing diversified dementia services to meet the preferences and needs of PWD (Qingdao Municipal Bureau of Human Resources and Social Security 2016).

Evaluating the outcomes of LTCI

Since the implementation of LTCI, Qingdao has seen an increase in the number of LTCI participants. The number of LTCI participants increased from about 3.65 million people in July 2013 (Qingdao Morning Post 2013) to 8.1 million people in 2016 (People's Daily 2016) and more than 8.5 million people in 2018 (Zhang 2018). In 2019, Qingdao had 8.6 million LTCI participants (Qingdao Daily 2019). About 3.74 million of them were urban employees, while 4.86 million of them were residents (Qingdao Daily 2019). The average age of LTCI beneficiaries in Qingdao was 79.3 years old (Mi *et al.* 2019: 30). The person of oldest age to receive LTC services in Qingdao was 109 years old (Mi *et al.* 2019: 30). The outcomes of LTCI in Qingdao can be evaluated in terms of five criteria: utilization of medical resources, cost, equity, quality of care, and sustainability.

Utilization of medical resources

Before the implementation of LTCI, the problem of social hospitalization or 'socialization of elderly hospitalization' was serious in Qingdao (People's Daily 2016). It refers to the reliance on hospitalization instead of elderly care institutions for caring for older adults in need of LTC (Dai 2018: 795; Dai and Lu 2018: 518). This would cause an immense waste of medical health resources (Dai 2018), create a severe drain on medical insurance funds (Dai and Lu 2018), place older adults and their family members at risk of debt or poverty, reduce the ability of older adults to take care of themselves on a daily basis due to lengthy stays in the hospitals, and increase work stress among hospital nursing staff (Dai 2018: 795).

According to Qingdao Health Bureau, over 50 percent of older adults with disability received medical and nursing care at hospitals before the implementation of LTCI (Qingdao Morning Post 2013). The implementation of LTCI helped address the problem of social hospitalization because older adults were diverted to different care settings based on the LTC needs assessment result.

For example, as of July 2013, there were 10,634 bedridden LTCI beneficiaries (Qingdao Morning Post 2013). About 8,867 of them received home care, while 1,269 of them received nursing home care and 498 of them received intensive care at Grade II or Grade III hospitals (Qingdao Morning Post 2013). Proper LTC was achieved through home care or nursing home care and hence, only about 4.7 percent of bedridden LTCI beneficiaries received care at Grade II or Grade III hospitals in Qingdao. From 2012 to 2018, the LTCI accumulated expenditure in Qingdao reached RMB 1.5 billion (Zhang 2018). Such accumulated expenditure was used to purchase 25.04 million days of LTC services for people with disability and PWD (Zhang 2018). The same amount of accumulated expenditure could purchase only about 1.7 million days of inpatient care at Grade II or Grade III hospitals (Zhang 2018). Hence, implementing LTCI enhances efficient allocation and utilization of medical resources (Qingdao Morning Post 2013). It can facilitate better utilization of LTCI funds and the provision of more diversified services for LTCI beneficiaries.

Cost

In China, '[a] one-time hospitalization usually costs over half of urban residents' annual per capita income, or 1.5 times of rural residents' annual per capital income' (Dai and Lu 2018: 522). Implementing LTCI can greatly reduce the financial costs borne by older adults and their family members because of two main reasons. First, LTC services can be obtained in different settings such as home or nursing homes without heavy reliance on hospitalization. A per diem rate for LTC is 'much lower compared to the cost of equivalent care provided at hospitals' (Yang *et al.* 2021: 162). For example, a chronically ill older person who received inpatient care for six times had to pay over RMB 20,000 on his own before the implementation of LTCI in Qingdao ('Parents Enjoy Home Care' 2015). After implementing LTCI, however, he had received two-year home care that cost him only about RMB 2,000 to RMB 3,000 ('Parents Enjoy Home Care' 2015). According to Qingdao Municipal Bureau of Human Resources and Social Security, the average annual expenditure of home care and nursing home care per capita was RMB 2,000, which was three times lower than the average annual expenditure of intensive care at designated Grade II or Grade III hospitals per capita (People's Daily 2016). This may explain why home care has gone mainstream in LTC in Qingdao. From 2012 to 2017, 82.4 percent of LTCI beneficiaries received home care (Mi *et al.* 2019: 33). During the same period, only 9.6 percent of LTCI beneficiaries received nursing home care, 4.1 percent received intensive care at hospitals, and 3.9 percent received services through community-based mobile clinic (Mi *et al.* 2019: 33) (See Table 5.5). As of July 2018, home care accounted for 89.6 percent of all the LTC services provided in the city (Zhang 2018).

Second, the reimbursement rate is high for LTCI-covered services. This helps significantly reduce out-of-pocket (OOP) payments. For example, before the implementation of LTCI in Qingdao, a 77-year-old patient with ischemic stroke had to pay almost RMB 10,000 for eight days of inpatient care (People's Daily

Table 5.5 Number of LTC beneficiaries from 2012 to 2017

	2012	2013	2014	2015	2016	2017	Total	Percentage (%)
Home care	6,629	11,027	8,226	1,473	1,175	60	28,590	82.4
Nursing home care	1,377	725	451	280	491	12	3,336	9.6
Intensive care at hospitals	560	440	425	0	0	0	1,425	4.1
Community-based mobile clinic	0	0	0	443	891	20	1,354	3.9
Total	8,566	12,192	9,102	2,196	2,557	92	34,705	100

Source: Mi, H., Ji, M. and Liu, W. G. (2019) *Research on Long-term Care Insurance in Qingdao, China* (Chinese version), China: China Labour and Social Security Publishing House, p. 33.

2016). After the implementation of LTCI, however, he had to pay only RMB 822 on his own for 148 days of inpatient care that cost RMB 8,223 (People's Daily 2016). Another example was that the cost of nursing home care was RMB 5949.50 per month for a 76-year-old bedridden patient after having a tracheostomy surgery in Qingdao (China Daily 2020). But she had to pay only RMB 2583.55 per month because over half of costs (including medical care and daily personal care expenses) were covered by LTCI (China Daily 2020). As of July 2018, every LTCI beneficiary in Qingdao received an average of 822 days of care according to a study jointly conducted by Zhejiang University, Qingdao Municipal Bureau of Human Resources and Social Security, and Qingdao Municipal Bureau of Finance (Zhang 2018). The average charges per day was RMB 77.6 per capita, but a LTCI beneficiary paid only an average RMB 8.3 per day (Zhang 2018). As a result, more people can benefit from the low-cost LTC coverage.

Nevertheless, a study found that the direct cost and total cost of EoL care paid by social insurance were about 62.7 percent and 43.9 percent higher than the direct cost and total cost of EoL care paid by families in China (Gong and Zhou 2018). This is because social insurance drives up demand for EoL care, and formal care is a substitute for informal care (Gong and Zhou 2018). Whether LTCI in Qingdao would drive up demand for LTC services (e.g. nursing home care, EoL care) and increase LTC costs in the long run needs further examination in future. LTC cost may increase when the supply of formal LTC services is inadequate to meet the increasing demand of LTC services caused by population ageing and increased disability prevalence.

Equity

The LTCI has been extended to cover more segments of population over time in Qingdao. It initially covered employees and residents in urban areas. Then, the coverage was extended to rural residents and PWD. Nevertheless, UEBMI participants enjoy better coverage than residents according to Article 20 of *Long-term Care Insurance Approach in Qingdao* (Office of the Qingdao Municipal People's Government 2020). For UEBMI participants, LTCI covers their expenses incurred by medical care, nursing care, and ADL care (Office of the Qingdao Municipal People's Government 2020). For residents, however, LTCI covers only their expenses incurred by medical care and nursing care (Office of the Qingdao Municipal People's Government 2020). This means that residents have to bear the expenses incurred by ADL care on their own (Sun 2020: 84). Those who are housewives, have no formal employment, or have no pension may have financial difficulty in paying the expenses out of pocket or encounter access barriers (Yang *et al.* 2021).

Besides, there is disparity in reimbursement rate among different segments of population. In 2015, UEBMI participants enjoyed the highest LTCI reimbursement rate (i.e. 90%), which was 10 percent higher than that of urban residents and 50 percent higher than that of rural residents. Urban and rural residents who enjoyed lower reimbursement rate had to bear higher OOP expenses when obtaining LTC services. But there was the problem of income disparity in Qing-dao. In 2015, the average annual income of urban employees was RMB 53,715 per capita (Qingdao Evening News 2016). In the same year, the average annual disposable income of urban residents was RMB 40,370, while that of rural residents was RMB 16,730 (Qingdao Municipal Statistics Bureau and National Bureau of Statistics Survey Office in Qingdao 2016). The average annual disposable income of rural residents was 2.41 times and 3.21 times lower than that of urban residents and urban employees. Due to income disparity, rural residents who had lower incomes may not have sufficient financial means to pay for LTC services. In 2018, the reimbursement rate for rural resident increased to 70 percent, while the reimbursement rate for UEBMI participants and urban residents remained the same. This helped reduce rural residents' OOP expenses for LTC services. But disparity in reimbursement rate among different segments of population still exists. As a result of the differences in reimbursement rate, a large proportion of service users at nursing homes and Grade II and Grade III hospitals are the UEBMI participants (Yang *et al.* 2021: 161).

In Qingdao, there is inequality in access to home care in urban districts. The eligibility policy states that LTCI beneficiaries 'can only choose a home care provider within 4 km away from their home and from the same district' (Chang *et al.* 2020). A study found that home care services in four districts (i.e. Shibei, Shinan, Licang, and Laoshan) were not distributed according to population needs (Chang *et al.* 2020). Although the demand for home care services was high, these services were not always available to those who lived in districts with high concentration of older people (e.g. Shibei, Shinan) (Chang *et al.* 2020). This led to a large amount of LTCI beneficiaries eligible for home care having no access to home care services (Chang *et al.* 2020). Similarly, another study found that people in Qingdao did not have equal access to home care, nursing home care, and intensive care at designated hospitals because these care services were unevenly distributed in six districts (i.e. Shinan, Shibei, Licang, Cheng-yang, Laoshan, and Huangdao) (Li 2015: 21). For example, there were about 16 home care providers for every 10,000 people living in Shibei District (Li 2015: 21). However, there were only about three home care providers for every 10,000 people living in Chengyang District (Li 2015: 21). It means that disabled people's demand for home care in Chengyang District is less likely to be met due to insufficient home care providers.

There is also urban–rural disparity in LTC. In Qingdao, about 67 percent of disabled elderly lived in rural areas (Li 2016). According to Qingdao Municipal Social Insurance Bureau, disabled elderly in rural areas had greater demand for LTC services than their urban counterparts due to having very low incomes and multiple illnesses (Li 2016). Compared with their urban counterparts, however, disabled elderly in rural areas had poorer access and poorer quality of medical care and LTC due to the lack of sufficient and qualified LTC facilities and workers (e.g. doctors, nurses, physiotherapists). Most of them could rely on only mobile clinics or home care. Mobile medical care in rural areas is delivered by over 4,000 village clinics (People's Daily 2016). Home care in rural areas is delivered by day care centres. A study conducted in a rural district in Qingdao found that home care services provided by a day care centre were limited to the delivery of three meals a day to disabled elderly, maintaining household hygiene, and doing the laundry for the disabled elderly (Zhang 2017: 23). But most of the disabled elderly interviewed in the study said that they wanted to receive more diversified home care services that could meet their needs, including medical care services (e.g. medical consultation, bedsore treatment), prescription delivery, and rehabilitation (Zhang 2017: 23). Also, the study found that most of the nursing homes in rural areas refused to accept disabled elderly by using shortage of nursing home beds as an excuse (Zhang 2017: 21). This was due to the lack of qualified LTC workers, more time needed to care for disabled elders, and higher risks borne by nursing homes and LTC workers when caring for disabled elders who had poorer health (Zhang 2017: 21). Hence, disabled elders may encounter more difficulty in obtaining nursing home care. Another study found that the underdevelopment of LTC facilities, especially in rural areas, led to low expenditure of the residents' LTCI funds in Qingdao in 2017 (Yu 2019: 53). Although RMB 300 million were raised for the residents' LTCI funds in 2017, only about RMB 20 million were used (Yu 2019: 53). In fact, living scattered in villages also increases the difficulty in delivering LTC to the disabled elderly in Qingdao (Li 2016). In sum, the healthcare and LTC needs of disabled elders in rural areas are less likely to be met by the current situation. How to boost LTC access in rural areas will be an important task for the government.

Quality of care

The '4+3' service approach is adopted to provide LTC for people with mild or severe disability and PWD. An annual assessment is carried out to evaluate LTC service providers against criteria set out in *Evaluation Standards for Designated Long-term Care Insurance Service Providers in Qingdao*. Since the result of the annual assessment would affect the rating of the designated LTC service providers, the appropriation and deduction of the assessment deposit, and the renewal of the service agreement, LTC service providers strive to meet or exceed service performing standards. They serve disabled persons in the best way possible by understanding their needs and meeting their expectations.

The '4+3' service approach can triage care needs. Home care enables disabled persons, particularly bedridden ones, to receive nursing care, ADLs care, or rehabilitation through on-call services and longer hours of home visits (Yang *et al.* 2021: 162). Some basic training is given to family members by home care providers so that family members can manage some care conditions of disabled persons at home (Yang *et al.* 2021: 162). Home care enables disabled persons to access care in the comfort, convenience, and privacy of familiar surroundings.

As regards community-based mobile clinics, they enable the chronically ill, homebound, bedridden older persons and those with mobility issue to receive timely and necessary medical care such as medical consultation, physical examinations, prescriptions, and refills at home. They help manage chronic conditions of older adults, reduce their emergency room visits and hospitalizations, lower the cost of care, improve older adults' safety and their quality of life, and give family caregivers peace of mind. For example, mobile clinics in Pingdu, a county-level city in Qingdao, provided regular medical care to rural bedridden or wheelchair-bound elders who usually delayed in seeking medical care due to having no family companionship (Li 2016). Community-based mobile clinics help disabled elders overcome barriers (e.g. geography, time, transportation) to health service access.

Nursing home care that integrates medical and elderly services enables disabled elderly residents who require repeated treatments to obtain quality medical care and other services (e.g. ADLs care, rehabilitation, preventive care, psychological counselling, health education and management, physical, recreational and cultural learning activities, and EoL care) at nursing homes without going to different places (Si *et al.* 2020). A recent study found that older residents in 43 nursing homes in Qingdao had high demand for medical care (about 88%), ADLs care (about 76%), and health management (about 74%) (Si *et al.* 2020). About 90 percent of older residents said in the survey that they were satisfied with the medical and elderly services they obtained at nursing homes (Si *et al.* 2020). In Qingdao, EoL care services at nursing homes could meet the psychological and spiritual needs of over 10,000 terminally ill elderly patients so that the patients died with dignity (People's Daily 2016).

Intensive care at designated Grade II or Grade III hospitals provides round-the-clock medical care and ADLs care for critically ill elders. This ensures that elderly patients who are at risk when left alone unattended have the attention, assistance, and support they need all the time. Short-term respite care and day respite care enable PWD to receive care in a safe, supportive environment while letting caregivers have a temporary rest ('Respite Care' n.d.). LTC for PWD enables PWD to receive round-the-clock care in dementia special care units so that their social, emotional, and psychological needs can be met by a professional care team.

However, there are several factors affecting quality of care. First, there is the shortage of LTC beds. In 2015, Qingdao had about 50,000 LTC beds (Shang *et al.* 2020). It had only 30 LTC beds per 1,000 older population, which was far below the standard of developed countries that have 50–70 beds per 1,000 older population (Shang *et al.* 2020). Inadequate LTC beds lead to disabled elders enduring lengthy waits to be admitted to nursing homes or other residential care facilities. Those with severe disability may not be able to get professional care and assistance they need if they continue to stay at home. Also, there is the shortage of LTC workers. At present, Qingdao has only about 6,000 LTC workers (Xiao 2019). There is a shortfall of at least 14,000 LTC workers in the city (Xiao 2019). A LTC worker has to take care of 8–10 older residents in some nursing homes (Xiao 2019). Working in the LTC sector is physically and emotionally demanding. Staffing shortage increases the workload of existing LTC workers, their risk for injury, stress and burnout levels while reducing their morale and job satisfaction. This in turn may make it difficult if not impossible to deliver timely, responsive, and high-quality care to older residents. Third, income level can affect the quality of care received by LTCI beneficiaries. A recent study found that LTCI beneficiaries with lower income in urban districts were more likely to choose a nursing home with low service costs albeit poor quality services (Chang *et al.* 2020: 112667). Services with better quality but higher service cost were primarily utilized by LTCI beneficiaries with higher income (Chang *et al.* 2020: 112667). Fourth, care providers' cost-saving and cream skimming practice also affect the quality of care. A study which drew data from 47 in-depth interviews in Qingdao found that poorer quality of care was the result of LTC service providers' intention to provide care at the least cost and their cream skimming practice (Yang *et al.* 2021: 162). Since care providers are paid at fixed costs, they may not always provide appropriate treatment for service recipients or may deliver less than needed of care to service recipients with severe LTC needs to avoid running a deficit (Yang *et al.* 2021: 162). For example, some home care providers control costs by controlling the use of incontinence pads by patients (Yang *et al.* 2021: 162). Another example is that some nursing home care providers are inclined to prescribe relatively low-cost medicines without considering their clinical efficacy (Yang *et al.* 2021: 162). The result of cream skimming by care providers is that resources are usually directed to people with mild or moderate disability (Yang *et al.* 2021). Care providers would avoid admitting eligible LTCI beneficiaries who are likely to incur high costs, such as those who constantly get infections and need antibiotics to control them, and suggest these LTCI beneficiaries be transferred to hospitals (Yang *et al.* 2021: 162).

Sustainability

In Qingdao, the number of LTCI beneficiaries have increased over time. It rose from 13,311 in July 2013 (Qingdao Morning Post 2013) to 43,000 in 2017 (Yu 2019). In 2019, there were over 60,000 LTCI beneficiaries (Qingdao Daily 2019), who accounted for 20 percent of all the people with disability and PWD in Qingdao (Sun 2020). The annual revenue for the urban employees' LTC insurance fund was about RMB 1 billion, while the annual revenue for the residents' LTC insurance fund was about RMB 300 million (Liu *et al.* 2019: 37). The LTC accumulated expenditure rose from 108 million in 2013 (Qingdao Morning Post 2013) to RMB 970 million in 2016 (People's Daily 2016), RMB 1.5 billion in 2018 (Zhang 2018), RMB 1.7 billion in 2019 (Qingdao Daily 2019), and RMB 2.4 billion in 2020 (Qingdao Municipal Medical Insurance Bureau 2020).

The implementation of LTCI does not require any premium contributions from employers, employees, and residents because the source of finance for both the urban employees' and residents' LTCI funds mainly relies on money transferred from the medical insurance fund (Feng *et al.* 2018: 114). While this funding method can avoid imposing a financial burden on employers, employees, and residents, it may affect the financial stability and sustainability of the LTCI funds in the long run. For example, the LTCI fund for employees may become financially unsustainable if there is a drastic decrease in the number of UEBMI participants due to the shrinking workforce or the deficit in the UEBMI fund due to a drastic increase in medical expenses. A study which developed an actuarial model based on China's 2010 population census to examine the financial sustainability of the LTCI fund in Qingdao found that the LTCI fund would become financially unsustainable in 2023 (Yang 2019). This was because ageing population would lead to the LTCI expenditure growing faster than the LTCI revenue (Yang 2019). The deficit of RMB 1.86 billion in the LTCI fund would occur in 2023 and the deficit would significantly increase to about RMB 8.7 billion in 2024 and RMB 14.3 billion in 2025 (Yang 2019: 187). An increase in the amount of money transferred from the medical insurance fund to support the LTCI fund may lead to the collapse of the medical insurance fund (Yang 2019). Another study which used the LTCI data from 2012 to 2017 in Qingdao to develop an actuarial model to predict the LTCI expenditure in future found that the growth of the LTCI expenditure was affected by the disability rate (Sun *et al.* 2020). The LTCI expenditure would increase from RMB 520 million in 2018 to RMB 4.495 billion in 2050 if there was low disability rate of 4.86 percent (Sun *et al.* 2020: 59). The LTCI expenditure as a share of GDP would increase from 0.04 percent in 2018 to 0.37 percent in 2050 (Sun *et al.* 2020: 59). However, the LTCI expenditure would increase from about RMB 1.29 billion in 2018 to RMB 10.2 billion in 2050 if there was high disability rate of 11.89 percent (Sun *et al.* 2020: 60). The LTCI expenditure as a share of GDP would increase from 0.11 percent in 2018 to 0.85 percent in 2050 (Sun *et al.* 2020: 60). The study also found that employees' LTCI expenditure grew faster than residents' LTCI expenditure no matter whether the disability rate was low or high in Qingdao (Sun *et al.* 2020: 61). The LTCI fund in Qingdao may not be financially sustainable in the long run if the disability rate keeps on increasing and its source of finance heavily relies on the medical insurance fund.

Recommendations

The Qingdao government needs to establish an independent financing system for LTCI to ensure its financial sustainability in the long run (Gao 2019: 42). The independent financing system can diversify sources of finance by constituting individual contribution, government subsidies, and social donation. Besides, the government needs to improve older adults' access to LTC services in urban districts. More professional LTC facilities should be constructed in urban districts where there is higher concentration of older adults. In rural areas, it is challenging to improve the delivery of LTC to older adults. It may be easier to deliver home care to older adults through community-based mobile clinics. The number of elder care workers in community-based mobile clinics can be increased and their level of competency needed to effectively care for older adults can be improved by receiving basic geriatric care training. A new policy should be formulated to develop a standardized training curriculum for people who want to become elder care workers so that trainees can demonstrate competency in caring for older adults. The training curriculum should include basic technical skills (e.g. transferring skills), personal care skills, mental health of older adults, nutrition, infection control, fall prevention, dementia care, communication and interpersonal skills, and emergency management skills. Besides, a certification system should be developed to recognize the qualification of elder care workers who complete the training and pass the assessment within a reasonable time frame so that workers feel respected and motivated to deliver LTC to older people. The pay rate for elder care workers should be raised to attract people to join and stay in the LTC sector.

Conclusion

To conclude, the implementation of LTCI in Qingdao enables people with moderate and severe disability and PWD to receive different types of LTC services to meet their specific needs. However, the access to LTC needs to be improved by increasing the number of professional LTC facilities. The quality of care needs to be improved by increasing the number of LTC workers and the level of competency of elder care workers. The financial sustainability of LTCI can be achieved through establishing an independent financing system in the long run.

References

Chang, S., Yang. W. and Deguchi, H. (2020) 'Care Providers, Access to Care, and the Long-Term Care Nursing Insurance in China: An Agent-Based Simulation', *Social Science & Medicine*, 244: 112667.

Charoenporn, P. (2012) *Growing China and Lessons to Thailand*. Online. Available HTTP: wwwbiz.meijo-u.ac.jp/SEBM/ronso/no12_4/17_CHAROENPORN.pdf (accessed 2 January 2021).

China Daily (2020) 'Moving Towards a Xiaokang Society: Qingdao Introduces a Long-Term Care Insurance System and Integrates Medical and Elderly Services', (Chinese version), *China Daily*, 24 July. Online. Available HTTP: https://baijiahao.baidu.com/s?id=1673081357032179208&wfr=spider&for=pc (accessed 20 February 2020).

Chung, J. H. (1999) 'A Sub-Provincial Recipe of Coastal Development in China: The Case of Qingdao', *The China Quarterly*, 160: 919–52.

Dai, W. (2018) 'Is China Facing the Social Risks Associated with Reliance on Hospitalization for the Care of the Elderly with Chronic Diseases?', *The International Journal of Health Planning and Management*, 34 (2): 794–805.

Dai, W. and Lu, S. (2018) 'The "Socialization of Elderly Hospitalization" in China: Development, Problems, and Solutions', *Journal of Social Service Research*, 44 (4): 518–28.

Dazhong Daily (2019) 'Community-Based Mobile Clinic Is Good: The Disabled Elderly Can Receive Medical Care at Their Own Homes', (Chinese version), *Dazhong Daily*, 16 October. Online. Available HTTP: www.163.com/dy/article/ERKLEQ7M0530WJTO.html (accessed 16 January 2021).

Dazhong Web (2016) *Introduction to the People's Hospital of Shinan District* (Chinese version). Online. Available HTTP: http://qingdao.dzwww.com/jiankang/xw/201611/t20161110_15124975.htm (accessed 24 February 2021).

Eng, J. Y. (2005) *China Investment Environment & Strategies: The Key to Winning in the Greater China Market*. Lincoln, NE: iUniverse, Inc.

Feng, G. G., Mi, H. and Zhang, Y. J. (2018) 'Analysis on Long-Term Care Insurance System Its Implications', (Chinese version), *Public Governance Review*, 1: 111–20.

Gao, N. (2019) 'Long-Term Care Insurance in Qingdao: Policy Analysis, Implementation Status and Path Optimization', (Chinese version), *World of Labor Security*, 24: 41–3.

Gong, X. and Zhou, W. (2018) 'Government Subsidies, Insurance Payment and the Cost of End-of-Life Care for Elders: Analysis Based on Data from the 2002–2014 Chinese Longitudinal Healthy Longevity Survey (CLHLS)', *Southern Economy*, 9: 68–85.

Ju, J. Y., Zhou, Q. M and Yang, J. (2011) *Survey Report on Ageing and Elderly Service in Qingdao* (Chinese version). Online. Available HTTP: www.wenmi.com/article/pyfxx100bct0.html (accessed 5 January 2021).

Li, B. (2018) 'A Comparative Study of Long-Term-Care Insurance for the Elderly in Qingdao, Nantong and Shanghai', *Advances in Economics, Business and Management Research (AEBMR)*, 60: 139–44. Online. Available HTTP: www.atlantis-press.com/proceedings/icmesd-18/25898599 (accessed 11 January 2021).

Li, L. L. (2016) 'How Can Disabled Elderly Age with Dignity?', (Chinese version), *Qingdao Daily*, 3 August. Online. Available HTTP: www.dailyqd.com/news/2016-08/03/content_344154.htm (accessed 21 February 2021).

Li, X. (2015) 'Evaluation of Fairness, Sustainability and Appropriateness of Qingdao's Long-Term Medical Care Insurance System', (Chinese version), *World of Labor and Social Security*, 30: 20–1, 23.

A List of Dementia Diagnosis Centres for Long-Term Care Insurance in Qingdao (Chinese version) (2017) Online. Available HTTP: https://qingdao.chashebao.com/yiliao/17001.html (accessed 1 February 2021).

Liu, W. G., Liu, L. R. and Zhang, Y. J. (2019) 'An Exploratory Study on Qingdao's Long-Term Care Insurance', (Chinese version), *China Health Insurance*, 3: 36–9.

Liu, X. X. and Liu, X. L. (2019) 'The Number of Elderly Population Has Reached over 1.835 Million, Accounting for 22 Percent of the Total Population in Qingdao', (Chinese version), *Bandao Metropolis*, 8 October. Online. Available HTTP: http://news.bandao.cn/a/289680.html (accessed 21 February 2021).

Lou, H. (2018) *Old-Age Population Was over Two Million in Qingdao, Accounting for 21.8 Percent of the Total Population* (Chinese version). Peninsula Metropolitan Post (*Bandao Dou Shi Bao*). Online. Available HTTP: http://news.bandao.cn/a/132684.html (accessed 5 January 2021).

Lu, B., Mi, H., Zhu, Y. and Piggott, J. (2017) 'A Sustainable Long-Term Health Care System for Aging China: A Case Study of Regional Practice', *Health Systems & Reform*, 3 (3): 182–90.

Lu, J., Zhang, X. and Sun, X. (2009) 'Population Ageing and Its Impact on the Development of Economy and Society in Qingdao', (Chinese version), *City*, 2: 57–61.

Mi, H., Ji, M. and Liu, W. G. (2019) *Research on Long-Term Care Insurance in Qingdao, China* (Chinese version). China: China Labour and Social Security Publishing House.

Ministry of Civil Affairs (2013) *Ability Assessment for Older Adults* (Chinese version). Online. Available HTTP: www.yanglaocn.com/shtml/20171019/1508362978112930.html (accessed 25 January 2021).

National Health Commission of the People's Republic of China (2015) *Qingdao Explores Long-Term Care System and Actively Promotes the Integration of Medical and Elderly Care Services* (Chinese version). Online. Available HTTP: www.nhc.gov.cn/wjw/dfxw/201504/ba34fcb2ecc84e6488b18dcd24db8477.shtml (accessed 16 January 2021).

Office of the Qingdao Municipal People's Government (2014) *Social Health Insurance Measures in Qingdao* (Qingdao Municipal Order No. 235) (Chinese version). Online. Available HTTP: www.huangdao.gov.cn/n10/upload/191017141522605104/191017141522622370.pdf (accessed 11 January 2021).

Office of the Qingdao Municipal People's Government (2020) *Long-Term Care Insurance Approach in Qingdao* (Chinese version). Online. Available HTTP: www.huangdao.gov.cn/n10/upload/201125135347487353/201125135856330388.pdf (accessed 25 January 2021).

Parents Enjoy Home Care (2015) Online. Available HTTP: http://m.dzwww.com/d/news/13340658.html (accessed 18 February 2021).

People's Daily (2016) 'Qingdao Has Been Implementing Long-Term Care Insurance for Almost Four Year: Older People with Disability Are Covered by Long-Term Care Insurance', (Chinese version), *People's Daily*, 27 March. Online. Available HTTP: https://china.huanqiu.com/article/9CaKrnJUPvw (accessed 18 February 2021).

Qingdao Daily (2019) 'Qingdao Takes the Lead in Establishing a Long-Term Care Insurance System in China and the System Has Covered 8.6 Million People', (Chinese version), *Qingdao Daily*, 19 August. Online. Available HTTP: http://insurance.cngold.org/c/2019-08-19/c6528276.html (accessed 19 February 2021).

Qingdao Evening News (2013) 'The Number of Fully Disabled and Partially Disabled People Has Increased by 50,000 in Two Years and the Expenditure of the Long-Term Care Insurance Reached Reminbi 100 Million', (Chinese version), *Qingdao Evening News*, 25 July. Online. Available HTTP: http://news.bandao.cn/news_html/201307/20130725/news_20130725_2226772.shtml (accessed 21 February 2021).

Qingdao Evening News (2016) 'The Average Annual Income of Urban Employees Was Renminbi 53,715 in Qingdao Last Year', (Chinese version), *Qingdao Evening News*, 26 May. Online. Available HTTP: http://news.qtv.com.cn/system/2016/05/26/013444451.shtml (accessed 21 February 2021).

Qingdao Financial Daily (2018) 'The Number of "Dementia Special Care Units" for Long-Term Care Increased to 11 in Qingdao', *Qingdao Financial Daily*, 5 January. Online. Available HTTP: http://qingdao.sdchina.com/show/4250755.html (accessed 1 February 2021).

Qingdao Morning Post (2013) 'Over 10,000 People Enjoyed Long-Term Care Insurance Benefits in Qingdao and the Long-Term Care Insurance Fund Has Raised 108 Million Renminbi', (Chinese version), *Qingdao Morning Post*, 18 July. Online. Available HTTP: http://finance.qingdaonews.com/content/2013-07/18/content_9864985.htm (accessed 19 February 2021).

Qingdao Morning Post (2014) 'Home-Based Care Has Gradually Gone Mainstream in Qingdao', (Chinese version), *Qingdao Morning Post*, 6 October. Online. Available HTTP: www.shandongmedia.com/news/zonghe/2014-10-06/10498.html (accessed 18 February 2021).

Qingdao Municipal Bureau of Human Resources and Social Security (2016) *Opinion on Including People with Advanced Dementia in the Long-Term Care Insurance and Ways to Manage Dementia Special Units* (Chinese version). Online. Available HTTP: www.qingdao.gov.cn/n172/n24624151/n24626255/n24626269/n24626283/170103092321087843.html (accessed 1 February 2021).

Qingdao Municipal Bureau of Human Resources and Social Security (2018) *Notification on Ways to Assess Designated Long-Term Care Service Institutions in Qingdao (Trial Implementation)* (Chinese version). Online. Available HTTP: www.qingdao.gov.cn/n172/n68422/n31280679/n31280695/200703163218922223.html (accessed 8 February 2021).

Qingdao Municipal Bureau of Human Resources and Social Security (2019) *Analysing Interim Measures for Long-Term Care in Qingdao* (Chinese version). Online. Available HTTP: www.qingdao.gov.cn/n172/n24624151/n31284614/n31284615/n31284623/190910135925004617.html (accessed 22 January 2021).

Qingdao Municipal Bureau of Human Resources and Social Security, Qingdao Municipal Health and Family Planning Commission and Qingdao Civil Affairs Bureau (2018a) *Notification on Implementation Measures of Qingdao Long-Term Care Needs Assessment* (Chinese version). Online. Available HTTP: www.qingdao.gov.cn/n172/n24624151/n24626255/n24626269/n24626283/180316194933717664.html (accessed 22 January 2021).

Qingdao Municipal Bureau of Human Resources and Social Security, Qingdao Municipal Health and Family Planning Commission and Qingdao Civil Affairs Bureau (2018b) *Notification on Ways to Manage Designated Long-Term Care Service Providers in Qingdao* (Chinese version). Online. Available HTTP: www.qingdao.gov.cn/n172/n24624151/n24626255/n24626269/n24626283/180316201831340483.html (accessed 8 February 2021).

Qingdao Municipal Medical Insurance Bureau (2019) *Notification on Addressing Agreed Management Issues of Dementia Special Care Units for Long-Term Care Insurance* (Chinese version). Online. Available HTTP: http://ybj.qingdao.gov.cn/n28356081/n32567782/n32567784/n32569020/200103095702458348.html (accessed 8 February 2021).

Qingdao Municipal Medical Insurance Bureau (2020) *The 13th Five-Year Plan Assessment Report of Qingdao Municipal Medical Insurance Bureau* (Chinese version). Online. Available HTTP: www.qingdao.gov.cn/zwgk/xxgk/ybj/gkml/ghjh/202011/t20201102_2062334.shtml (accessed 18 February 2021).

The Qingdao Municipal People's Government (2012) *Notification of Opinions on the Establishment of Long-Term Care Medical Insurance System (Trial)* (Chinese version). Online. Available HTTP: http://qd.bendibao.com/live/2014821/43379.shtm (accessed 11 January 2021).

The Qingdao Municipal People's Government (2018) *Interim Measures for Long-Term Care in Qingdao* (Chinese version). Online. Available HTTP: www.yanglaocn.com/shtml/20180320/1521532406114318.html (accessed 22 January 2021).

Qingdao Municipal Statistics Bureau (2019) *Gross Domestic Product in Q4 2019.* Online. Available HTTP: http://qdtj.qingdao.gov.cn/n28356045/n32561056/n32561069/n32561125/n32562280/200402100656390441.html (accessed 2 January 2021).

Qingdao Municipal Statistics Bureau and National Bureau of Statistics Survey Office in Qingdao (2016) *Statistical Bulletin of Qingdao's Economic and Social Development in 2015* (Chinese version). Online. Available HTTP: http://qdsq.qingdao.gov.cn/n15752132/n20546841/n32208957/n32209705/170630111459138305.html (accessed 21 February 2021).

Qingdao Municipal Statistics Bureau and National Bureau of Statistics Survey Office in Qingdao (2018) *Qingdao Statistical Yearbook 2018.* Beijing: China Statistics Press.

Qingdao Municipal Statistics Bureau and National Bureau of Statistics Survey Office in Qingdao (2020) *Statistical Communique of Qingdao on the 2019 National Economic and Social Development* (Chinese version). Online. Available HTTP: http://qdtj.qingdao.gov.cn/n28356045/n32561056/n32561070/200327102041515838.html (accessed 2 January 2021).

Qingdao News (2010) *There Will Be 'Zero Population Growth' in Qingdao 20 Years Later* (Chinese version). Online. Available HTTP: http://epaper.qingdaonews.com/html/qdwb/20100802/qdwb123516.html (accessed 5 January 2021).

Respite Care (n.d.) Online. Available HTTP: www.alz.org/help-support/caregiving/care-options/respite-care (accessed 24 February 2021).

Shang, Q. Y., Tang, S. K. and Jiao, T. S. (2020) 'Problems and Solutions to the Long-Term Care Insurance System in Qingdao', (Chinese version), *Education Digest*, 7. Online. Available HTTP: www.qikanchina.net/thesis/view/4678439 (accessed 25 February 2021).

Si, M., Shao, M. Su, Y., Liang, D., Wu, Y., Li, L., Ge, D. and Yang, L. (2020) 'A Survey on Utilization of and Demands for Integrated Medical and Nursing Services among Elderly in Qingdao', *Chinese Journal of Public Health*, 36 (4): 537–41.

Sun, J. H. (2020) 'The Current Situation, Problems and Countermeasures to the Pilot Long-Term Care Insurance System: The Case Study of Qingdao', (Chinese version), *Journal of Shandong Administration Institute*, 1: 81–7.

Sun, L. X., Feng, G. G. and Mi, H. (2020) 'A Study on the Financial Sustainability of the Long-Term Care Insurance Fund in China: The Case Study of Qingdao', *Dong Yue Tribune*, 41 (5): 52–62.

Wang, X. X. (2016) *Six Models of Integrating Medical and Elderly Care Services* (Chinese version). Online. Available HTTP: http://xinbao.qdxin.cn/html/20160122/7.html (accessed 8 February 2021).

Xiao, L. L. (2019) *There Is a Shortfall of at Least 14,000 Long-Term Care Workers in Qingdao* (Chinese version). Online. Available HTTP: http://news.bandao.cn/a/240200.html (accessed 25 February 2021).

Yang, W., Chang, S., Zhang, W., Wang, R., Mossialos, E., Wu, X., Cui, D., Li, H. and Mi, H. (2021) 'An Initial Analysis of the Effects of a Long-Term Care Insurance on Equity and Efficiency: A Case Study of Qingdao City in China', *Research on Aging*, 4 (3):156–65.https://journals.sagepub.com/doi/pdf/10.1177/0164027520907346 (accessed 26 May 2021).

Yang, Y. L. (2019) 'The Financial Sustainability of Long-Term Care Insurance in Qingdao', (Chinese version), *Market Weekly*, 10: 185–8.

Yu, B. R. (2019) 'The Use of Long-Term Care Insurance to Address the Problem of "Social Hospitalization" in Qingdao', (Chinese version), *China Health*, 3: 53–5.

Zhang, L. (2015) *Managing the City Economy: Challenges and Strategies in Developing Countries.* London; New York, NY: Routledge, Taylor & Francis Group.

Zhang, M. and Rasiah, R. (2013) 'Qingdao', *Cities*, 31: 591–600.

Zhang, P. (2018) 'The First Long-Term Care Insurance Blue Book in Qingdao Was Published', (Chinese version), *Qingdao News*, 11 December. Online. Available HTTP: http://news.qingdaonews.com/qingdao/2018-12/11/content_20256838.htm (accessed 18 February 2021).

Zhang, X. M. (2017) *A Study on Delivering Elderly Care Services for Disabled Elderly in Rural Area: The Case Study of H District in Qingdao* (Chinese version). Master Thesis. Online. Available HTTP: www.cnki.net (accessed 21 February 2021).

6 The long-term care model in Nantong

Introduction

Nantong, which was named the first 'Capital of Longevity of the World', is a super-aged city in China. In 2015, Nantong implemented Basic Care Insurance, which provided long-term care (LTC) and financial protection for people with long-term disability in some urban districts. By the end of 2019, long-term care insurance (LTCI) was implemented in the whole city. At present, LTCI has almost achieved full coverage in the city. It covers 98 percent of the population, including urban employees, urban residents, and rural residents. A credit rating system is established to measure the integrity and service quality of designated LTC service providers. This chapter gives a detailed account of the development of LTCI in Nantong. It evaluates the outcomes of LTCI in terms of five criteria: utilization of medical resources, cost, equity, quality of care, and financial sustainability. It finds that the government needs to build and grow its pool of professional elder care workers so as to meet the growing demand for LTC, introduce more comprehensive home care service packages, develop a pay range pegged to the level of certification elder care workers received, and establish an LTCI funding system that can be independent from the medical insurance system. Further, a volunteering system that promotes time banking should be promoted in the city.

Background

Nantong is a prefecture-level city in the east of Jiangsu province with a population of about 7.72 million. In 1984, Nantong was selected by the central government as one of the 14 coastal cities opened to foreign investment. By the end of 2011, over 1,000 projects in Nantong were foreign invested and the realized amount of foreign investment in Nantong exceeded USD$22 billion (Deloitte 2012: 7). Foreign investment is an accelerator for economic growth in the city (Deloitte 2012: 7). At present, Nantong is the largest home textile industry base in China (China Daily 2018) and a famous textile and garment export base in the country ('The Five Regions of Nantong' 2019). It has six pillar industries, including shipping and heavy equipment, electronics and information technology (IT), fine chemicals, textiles and apparel, light industry and food, and construction

DOI: 10.4324/9780429057199-6

(Deloitte 2012: 27). In 2020, the primary, secondary, and tertiary sectors represented 4.6 percent, 47.5 percent, and 47.9 percent respectively of Nantong's Gross Domestic Product (GDP) (Nantong Municipal Statistics Bureau 2021a). Nantong ranked twentieth in China in terms of GDP in 2020 (China Banking News 2021).

Nantong has been experiencing rapid population ageing. It became an ageing society in 1982, with persons aged 65 and above making up 7.2 percent of its total population (Yang *et al.* 2004: 49). It was 17 years ahead of China in becoming an ageing society. In 1990, there were 689,071 persons aged 65 and above, making up 8.98 percent of the total population in Nantong (Qian 2003: 23). In 2000, there were 934,717 persons aged 65 and above, making up 12.44 percent of the total population in Nantong (Qian 2003: 23). In 2010, Nantong became an aged society. It had about 1.2 million persons aged 65 and above, making up 16.5 percent of the total population (Nantong Municipal Statistics Bureau 2013). The share of the population aged 65 years or above in total population in Nantong was 5.62 percent higher than that of in Jiangsu province and 7.58 percent higher than the national level (Zhu 2012). In 2020, Nantong became a super-aged society. It had about 1.75 million persons aged 65 and above, making up 22.67 percent of the total population (Nantong Municipal Statistics Bureau 2021b).

In Nantong, the number of centenarians (people aged 100 and older) has increased over time. In 1990, Nantong had 69 centenarians, of whom seven were males and 62 were females (Qian 2003: 23). In 2000, Nantong had 191 centenarians, of whom 26 were males and 165 were females (Qian 2003: 23). In January 2003, Nantong had 449 centenarians (Yang *et al.* 2004: 50). Particularly, Rugao, a county-level city of Nantong, had the highest proportion of persons aged 100 and above (Yang *et al.* 2004: 50). It had 83 centenarians per 1,000,000 people (Yang *et al.* 2004: 50). In 2010, Nantong had 768 centenarians (Xie 2013: 88). There were 10 centenarians per 100,000 people in the city (Xie 2013: 88). In May 2014, Nantong was named the first 'Capital of Longevity of the World' (*shi jie chang shou zhi dou*) by International Naturopathic Medical Society and the Scientific Certification Committee for the World's Longevity Village (Xue and Wu 2014). At that time, Nantong had 1,031 centenarians, who accounted for 25 percent of centenarians in Jiangsu province (Zhang M. 2015: 22). The oldest centenarian in Nantong was 109 years old (Zhang M. 2015: 22). In 2018, Nantong had 1,321 centenarians (Xinhua Daily 2019). It is expected that the number of centenarians will continue to rise in Nantong in the coming years.

Nantong has been facing the problem of 'empty-nesters'. In 2013, there were almost 980,000 'empty-nesters', who accounted for over half of the elderly population in the city (Jianghai Evening News 2014). About 420,000 of them lived in urban areas, while 560,000 of them lived in rural areas (Jianghai Evening News 2014). The former accounted for 54 percent of urban elderly population in Nantong, while the latter accounted for 48 percent of rural elderly population in Nantong (Jianghai Evening News 2014). A study found that 'empty-nesters' in Nantong had poorer psychological well-being than 'non-empty-nesters' (Feng and Chen 2008: 202). It found that 49.7 percent of 'empty-nesters' felt that life was interesting, which was 19 percent lower than that of 'non-empty-nesters' (Feng and Chen 2008: 202). In addition, 46.2 percent of 'empty-nesters' felt that they were energetic in daily life, which was 19.5 percent lower than that of 'non-empty-nesters' (Feng and Chen 2008: 202). Also, the study found that 44.8 percent of 'empty-nesters' felt that they did not have any value, which was 20.9 percent higher than that of non-empty-nesters (Feng and Chen 2008: 202). And 33.8 percent of 'empty-nesters' reported that they had fear for unknown reasons, while 28.2 percent of 'empty-nesters' reported that they had anxiety (Feng and Chen 2008: 202). These raise concerns over ways to improve the psychological well-being of 'empty-nesters' in the city.

Another problem faced by Nantong was the need to care for partially and fully disabled elders. In 2015, newspaper reported that there were about 320,000 partially or fully disabled persons in need of LTC (Zhang Y. 2015). However, the government statistics showed that in the same year, the number of disabled persons in Nantong reached 394, 200 (Sheng 2016: 293). Recognizing that the medical insurance system would not be able to meet the increasing demand for medical and nursing care as well as activities of daily living (ADLs) care due to the growth in the number of disabled persons, the Nantong government began to examine the feasibility of implementing LTCI in the city (Zhang Y. 2015).

Development of LTCI

In fact, in response to the rapidly ageing population in Nantong, the government in 2000 established a home medical care system (*jiating bingchuang zhiduo*) to allow partially or fully disabled Urban Employee Basic Medical Insurance (UEBMI) participants to receive necessary medical care provided by doctors from designated hospitals in their residence (People's Government of Jiangsu Province 2015). The fees incurred from home medical care would be covered by medical insurance (People's Government of Jiangsu Province 2015). In 2012, the government allowed medical insurance to cover bedridden participants' expenses incurred from medical care, nursing care, rehabilitation, and end-of-life (EoL) care at nursing homes (People's Government of Jiangsu Province 2015).

In October 2015, the Nantong government issued *Opinions on Establishing the Basic Care Insurance System (Trial Implementation)* (hereafter *the 2015 Opinions*), which aimed to provide LTC and financial protection for people with long-term disability starting from 1 January 2016 (The Nantong Municipal People's Government 2015). According to *the 2015 Opinions*, LTCI mainly covered UEBMI participants and residents in two urban districts (i.e. Chongchuan, Gangzha) and Nantong Economic and Technological Development Area (NETDA) (The Nantong Municipal People's Government 2015). In 2018, LTCI was implemented in Rugao, which was a county-level city (Nantong Municipal Human Resources and Social Security Bureau 2018a). On 1 January 2019, LTCI was also implemented in Tongzhou District (Nantong Municipal Human Resources and Social

Security Bureau 2018a). By the end of 2019, LTCI was implemented in the whole city. It covered UEBMI participants as well as Urban and Rural Resident Basic Medical Insurance (URRBMI) participants.

The LTCI premium was set at renminbi (RMB) 100 per person annually, which was equivalent to 3 percent of urban residents' per capita disposable income in the previous year (The Nantong Municipal People's Government 2015). The premium was financed through three sources: RMB 30 came from individual contribution, RMB 30 came from the social pooling fund (SPF) of basic medical insurance (BMI) fund, and RMB 40 came from government subsidies (The Nantong Municipal People's Government 2015). For UEBMI participants, however, the individual contribution was actually covered by money transferred from the individual Medical Savings Account (MSA). On the other hand, URRBMI participants had to make contribution to the insurance on their own (The Nantong Municipal People's Government 2015). The government would fully subsidize the individual contribution for UEBMI participants coming from household in extreme poverty (*tekunhu*), URRBMI participants who were minors (including students), people coming from the minimum living standard guarantee (*dibao*) household, and people with severe disability (i.e. those who mostly or fully lost physical work ability) (The Nantong Municipal People's Government 2015). In addition, LTCI was financed by money from the welfare lottery fund annually and donation from individuals, enterprises, or charity organizations (The Nantong Municipal People's Government 2015).

The Barthel Index (BI) was adopted to assess an applicant's performance in ADL and mobility (See Table 6.1). It yielded a total score out of 100 (Nantong Municipal Human Resources and Social Security Bureau 2016). Higher scores indicated a higher level of independence. A score of less than 40 marks suggested total dependence, 41–60 moderate dependence, 61–99 slight dependence, and 100 fully independent (Nantong Municipal Human Resources and Social Security Bureau 2016). Applicants who had been receiving treatment for at least six months and had been assessed as being severely disabled were eligible for receiving LTC (The Nantong Municipal People's Government 2015).

Starting from 1 January 2017, applicants were required to pay assessment fees (Nantong Municipal Human Resources and Social Security Bureau 2016). Assessment fee was RMB 200 each time for those who applied for LTC provided in nursing homes or hospitals (Nantong Municipal Human Resources and Social Security Bureau 2016). Meanwhile, assessment fee should not exceed RMB 300 each time for those who applied for home care (Nantong Municipal Human Resources and Social Security Bureau 2016). In addition, there would be a video recording of on-site assessment on an applicant's performance in ADL care and mobility using the BI (Nantong Municipal Human Resources and Social Security Bureau 2016). Applicants who had been receiving treatment for at least six months and had been assessed as being moderately dependent (i.e. only those who scored between 41 and 50) or totally dependent (those who scored less than 40 marks) were eligible for receiving LTC (Nantong Municipal Human Resources and Social Security Bureau 2016). Eligible beneficiaries would receive a Disability Assessment

Table 6.1 Barthel Index for ADLs (Nantong version)

Items	Degree of independence	Scores
[1] Feeding	Rather dependent on others/Fully dependent	0
	Needs help	5
	Fully independent	10
[2] Bathing	Dependent	0
	Independent	5
[3] Grooming	Dependent	0
	Independent (e.g. face washing/hair washing/tooth brushing/shaving)	5
[4] Dressing	Dependent	0
	Needs help, but can do about half unaided	5
	Independent (including buttons, zips, and laces)	10
[5] Bowels	Incontinent	0
	Occasional accident (once per week)	5
	Continent	10
[6] Bladder	Incontinent or catheterized	0
	Occasional accident (maximum once per 24 hours; more than once per week)	5
	Continent	10
[7] Toilet use	Dependent	0
	Needs some help	5
	Independent	10
[8] Transfer from a bed to a chair	Fully independent	0
	Major help (two people, physical), can sit	5
	Minor help (one person)	10
	Independent	15
[9] Mobility	Immobile	0
	Wheelchair independent	5
	Walks with help of one person (physical or verbal)	10
	Independent (but may use any aid)	15
[10] Stairs	Unable	0
	Needs help	5
	Independent up and down	10
Total		100

Remarks: The Barthel Index yields a total score out of 100. It is divided into total dependence, moderate dependence, slight dependence, and full independence. A score of less than 40 marks suggests total dependence, 41–60 moderate dependence, 61–99 slight dependence, and 100% no dependence.

Source: Nantong Municipal Human Resources and Social Security Bureau (2016) *Notification on Distributing the Implementation Details of Basic Care Insurance in Nantong, Annex 2* (Chinese version). Online. Available HTTP: http://ylbzj.nantong.gov.cn/ntsylbzj/bmwj/content/dc782759-2d09-4dd6-85fc-93a71c00d676.html (accessed 2 June 2021).

Result of the Basic Care Insurance Participant in Nantong (hereafter 'the Disability Assessment Result') issued by Nantong Labor Ability Appraisal Center (Nantong Municipal Human Resources and Social Security Bureau 2016). They would be assessed again every two years to see if they were eligible for continuously receiving LTC.

Eligible beneficiaries could receive LTC services at home, nursing homes, or designated hospitals (The Nantong Municipal People's Government 2015). The government encouraged people to receive home care (The Nantong Municipal People's Government 2015). At first, two types of home care service packages were introduced for eligible beneficiaries to choose (Nantong Municipal Medical Insurance Bureau 2016). The monthly charge for each service package was RMB 500 (Nantong Municipal Medical Insurance Bureau 2016) (See Table 6.2).

In October 2017, six types of home care service packages were introduced for eligible beneficiaries to choose (Nantong Municipal Human Resources and Social Security Bureau 2017a) (See Tables 6.3–6.5). Charges for these home care service packages ranged from RMB 390/4 times to RMB 500/4 times,

Table 6.2 Two types of home care service packages in Nantong (2016)

Home care service package A1			Home care service package A2		
Item	Types of services	Frequency of services	Item	Types of services	Frequency of services
1	Changing bedsheets	Once every two weeks	1	Changing bedsheets	Once every two weeks
2	Washing face/ shaving	Once a week	2	Washing face/ shaving	Once a week
3	Washing hair	Once a week	3	Washing hair	Once a week
4	Foot soak assistance	Once a week	4	Foot soak assistance	Once a week
5	Assist older adults to turn over in bed	Once a week	5	Assist older adults to turn over in bed	Once a week
6	Removal of earwax	Once every two weeks	6	Removal of earwax	Once every two weeks
7	Trim fingernails	Once every two weeks	7	Trim fingernails	Once every two weeks
8	Trim toenails	Once every two weeks	8	Trim toenails	Once every two weeks
9	Haircut	Once a month	9	Haircut	Once a month
10	Bed bath	Once a week	10	Bathing	Once a week
11	Pressure ulcer care	Once a week			
12	Measuring and recording vital signs (i.e. blood pressure, pulse rate, respiration rates, body temperature)	Once a week			

Source: Nantong Municipal Medical Insurance Bureau (2016) *Opinions on Providing Home Care Services under Basic Care Insurance in Nantong (Trial Implementation)* (Chinese version). Online. Available HTTP: http://ylbzj.nantong.gov.cn/ntsylbzj/bmwj/content/ee4a7387-74e5-4158-9721-5230c63c8d83.html (accessed 5 June 2021).

depending on the types of services provided by the package. The length of service lasted for 1–1.5 hours each time. Fully dependent beneficiaries were required to co-pay RMB 10 for home care services each time, while moderately dependent

Table 6.3 Home care service packages (*Ankang 1 and Ankang 2*) in Nantong (2017)

Home care service package (Ankang 1)			*Home care service package* (Ankang 2)		
Item	Types of services	Frequency of services	Item	Types of services	Frequency of services
1	Changing bedsheets	Once every two weeks	1	Changing bedsheets	Once every two weeks
2	Washing face/shaving	Once a week	2	Washing face/shaving	Once a week
3	Washing hair	Once a week	3	Washing hair	Once a week
4	Foot soak assistance	Once a week	4	Foot soak assistance	Once a week
5	Assist older adults to turn over in bed	Once a week	5	Assist older adults to turn over in bed	Once a week
6	Removal of earwax	Once every two weeks	6	Removal of earwax	Once every two weeks
7	Trim fingernails	Once every two weeks	7	Trim fingernails	Once every two weeks
8	Trim toenails	Once every two weeks	8	Trim toenails	Once every two weeks
9	Haircut	Once a month	9	Haircut	Once a month
10	Bed bath	Once a week	10	Bathing	Once a week
11	Pressure ulcer care	Once a week			
12	Measuring and recording vital signs (i.e. blood pressure, pulse rate, respiration rates, body temperature)	Once a week			

Length of service: 1–1.5 hours every time

Length of service: 1–1.5 hours every time

Charge: RMB 500/4 times

Charge: RMB 500/4 times

Co-payment for fully dependent beneficiaries: RMB 10 per time per person

Co-payment for fully dependent beneficiaries: RMB 10 per time per person

Co-payment for moderately dependent beneficiaries: RMB 20 per time per person

Co-payment for moderately dependent beneficiaries: RMB 20 per time per person

Source: Nantong Municipal Human Resources and Social Security Bureau (2017a) *Opinions on Home Care Services under Basic Care Insurance in Nantong, Annex 1 and Annex 2* (Chinese version). Online. Available HTTP: http://ylbzj.nantong.gov.cn/ntsylbzj/bmwj/content/5bfcbcf2-450f-415d-9158-6af304abeb9a.html (accessed 5 June 2021).

Table 6.4 Home care service packages (*Hukang 1 and Hukang 2*) in Nantong (2017)

Home care service package (Hukang 1)			Home care service package (Hukang 2)		
Item	Types of services	Frequency of services	Item	Types of services	Frequency of services
1	Washing face/ shaving	Once a week	1	Washing face/ shaving	Once a week
2	Washing hair	Once a week	2	Washing hair	Once a week
3	Haircut	Once a month	3	Haircut	Once a month
4	Removal of earwax	Once every two weeks	4	Removal of earwax	Once every two weeks
5	Trim fingernails	Once every two weeks	5	Trim fingernails	Once every two weeks
6	Trim toenails	Once every two weeks	6	Trim toenails	Once every two weeks
7	Foot soak assistance	Once a week	7	Foot soak assistance	Once a week
8	Bed bath	Once a week	8	Bathing	Once a week
9	Oral care	Once a week	9	Oral care	Once a week
10	Assist older adults to turn over in bed	Once a week	10	Assist older adults to turn over in bed	Once a week
11	Pressure ulcer care	Once a week			
12	Measuring and recording vital signs (i.e. blood pressure, pulse rate, respiration rates, body temperature)	Once a week			

Length of service: 1–1.5 hours every time

Charge: RMB 500/4 times

Co-payment for fully dependent beneficiaries: RMB 10 per time per person

Co-payment for moderately dependent beneficiaries: RMB 20 per time per person

Length of service: 1–1.5 hours every time

Charge: RMB 480/4 times

Co-payment for fully dependent beneficiaries: RMB 10 per time per person

Co-payment for moderately dependent beneficiaries: RMB 20 per time per person

Source: *Nantong Municipal Human Resources and Social Security Bureau (2017a) Opinions on Home Care Services under Basic Care Insurance in Nantong, Annex 3 and Annex 4* (Chinese version). Online. Available HTTP: http://ylbzj.nantong.gov.cn/ntsylbzj/bmwj/content/5bfcbcf2-450f-415d-9158-6af304abeb9a.html (accessed 5 June 2021).

beneficiaries were required to co-pay RMB 20 for home care services each time (Nantong Municipal Human Resources and Social Security Bureau 2017a).

In late December 2017, three more types of home care service packages were introduced for eligible beneficiaries to choose from (Nantong Municipal Human Resources and Social Security Bureau 2017b). They focused on

Table 6.5 Home care service packages (*Hukang 3 and Hukang 4*) in Nantong (2017)

Home care service package (Hukang 3)			Home care service package (Hukang 4)		
Item	Types of services	Frequency of services	Item	Types of services	Frequency of services
1	Washing face/ shaving	Once a week	1	Washing face/ shaving	Once a week
2	Washing hair	Once a week	2	Washing hair	Once a week
3	Haircut	Once a month	3	Haircut	Once a month
4	Bed bath	Once a week	4	Bathing	Once a week
5	Oral care	Once a week	5	Oral care	Once a week
6	Assist older adults to turn over in bed	Once a week	6	Measuring and recording vital signs (i.e. blood pressure, pulse rate, respiration rates, body temperature)	Once a week
7	Pressure ulcer care	Once a week	7	Glucose monitoring	Once a week
8	Measuring and recording vital signs (i.e. blood pressure, pulse rate, respiration rates, body temperature)	Once a week			
9	Glucose monitoring	Once a week			
Length of service: 1–1.5 hours every time			Length of service: 1–1.5 hours every time		
Charge: RMB 470/4 times			Charge: RMB 390/4 times		
Co-payment for fully dependent beneficiaries: RMB 10 per time per person			Co-payment for fully dependent beneficiaries: RMB 10 per time per person		
Co-payment for moderately dependent beneficiaries: RMB 20 per time per person			Co-payment for moderately dependent beneficiaries: RMB 20 per time per person		

Source: Nantong Municipal Human Resources and Social Security Bureau (2017a) Opinions on Home Care Services under Basic Care Insurance in Nantong, Annex 5 and Annex 6 (Chinese version). Online. Available HTTP: http://ylbzj.nantong.gov.cn/ntsylbzj/bmwj/content/5bfcbcf2-450f-415d-9158-6af304abeb9a.html (accessed 5 June 2021).

personal hygiene, pressure ulcer care, and vital sign monitoring. Their charges ranged from RMB 280/4 times to RMB 320/4 times (Nantong Municipal Human Resources and Social Security Bureau 2017b). The length of service lasted for 20–50 minutes each time. Fully dependent beneficiaries were required to co-pay RMB 5 for home care services each time, while moderately dependent beneficiaries were required to co-pay RMB 10 for home care services each time (See Table 6.6) (Nantong Municipal Human Resources and Social Security Bureau 2017b).

In addition, eligible beneficiaries receiving home care could rent six types of auxiliary aids such as wheelchairs, nursing beds, and robot nurses (Xu and Gu 2020). Rentals ranged from RMB 1 to RMB 10 per day (Xu and Gu 2020). One-stop services including the delivery, installation, recycling, disinfection, and storage

Table 6.6 Home care service packages (i.e. personal hygiene, pressure ulcer care, and vital sign monitoring) in Nantong (2017)

Home care service package	Types of services	Charge	Length of service
'Personal hygiene' package	[1] Washing face/shaving (once a week) [2] Washing hair (once a week) [3] Bathing (once a week) [4] Oral care (once a week) [5] Haircut (once a month)	RMB 280/4 times	20–50 minutes each time
'Pressure ulcer care' package	[1] Turn over in bed [2] Tap the back (to prevent lung infection) [3] Pressure ulcer care [4] Skin care for pressure ulcers [5] Assist in dressing and undressing a person (All services provided once a week)	RMB 320/4 times	30–50 minutes each time
'Vital sign monitoring' package	[1] Blood pressure monitoring [2] Pulse rate monitoring [3] Respiration rate monitoring [4] Body temperature monitoring [5] Glucose monitoring [6] Medication management [7] Excretion care [8] Safety guidance (All services provided once a week)	RMB 320/4 times	20–50 minutes each time

Source: Nantong Municipal Human Resources and Social Security Bureau (2017b) *Notification on Introducing More Home Care Service Packages in Nantong* (Chinese version). Online. Available HTTP: http://ylbzj.nantong.gov.cn/ntsylbzj/bmwj/content/9c18f98b-bbf9-4673-a92d-033a95963dfe.html (accessed 6 June 2021).

of auxiliary aids would be provided by professional companies (Nantong Net 2018). Eligible beneficiaries could also buy 15 types of nursing and healthcare consumables such as diapers, nursing pads, commode chairs, and walking aids below market prices (Xu and Gu 2020).

As regards LTC at designated hospitals, it was mainly for coma patients, long-term ventilator-dependent patients, patients with complete paralysis, hemiplegia or paraplegia, and patients with long-term use of gastrostomy tube, tracheostomy cannulae, external biliary drainage catheter or other tubes (The Nantong Municipal People's Government 2015). Services covered by LTCI included ADLs care (e.g. personal hygiene, feeding, excretion care), safety care, sleeping care, caring for tubes (e.g. gastrostomy tube), clinical observation, rehabilitation services, cleaning, and disinfection (The Nantong Municipal People's Government 2015).

Beneficiaries who were eligible for nursing home care or hospitalization care could choose the designated nursing home or medical institution they preferred. They were required to check in to the designated nursing home or medical institution by presenting their social insurance card and the Disability Assessment Result (Nantong Municipal Human Resources and Social Security Bureau 2016). Beneficiaries who were eligible for receiving home care had to bring their social insurance card and the Disability Assessment Result to a designated service agency and sign a service user's contract with the designated service agency (Nantong Municipal Human Resources and Social Security Bureau 2016). The contract should clearly state all agreed services to be provided, frequency of services provided, when the service would be provided, the rights and obligations of the service user, the rights and obligations of the care provider, and an exemption clause (Nantong Municipal Human Resources and Social Security Bureau 2016).

In order to provide LTCI beneficiaries with personalized care that could meet their needs, care service providers were required by Nantong Municipal Human Resources and Social Security Bureau to conduct a comprehensive assessment on LTCI beneficiaries they cared for based on seven dimensions: basic conditions (e.g. personal information, personal health history, family health history, history of food and drug allergies), daily life (e.g. ADLs, smoking, drinking alcohol), vital signs, psychosocial assessment, fall risk assessment, physical examination, and catheterization and treatment (Nantong Municipal Human Resources and Social Security Bureau 2017c). Care service providers had to formulate a personalized care plan (i.e. any major health issues, any major care issues, concrete service plan, service provision period, frequency of services provided, expected goals) based on the comprehensive assessment result by filling in a care service plan and an evaluation form (Nantong Municipal Human Resources and Social Security Bureau 2017c). Besides, care service providers were required to establish a service user satisfaction evaluation system to collect the views of LTCI beneficiaries on the services they received through questionnaires, telephone interviews, face-to-face interviews, user complaints, or reports (Nantong Municipal

Human Resources and Social Security Bureau 2017c). Service user satisfaction would become one of the criteria used by the government to evaluate the performance of care service providers (Nantong Municipal Human Resources and Social Security Bureau 2017c).

LTCI covered service charges, the cost of bed occupancy, and the cost of using nursing equipment and consumables (The Nantong Municipal People's Government 2015). At first, LTCI covered up to RMB 1,200 per month for home care services provided by designated service agencies (The Nantong Municipal People's Government 2015). Meanwhile, it covered 50 percent of the cost of LTC provided in designated nursing homes (The Nantong Municipal People's Government 2015). It covered 60 percent of the cost of LTC provided in designated hospitals, and beneficiaries could still enjoy hospitalization benefits in accordance with the basic medical insurance system (The Nantong Municipal People's Government 2015). Starting from 1 January 2017, however, fixed payment was adopted for reimbursement. Besides, totally dependent beneficiaries enjoyed higher reimbursement and care subsidies than moderately dependent beneficiaries. For nursing home care, LTCI covered RMB 10 per day for every moderately dependent beneficiary and RMB 40 per day for every totally dependent beneficiary (Nantong Municipal Human Resources and Social Security Bureau 2016). For LTC provided in designated hospitals, LTCI covered RMB 10 per day for every moderately dependent beneficiary and RMB 50 per day for every totally dependent beneficiary (Nantong Municipal Human Resources and Social Security Bureau 2016). Eligible LTCI beneficiaries could not enjoy any LTCI benefits when they were enjoying the hospitalization benefits covered by the medical insurance in designated medical institutions (Nantong Municipal Human Resources and Social Security Bureau 2016). For home care, care subsidies of RMB 8 per day would be given to every moderately dependent beneficiary while care subsidies of RMB 15 per day would be given to every totally dependent beneficiary (Nantong Municipal Human Resources and Social Security Bureau 2016). Table 6.7 summarizes the LTCI reimbursement and care subsidies for moderately and totally dependent beneficiaries in 2017.

Table 6.7 LTCI reimbursement and care subsidies for moderately and totally dependent beneficiaries (2017)

Eligible LTC beneficiaries	Moderately dependent	Totally dependent
The Barthel Index (BI)	Score: 41–50	Score: below 40
Reimbursement (nursing home care)	RMB 10 per day	RMB 40 per day
Reimbursement (hospitalization care)	RMB 10 per day	RMB 50 per day
Care subsidies	RMB 8 per day	RMB 15 per day

Source: Nantong Municipal Human Resources and Social Security Bureau (2016) *Notification on Distributing the Implementation Details of Basic Care Insurance in Nantong* (Chinese version). Online. Available HTTP: http://ylbzj.nantong.gov.cn/ntsylbzj/bmwj/content/dc782759-2d09-4dd6-85fc-93a71c00d676.html (accessed 2 June 2021).

In 2018, there was higher LTCI coverage for nursing home care and LTC provided in designated hospitals. For nursing home care, LTCI covered RMB 30 per day for every moderately dependent beneficiary and RMB 50 per day for every totally dependent beneficiary (Office of Nantong Municipal Government 2018a). For LTC provided in designated hospitals, LTCI covered RMB 30 per day for every moderately dependent beneficiary and RMB 70 per day for every totally dependent beneficiary (Office of Nantong Municipal Government 2018a). Besides, care subsidies of RMB 2,100 per month per head would be given to LTCI beneficiaries at designated nursing homes and hospitals (Nantong Municipal Human Resources and Social Security Bureau 2018b).

Starting from 1 January 2019, LTCI was extended to cover people with dementia (PWD). An applicant could bring his/her identity card or social insurance card to a care service centre to submit a dementia assessment application form together with a copy of the relevant medical examination report as well as sign an integrity commitment letter (Nantong Municipal Human Resources and Social Security Bureau 2018b). The care service centre would help the applicant schedule an appointment at Nantong Fourth People's Hospital (also known as Nantong Mental Health Centre) to undergo dementia assessment (Nantong Municipal Human Resources and Social Security Bureau 2018c). It could also help the applicant with mobility difficulty to arrange dementia assessment to be conducted by specialists at his/her home (Nantong Municipal Human Resources and Social Security Bureau 2018c). The applicant would be assessed by Mini-Mental State Examination (MMSE). A score of 10–20 suggested moderate dementia and a score of 0–9 indicates severe dementia ('Who can enjoy long-term care benefits?' 2021). At first, only applicants with severe dementia could receive LTC (Nantong Municipal Human Resources and Social Security Bureau 2018c). Later, those with moderate dementia were also eligible for receiving LTC ('Who can enjoy long-term care benefits?' 2021).

People with severe dementia could receive LTC at dementia care wards of designated nursing homes or hospitals (Nantong Municipal Human Resources and Social Security Bureau 2018c). Every dementia care ward had about nine beds and three medical personnel or elder care workers who had received dementia care training (Office of Nantong Municipal Government 2018b). Dementia care wards were closed, safe places with spaces for activities (Office of Nantong Municipal Government 2018b). They were monitored by closed-circuit televisions (CCTVs) (Office of Nantong Municipal Government 2018b). For LTC at dementia care wards of designated hospitals, LTCI covered RMB 70 per day per head for people with severe dementia and RMB 50 per day per head for people with moderate dementia (China Daily 2020). At the same time, basic medical insurance would cover the hospitalization expenses of PWD at dementia care wards. For LTC at dementia care wards of designated nursing homes, LTCI covered RMB 50 per day per head for people with severe dementia and RMB 40 per day per head for people with moderate dementia (China Daily 2020). PWD could also receive LTC at their homes. The annual maximum fee for home care was capped at RMB 8,000 for people with severe dementia and RMB 6,000 for people with moderate dementia (China Daily 2020). LTCI covered 80 percent of the annual maximum fee, with the remainder paid by PWD out of pocket (China Daily 2020). In addition, home care subsidies of RMB 15 per day per head and RMB 8 per day per head would be given to people with severe dementia and people with moderate dementia respectively (China Daily 2020). PWD receiving home care could rent six types of auxiliary aids such as wheelchairs, nursing beds, and robot nurses (Xu and Gu 2020). Rentals ranged from RMB 1 to RMB 10 per day (Xu and Gu 2020). They could also buy 15 types of nursing and healthcare consumables such as diapers, nursing pads, commode chairs, and walking aids below market prices (Xu and Gu 2020).

LTC providers in Nantong

In Nantong, LTC services are provided by hospitals, nursing homes, and community healthcare service centres (The Nantong Municipal People's Government 2015). In 2016, there were only two designated LTC service agencies in Nantong (Huang and Yan 2020). In 2020, there were 254 designated LTC service agencies, with the total investment exceeding RMB 2.36 billion (Huang and Yan 2020). As of October 2020, there were 157 designated institutions providing home care services (Nantong Net 2020). They trained and employed over 8,000 people (Nantong Net 2020). Some of the employees obtained Level 5 and above Certificate in Aged Care Work (Nantong Net 2020).

To ensure service quality, LTC bed services in hospitals and nursing homes would be evaluated annually while home care services would be evaluated monthly (Nantong City Medical Insurance Fund Management Center 2017). LTC service providers that were ranked as excellent would be praised and announced to the public (Nantong City Medical Insurance Fund Management Center 2017). Those that did not pass the evaluation were required to rectify their practices (Nantong City Medical Insurance Fund Management Center 2017). If LTC service providers failed to meet the requirements after rectification, they would be required to suspend their service for one to six months (Nantong City Medical Insurance Fund Management Center 2017). If they failed to pass the evaluation in the subsequent year, they would be required to terminate their service (Nantong City Medical Insurance Fund Management Center 2017). Their service agreement with the government would also be terminated (Nantong City Medical Insurance Fund Management Center 2017).

In June 2020, a credit rating system was established to measure the integrity and service quality of designated LTC service providers, such as hospitals, nursing homes, home care service providers, and companies that provided auxiliary aids (Office of the Nantong Municipal Medical Insurance Bureau 2020). A rating of A, B, or C would be assigned to a LTC service provider after comprehensive analysis of its ability to execute service agreement, ensure data security of the care insurance information system properly, provide services with integrity, adopt a reasonable user charge, maintain a good public reputation, and comply with relevant rules and regulations (Office of the Nantong Municipal

Medical Insurance Bureau 2020). A rating of 'A' meant excellent integrity and service quality (i.e. obtain less than 15 marks), 'B' meant good integrity and service quality (i.e. obtain less than 20 marks), 'C' meant integrity and service quality not meeting the expectations or failure of performance appraisal (i.e. obtain more than 20 marks) (Office of the Nantong Municipal Medical Insurance Bureau 2020). A rating of 'C' would also be given to newly established LTC service providers (Office of the Nantong Municipal Medical Insurance Bureau 2020). Any designated LTC service providers which violated relevant rules and regulations or service agreement may face rating downgrades, suspension of service, or termination of service agreement (Office of the Nantong Municipal Medical Insurance Bureau 2020). A rating of 'A' or 'B' would not be assigned to any designated LTC service providers in the subsequent two years once they were asked to suspend services (Office of the Nantong Municipal Medical Insurance Bureau 2020). In addition, a rating of 'A' or 'B' would not be assigned to any LTC service providers in the subsequent three years if they faced termination of service agreement (Office of the Nantong Municipal Medical Insurance Bureau 2020). The credit ratings of LTC service providers would be posted on the website of Nantong Municipal Medical Insurance Bureau and the mobile application (Office of the Nantong Municipal Medical Insurance Bureau 2020).

In order to supplement the current elder care workforce, the Nantong government in April 2018 established a volunteer system to provide LTC services. It encouraged people to register as volunteers through the Nantong LTCI mobile application (Nantong Municipal Human Resources and Social Security Bureau 2018b). Volunteers could provide diversified services for LTC beneficiaries staying at homes, nursing homes, or hospitals, depending on their abilities and talents or the demands of LTC beneficiaries (Nantong Municipal Human Resources and Social Security Bureau 2018b). These services could be reading books or newspapers to LTC beneficiaries, chatting with LTC beneficiaries, vital sign measurement (e.g. blood pressure, glucose), providing ADLs care (e.g. personal hygiene) or respite care (Nantong Municipal Human Resources and Social Security Bureau 2018b). Through the mobile application, volunteers could choose which LTC beneficiaries they wanted to serve, which types of services they could offer, and when to deliver the services to LTC beneficiaries (Nantong Municipal Human Resources and Social Security Bureau 2018b). After receiving the services, LTC beneficiaries or their family members could give a rating (i.e. excellent, good, fair, or poor) to volunteers through the mobile application (Nantong Municipal Human Resources and Social Security Bureau 2018b). The rating would be one of the important data for the municipal care insurance service centres to track the quality of service provided by volunteers and reward volunteers (Nantong Municipal Human Resources and Social Security Bureau 2018b).

A point system similar to time banking was adopted to motivate volunteers. Ten points would be given to a volunteer for every hour of his/her volunteer time (Nantong Municipal Human Resources and Social Security Bureau 2018b).

The number of hours volunteers provided and the number of points they earned would be recorded in the care insurance information system (Nantong Municipal Human Resources and Social Security Bureau 2018b). An honorary certificate would be awarded to volunteers who obtained 3,000 points (Nantong Municipal Human Resources and Social Security Bureau 2018b). Points accumulated would be valid for lifetime and could be inherited by direct dependents (Nantong Municipal Human Resources and Social Security Bureau 2018b). Volunteers could share their points among family members or redeem the points to obtain corresponding LTC benefits when they or their family members had moderate or severe disability in future (Nantong Municipal Human Resources and Social Security Bureau 2018b). For example, 100 points could be used to obtain one hour of LTC service provided by professional care agencies or rent auxiliary aids that cost RMB 100 (Nantong Municipal Human Resources and Social Security Bureau 2018b). In addition, points earned through volunteering would be considered by potential employers during the hiring process if volunteers applied for civil service jobs or jobs in public institutions (Wang and Yu 2018).

Evaluating outcomes of LTCI

By the end of 2016, LTCI in Nantong covered over 1.1 million people, with an annual revenue of RMB 110 million ('The Operation of Long-term Care Insurance in Nantong' 2017). More than 2,000 people could enjoy LTCI benefits and the usage of LTCI fund was about 10 percent ('The Operation of Long-term Care Insurance in Nantong' 2017). Among these LTCI beneficiaries, about 10 percent of them were aged below 60, 30 percent of them were aged between 60 and 80, and 60 percent of them were aged 80 and above ('The Operation of Long-term Care Insurance in Nantong' 2017). In 2018, LTCI in Nantong covered 1.2 million people (Office of Nantong Municipal Government 2018a), with an annual revenue of RMB 120 million (Nantong Net 2018). As of November 2020, LTCI covered about 7.19 million people (Zhang *et al.* 2021: 15). Coverage had reached 98 percent of the population in Nantong (Zhang *et al.* 2021: 15). As of November 2018, a total of 6,086 people enjoyed LTC benefits (Nantong Net 2018). From 2016 to 2018, professional nursing care institutions provided home care for about 220,000 times (Office of Nantong Municipal Government 2018a). In 2020, nursing homes and other care service agencies provided home care services for about 1.84 million times (He 2021). In 2018, more than 5,223 disabled people and PWD enjoyed the auxiliary aids services (Guo 2020). In 2020, a total of 3,851 disabled people enjoyed the auxiliary aids services (He 2021). As of October 2020, a total of 25,727 people enjoyed LTC benefits (Huang and Yan 2020). Among these LTCI beneficiaries, 84 percent received home care while the rest received LTC at designated nursing homes or hospitals (Huang and Yan 2020). Besides, 64 percent of LTCI beneficiaries were 80 years old and above (Nantong Net 2020). The oldest LTCI beneficiary was 108 years old (Nantong Net 2020). By the end of 2020, the LTCI expenditure reached about RMB 114.5 million (He 2021).

Medical resources and medical costs

Before the implementation of LTCI in Nantong, some of the disabled people delayed discharge from hospitals due to the anxiety of not being taken care of after returning home (Zhang *et al*. 2021: 17). This led to unnecessary medical expenses (Zhang *et al*. 2021: 17) and inefficiency in the use of hospital beds. After the implementation of LTCI, however, there is more reasonable use of medical resources in Nantong (Huang and Yan 2020). About 19 percent of disabled persons who were originally in long-term hospitalization moved to nursing homes to receive care (Huang and Yan 2020). The average medical cost in nursing homes was much lower than the average medical costs at hospitals. The cost of the former was only RMB 745 while that of the latter was RMB 18,426 (Nantong Municipal Medical Insurance Bureau 2020; Zhang *et al*. 2021: 17). Hence, receiving medical care at nursing homes could help efficiently manage hospital beds and save the medical expenses of RMB 269 million (Nantong Municipal Medical Insurance Bureau 2020; Nantong Net 2020; Zhang *et al*. 2021: 17). Besides, a lot of medical insurance fund was saved (Nantong Net 2020). The implementation of LTCI helped solve the problems of using medical care to substitute LTC and social hospitalization (Zhang *et al*. 2021: 17).

Cost

The implementation of LTCI helps reduce the financial burden of disabled people and their family caregivers in several ways. First, the medical expense decreased drastically for LTCI beneficiaries. For example, average expenses per inpatient day was RMB 1,247 for a stroke elder who stayed in a Grade II hospital for 132 days (Xinhua Daily 2020). After enjoying LTCI, the stroke elder moved to a medical ward at a nursing home to receive care for 349 days (Xinhua Daily 2020). Average expenses per inpatient day at a nursing home were just RMB 145 (Xinhua Daily 2020). This was 8.6 times less expensive than average hospital expenses per inpatient day. The total amount of medical expenses at the nursing home was RMB 47,000 (Xinhua Daily 2020). However, the stroke elders bear only RMB 6,900 (Xinhua Daily 2020). Second, the care subsidy helped cover LTC expenses for beneficiaries. For example, the care subsidy of RMB 2,100 helped cover half of the accommodation fees of some nursing homes such as Evergreen and Healthy Ageing Nursing Home in Nantong (Huang and Yan 2020). Third, allowing LTCI beneficiaries, especially those who were long-term bedridden, to pay nominal fees to rent auxiliary aids they needed helped reduce their financial burden (Xinhua Daily 2020). For example, buying a manual wheelchair could cost a few hundred dollars, while an electric one could cost a few thousand dollars. But LTCI beneficiaries could use about RMB 200 to rent a wheelchair for six months, which made them worry-free and helped them save a lot of money (Xinhua Daily 2020). Fourth, allowing LTCI beneficiaries to buy 15 types of nursing and healthcare consumables below market price also helped reduce the financial burden of LTCI beneficiaries and their caregivers. For example, adult diapers could cost an elderly few hundred dollars a month (Xinhua Daily 2020). But LTCI beneficiaries were allowed to buy five packs of elderly diapers every month, which only cost RMB 4.5 per pack (Xinhua Daily 2020). This helped LTCI beneficiaries save a lot of money.

Equity

LTCI almost achieves full coverage in Nantong. It covers 98 percent of the population, including urban employees and urban and rural residents. The BI is used as a standardized measure of functional disability while the MMSE is used to measure cognitive impairment among the elderly. Initially, only those who were assessed as severely disabled persons were eligible for receiving LTC. Then, LTCI was extended to cover people who were assessed as moderately dependent (i.e. people with moderate disability). In early 2019, LTCI was further extended to cover people with severe and moderate dementia. The extension of LTCI coverage enables more people to receive care.

The Nantong government encourages LTCI beneficiaries to receive home care services. Compared to their urban counterparts, however, rural older adults may not have equal access to home care services due to uneven development of elder care facilities between urban and rural areas. The pace of establishing home care service stations in rural areas is slow and fails to cover many rural residents due to the lack of venues and money (Ji and Ruan 2015: 23). Some rural village committee offices put up a signage to indicate that their places are home care service stations (Ji and Ruan 2015: 23). But such stations do not operate normally (Ji and Ruan 2015: 23). Many home care service stations are unable to recruit sufficient number of elder care workers (Ji and Ruan 2015: 23). For example, a community in Chongchuan District had only one doctor and one nurse (Ji and Ruan 2015: 23). But these two medical staff were responsible for providing home care services for 600 elders (Ji and Ruan 2015: 23). It was impossible for them to provide home care services for all the elders every week (Ji and Ruan 2015: 23). In rural areas, many elder care workers are aged between 40 and 50 and they lack professional knowledge and skills to deliver LTC services (Ji and Ruan 2015: 23). This leads to poor service quality (Ji and Ruan 2015: 23). Due to shortage of elder care workers, some village cadres have to play the role of elder care workers, which is hard to meet the demand of rural elders in need of home care (Ji and Ruan 2015: 23).

Quality of care

The implementation of LTCI helped improve the quality care of disabled people and enabled family members to take a break and re-energize. For example, an 82-year-old man who experienced paralysis due to stroke regained his ability to communicate after receiving proper home-based rehabilitation services (Huang and Yan 2020). His wife could take a break from her caregiving duties and visited a park when an elder care worker visited her home twice a week to take care of her husband (Huang and Yan 2020). Another example was that of a 92-year-old bedridden elder who recovered from a pressure ulcer that was 26 centimetres in diameter after receiving home care services for six months (Zhang and Feng 2018). A nurse from Dasheng Nursing Home provided pressure ulcer care for the elder twice weekly (Zhang and Feng 2018). Based on the suggestions of the nurse, the elder switched from sleeping on a hard bed to sleeping on an air mattress (Zhang and Feng 2018). She also ate more high protein foods (Zhang and Feng 2018). Her family members knew how to care for her properly after learning the nursing care knowledge from the nurse (Zhang and Feng 2018).

Since the implementation of LTCI, most of the LTC service providers have complied with relevant rules and regulations. Only nine designated LTC service providers have undertaken a penalty payment of RMB 64,000 for breach of contract (Nantong Municipal Medical Insurance Bureau 2020; Nantong Net 2020). For example, a nursing home in Nantong was required to suspend its service for six months due to committing insurance fraud by fabricating care service record (Nantong City Medical Insurance Fund Management Center 2020). It received a rating downgrade from 'B' to 'C' for its home care service and undertook a penalty payment of RMB 12,000 for breach of contract (Nantong City Medical Insurance Fund Management Center 2020). According to Nantong Municipal Medical Insurance Centre, public satisfaction with LTCI reached 99 percent in 2020 (He 2021).

Nevertheless, shortage of elder care workers and a lack of professional training among elder care workers may affect the quality of care received by LTC beneficiaries in Nantong. Elder care workers had low pay and low social status in the city (Sheng 2016: 293). In 2017, there were only 3,431 elder care workers in Nantong (Nantong Municipal Civil Affairs Bureau 2018). About 56.7 percent of elder care workers in Nantong were aged between 46 and 65 (Sheng 2016: 293). The number of female elder care workers was three times more than the number of male elder care workers (Sheng 2016: 293). Over 54 percent of elder care workers were originally registered as unemployed persons and about 12 percent of them were land-lost farmers (Sheng 2016: 293). Most of them completed only junior high education (Sheng 2016: 293). They lack professional knowledge and skills in elder care (Sheng 2016: 293). The number of untrained workers was six times more than the number of trained workers in nursing homes (Sheng 2016: 293). A study found that low education level and long working hours were reasons why elder care workers in Chongchuan District, Nantong had lower demand for training (Xu *et al.* 2017). Elder care workers with low education level had poor learning ability (Xu *et al.* 2017: 46) and were afraid of receiving training. Meanwhile, those who had to work for 12 hours or 24 hours a day found themselves too tired to receive training (Xu *et al.* 2017: 46). Due to shortage of elder care workers, some nursing homes (e.g. Dasheng Nursing Home) which still had residential placement could not admit older people but put them on a wait list (Chen 2017). In rural areas, there were 92 geracomiums (*jinglaoyuan*) providing 23,483 nursing care beds (Gong 2017). However, due to poor management and service quality, the utilization rate of nursing care beds in geracomiums reached only 48 percent (Gong 2017), which was below the targeted utilization rate of 65 percent (Jiangsu China Net 2018).

In late December 2020, more than 600 elder care workers received a free skills training jointly organized by Civil Affairs Bureau and the Ministry of Human Resources and Social Security in Chongchuan District (Li and He 2020). Those who were awarded a certificate after passing the training assessment could receive a certification subsidy that ranged from RMB 1,000 to RMB 3,000 and a monthly job subsidy that ranged from RMB 300 to RMB 1,000 (Li and He 2020). But it is yet to know if this free skills training will be held regularly and similar training can be offered to elder care workers in different districts in the city.

Sustainability

LTCI in Nantong is financed by multiple sources, including individual contribution, individual MSA and the SPF of BMI, government subsidies, the welfare lottery fund, and donation from individuals, enterprises, or charity organizations. The fiscal responsibility is borne by individuals, the government, and society. At present, the funding of LTCI has yet to be totally separated from the medical insurance system because part of the funding comes from the SPF of BMI and money transferred from the individual MSA of UEBMI participants. According to Vice Minister of Medical Insurance Bureau, however, the rapidly ageing population in Nantong, an increase in the prevalence of chronic diseases, and the continuous increase in medical expenditure have significantly reduced the medical insurance fund reserve ratio and increased pressure on medical insurance expenditure (Wang 2019). The financial stability and sustainability of LTCI fund would be affected by the financial stability of the medical insurance fund. Besides, LTCI relies heavily on government subsidies. From 2016 to 2020, the municipal government injected RMB 282 million to LTCI fund, which accounted for 45 percent of the LTCI fund (Nantong Net 2020). Nevertheless, over reliance on government subsidies would also affect the financial stability and sustainability of the LTCI fund in the long run. Afterall, the ability of the Nantong government to continuously fund LTCI depends on its fiscal health and financial performance.

Recommendations

The Nantong government needs to build and grow its pool of professional elder care workers to meet the growing demand for LTC. It needs to develop a comprehensive training curriculum for skill certification. For example, it can learn from India, which developed a training curriculum for geriatric care assistant (Ministry of Health and Family Welfare 2017). To qualify as a geriatric care assistant, a candidate must receive a minimum duration of 700 hours of training (165 hours for theory, 360 hours for practical skills training, and 175 hours for internship) and pass the final examination (Ministry of Health and Family Welfare 2017: 4). The building of a pool of professional elder care workers enables the government to provide a diversified LTC service packages for disabled elders and PWD. At present, the home care service packages focus on providing ADL care for LTCI beneficiaries. But more comprehensive home care service packages including infection control, rehabilitation, and dementia care can be provided if elder care workers are equipped with relevant skills. Besides, it is important for the government to attract and retain elder care workers by providing them with better status and salary. The government can consider developing a pay range pegged to the level of certification elder care workers received. It can further promote a volunteering system that promotes time banking. Also, the government needs to establish a LTCI funding system that can be independent from the medical insurance system. It needs to explore the feasibility of asking employers and employees to jointly contribute to LTCI. It may be possible to do so if the government can reduce the amount of contribution by employers and employees to BMI. This can avoid increasing the financial burden of both parties.

Conclusion

To conclude, the implementation of LTCI in Nantong leads to better utilization of medical resources, save medical insurance fund, and greatly reduce the financial costs borne by care recipients and their family members. It can solve the problem of social hospitalization. However, the government needs to build and grow a pool of professional elder care workers, improve the quality of LTC workers, provide more comprehensive home care service packages, and establish a LTCI funding system independent from the medical insurance system.

References

Chen, K. (2017) *The Problem of Shortage of Manpower in Nursing Homes in Nantong Is Yet to Be Resolved* (Chinese version). Online. Available HTTP: http://jsnews. jschina.com.cn/nt/a/201705/t20170507_466222.shtml (accessed 16 June 2021).

China Banking News (2021) *Shanghai, Beijing and Shenzhen Top List of China's Top 50 Cities in Terms of 2020 GDP*. Online. Available HTTP: www.chinabankingnews. com/2021/01/08/shanghai-beijing-and-shenzhen-top-list-of-chinas-top-50-cities-in-terms-of-2020-gdp/ (accessed 29 May 2021).

China Daily (2018) 'High-End Textile Industry', *China Daily*, 27 July. Online. Available HTTP: http://en.nantong.gov.cn/2018-07/27/c_258508.htm (accessed 29 May 2021).

China Daily (2020) 'Using Five Years to Establish a Long-Term Care Insurance System: The Nantong Model', (Chinese version), *China Daily*, 10 October. Online. Available HTTP: http://ex.chinadaily.com.cn/exchange/partners/82/rss/channel/cn/ columns/j3u3t6/stories/WS5f818ebda3101e7ce97287ef.html (accessed 7 June 2021).

Deloitte (2012) *The Su-Tong Science and Technology Park Investment Environment Evaluation Report*. Online. Available HTTP: www2.deloitte.com/content/dam/ Deloitte/ca/Documents/international-business/csg-china-research-report-on-investment-environment-of-sutong-science-and-technology-park-en-2013.pdf (accessed 29 May 2021).

Feng, L. F. and Chen, Y. X. (2008) 'A Survey on the Psychological Well-Being of "Empty-Nesters" in Four Community Places in Nantong and Measures to Care for "Empty-Nesters"', *Chinese Journal of Modern Drug Application*, 2 (24): 202–3.

The Five Regions of Nantong Were Selected as the 'National Textile Industrial Cluster Pilot' (2019) Online. Available HTTP: www.sjfzxm.com/global/en/555890.html (accessed 29 May 2021).

Gong, D. (2017) *Eight Geracomiums Have Been Upgraded to Become Social Welfare Service Centres in Nantong* (Chinese version). Online. Available HTTP: http://jsnews.jschina.com.cn/nt/a/201711/t20171107_1172014.shtml (accessed 17 June 2021).

Guo, X. C. (2020) 'Long-Term Care Insurance in Nantong Covers 7.2 Million People', (Chinese version), *Xiao Xiang Daily*, 12 October. Online. Available HTTP: https://baijiahao.baidu.com/s?id=1680321938161417423&wfr=spider&for=pc (accessed 9 June 2021).

He, J. Y. (2021) *The Level of Public Satisfaction with Long-Term Care Insurance in Nantong Reached 99 Percent* (Chinese version). Online. Available HTTP: https://baijiahao.baidu.com/s?id=1700270213266350430&wfr=spider&for=pc (accessed 15 June 2021).

Huang, H. F. and Yan, L. (2020) *The Sixth Insurance Helps Us to Age with Dignity* (Chinese version). Online. Available HTTP: http://xh.xhby.net/pc/con/202010/12/content_835299.html (accessed 10 June 2021).

Ji, N. F. and Ruan, S. M. (2015) 'The SWOT Analysis of the Development of Home Care Service System in Rural Villages: The Case Study of Nantong', (Chinese version), *Liaoning Agricultural Sciences*, 5: 21–5.

Jianghai Evening News (2014) 'There Is One Elder for Every Four Persons in Nantong', (Chinese version), *Jianghai Evening News*, 1 October. Online. Available HTTP: http://epaper.ntrb.com.cn/new/jhwb/html/2014-10/01/content_267057.htm (accessed 30 May 2021).

Jiangsu China Net (2018) *Nantong Will Establish 252 Home Care Service Centre within a Year* (Chinese version). Online. Available HTTP: https://baijiahao.baidu.com/s?id=1591439998916299437&wfr=spider&for=pc (accessed 17 June 2021).

Li, T. and He, J. Y. (2020) *More Than 600 Eldercare Workers in Chongchuan District, Nantong Received a Free Skills Training: The Highest Amount of Subsidy Is RMB 3,000 for Those Who Get Certification* (Chinese version). Online. Available HTTP: https://baijiahao.baidu.com/s?id=1685019927241441819&wfr=spider&for=pc (accessed 18 June 2021).

Ministry of Health and Family Welfare (2017) *Short Term Training Curriculum Handbook: Geriatric Care Assistant*. Online. Available HTTP: https://main.mohfw.gov.in/sites/default/files/Short%20Term%20Training%20Curriculum%20Handbook_Geriatric%20Care%20Assistant_1%20June%202017_0.pdf (accessed 18 June 2021).

Nantong City Medical Insurance Fund Management Center (2017) *Nantong Conducts Performance Appraisal in Designated Care Service Institutions* (Chinese version). Online. Available HTTP: www.nantong.gov.cn/ntsrsj/gzdt/content/A74C00DF8BB54B408DE7AAFB0B144341.html (accessed 12 June 2021).

Nantong City Medical Insurance Fund Management Center (2020) *Notification on Temporarily Suspending the Provision of Care Services by Nantong North Nursing Home* (Chinese version). Online. Available HTTP: www.nantong.gov.cn/ntsylbzj/gggs/content/e4fd8369-e693-48d7-8371-2354fdd2ff61.html (accessed 14 June 2021).

Nantong Municipal Civil Affairs Bureau (2018) *Suggestions about Building Care Teams in Nursing Homes* (Chinese version). Online. Available HTTP: http://mzj.nantong.gov.cn/ntsmzzj/jytabljg/content/b8cad99f-4dd7-4402-a898-edd-30d1acb1c.html (accessed 16 June 2021).

Nantong Municipal Human Resources and Social Security Bureau (2016) *Notification on Distributing the Implementation Details of Basic Care Insurance in Nantong* (Chinese version). Available HTTP: http://ylbzj.nantong.gov.cn/ntsylbzj/bmwj/content/dc782759-2d09-4dd6-85fc-93a71c00d676.html (accessed 2 June 2021).

Nantong Municipal Human Resources and Social Security Bureau (2017a) *Opinions on Home Care Services under Basic Care Insurance in Nantong* (Chinese version). Online. Available HTTP: http://ylbzj.nantong.gov.cn/ntsylbzj/bmwj/content/5bfcbcf2-450f-415d-9158-6af304abeb9a.html (accessed 5 June 2021).

Nantong Municipal Human Resources and Social Security Bureau (2017b) *Notification on Introducing More Home Care Service Packages in Nantong* (Chinese version). Online. Available HTTP: http://ylbzj.nantong.gov.cn/ntsylbzj/bmwj/content/9c18f98b-bbf9-4673-a92d-033a95963dfe.html (accessed 6 June 2021).

Nantong Municipal Human Resources and Social Security Bureau (2017c) *Notification on Adopting Standardized Management of Medical Insurance and Care Insurance Services* (Chinese version). Online. Available HTTP: http://ylbzj.nantong.gov.cn/ntsylbzj/bmwj/content/12febec5-1c63-4f37-b464-a99f4e8609d8.html (accessed 5 June 2021).

Nantong Municipal Human Resources and Social Security Bureau (2018a) *Opinions on Establishing a Unified Basic Care Insurance System in the Whole City* (Chinese version). Online. Available HTTP: http://gzw.nantong.gov.cn/ntsrmzf/zcwj2/content/8d94b7e2-0a99-46b2-9224-5e1b875cead8.html (accessed 6 June 2021).

Nantong Municipal Human Resources and Social Security Bureau (2018b) *Press Conference on Launching Volunteer Services under Care Insurance in Nantong* (Chinese version). Online. Available HTTP: www.nantong.gov.cn/ntsrmzf/xwfbh/content/b2877d33-4126-4a63-9383-b6c72b6cf6b8.html (accessed 9 June 2021).

Nantong Municipal Human Resources and Social Security Bureau (2018c) *Policy Analysis on Extending the Coverage of Basic Care Insurance to People with Dementia* (Chinese version). Online. Available HTTP: www.nantong.gov.cn/ntsrmzf/bmjd2/content/fb933c75-2536-4505-8de8-78ca86f526af.html (accessed 6 June 2021).

Nantong Municipal Medical Insurance Bureau (2016) *Opinions on Providing Home Care Services under Basic Care Insurance in Nantong (Trial Implementation)* (Chinese version). Online. Available HTTP: http://ylbzj.nantong.gov.cn/ntsylbzj/bmwj/content/ee4a7387-74e5-4158-9721-5230c63c8d83.html (accessed 5 June 2021).

Nantong Municipal Medical Insurance Bureau (2020) *Press Conference on the Fifth Anniversary of Pilot Long-Term Care Insurance in Nantong* (Chinese version). Online. Available HTTP: http://czj.nantong.gov.cn/ntsrmzf/xwfbh/content/29839a60-5c6e-4388-8c29-c8edbd4a8ff7.html (accessed 13 June 2021).

The Nantong Municipal People's Government (2015) *Notification on Issuing and Distributing Opinions on Establishing the Basic Care Insurance System (Trial Implementation)* (Chinese version). Online. Available HTTP: http://ylbzj.nantong.gov.cn/ntsylbzj/bmwj/content/e72137da-ede3-4952-b5a7-fb7b344d4cb0.html (accessed 1 June 2021).

Nantong Municipal Statistics Bureau (2013) *Communiqué on Major Data of the Sixth National Population Census of Nantong City in 2010* (Chinese version). Online. Available HTTP: www.nantong.gov.cn/ntstj/tongjgb/content/2251717f-0248-433b-af6f-04479b2b74fe.html (30 May 2021).

Nantong Municipal Statistics Bureau (2021a) *Statistical Communiqué on the 2020 National Economic and Social Development in Nantong* (Chinese version). Online. Available HTTP: www.nantong.gov.cn/ntstj/tjgb/content/13a26b37-d232-464e-91d3-f66ea1e7a0eb.html (accessed 29 May 2021).

Nantong Municipal Statistics Bureau (2021b) *Press Conference on Major Data of the Seventh National Population Census of Nantong City* (Chinese version). Online. Available HTTP: www.nantong.gov.cn/ntstj/xwfbh/content/8887b73a-ce35-45cd-94a6-00a4f9473b08.html (accessed 30 May 2021).

Nantong Net (2018) *Nantong Takes the Lead in Implementing Care Insurance System and Brings Benefits to Disabled People* (Chinese version). Online. Available HTTP: http://news.jstv.com/a/20181104/1541302814943.shtml (accessed 9 June 2021).

Nantong Net (2020) *Designated Care Institutions Increased to More Than 250: Care Insurance in Nantong Has Covered More Than 7 Million People within Five Years* (Chinese version). Online. Available HTTP: www.china-insurance.com/insurdata/20201011/44578.html (accessed 9 June 2021).

Office of Nantong Municipal Government (2018a) *Nantong Plans to Achieve Universal Care Insurance Coverage in the Whole City by 2020* (Chinese version). Online. Available HTTP: www.jiangsu.gov.cn/art/2018/6/27/art_46502_7725753.html (9 June 2021).

Office of Nantong Municipal Government (2018b) *Basic Care Insurance in Nantong Covers People with Severe Dementia* (Chinese version). Online. Available HTTP: www.jiangsu.gov.cn/art/2018/12/14/art_46502_7962712.html (accessed 7 June 2021).

Office of the Nantong Municipal Medical Insurance Bureau (2020) *Measures for the Administration of the Credit Ratings of Integrity and Services of Designated Institutions for Care Insurance in Nantong* (Chinese version). Online. Available HTTP: www.nantong.gov.cn/ntsylbzj/upload/55423bfe-78b9-4574-8acc-df3de9719270.pdf (accessed 12 June 2021).

The Operation of Long-Term Care Insurance in Nantong and Its Implication (2017) (Chinese version). Online. Available HTTP: www.jianke.com/xwpd/4539806.html (accessed 14 June 2021).

People's Government of Jiangsu Province (2015) *Care for People with Long-Term Disability Would Be Protected by the System in Nantong* (Chinese version). Online. Available HTTP: www.jiangsu.gov.cn/art/2015/11/2/art_46501_2534865.html (accessed 9 June 2021).

Qian, X. F. (2003) 'The Development of Population Ageing in Nantong and Its Impact on Old-Age Security', (Chinese version), *Jiangsu Statistics* 1: 23–5.

Sheng, C. X. (2016) 'Analysis on the Present State of Manpower in Elder Care Industry: The Case of Nantong', (Chinese version), *Human Resource Management*, 12: 292–4.

Wang, J. L. (2019) *Nantong Comprehensively Promotes Municipal-Level Coordination of Medical Insurance for Residents: The Payment Standard Is RMB 1,200* (Chinese version). Online. Available HTTP: www.yangtse.com/zncontent/150555.html (accessed 18 June 2021).

Wang, Y. X. and Yu, W. D. (2018) *Nantong Plans to Provide Universal Care Insurance Coverage by 2020 So That Disabled People Can Live with Dignity* (Chinese version). Online. Available HTTP: http://news.2500sz.com/doc/2018/06/26/301403.shtml (accessed 11 June 2021).

Who Can Enjoy Long-Term Care Benefits? (2021) (Chinese version). Online. Available HTTP: www.nantong.gov.cn/tzqrmzf/wdzsk/content/4f5cff11-125d-439d-a66e-644d2b255b7b.html (accessed 7 June 2021).

Xie, Q. (2013) 'Research on Population Aging in the Process of Preliminary Modernization in Nantong', (Chinese version), *Modern Urban Research*, 5: 87–91.

Xinhua Daily (2019) 'The Percentage of Persons Aged 60 and above Has Accounted for 23 Percent of the Total Population in Jiangsu Province', (Chinese version), *Xinhua Daily*, 31 October. Online. Available HTTP: http://wjw.jiangsu.gov.cn/art/2019/10/30/art_75072_8748371.html (accessed 30 May 2021).

Xinhua Daily (2020) 'The Nantong Model of Long-Term Care', (Chinese version), *Xinhua Daily*, 22 May. Online. Available HTTP: https://baijiahao.baidu.com/s?id=1667374474178638136&wfr=spider&for=pc (accessed 16 June 2021).

Xu, J. L., Wang, Y. N., Song, H. L., Gu, T. Y., Geng, G. L. and Xu, B. (2017) 'Analysis on the Demand for Training among Elder Care Workers in Non-Profit Nursing Homes in Nantong and Its Influencing Factors', (Chinese version), *Journal of Nursing (China)*, 24 (4): 43–6.

Xu, S. N. and Gu, X. (2020) *Jiangsu Province Already Has 71,000 People Enjoying Long-Term Care Insurance Benefits and Reduced the Burden of Disabled People and People with Dementia* (Chinese version). Online. Available HTTP: http://app.myzaker.com/news/article.php?pk=5f7958be1bc8e06b7b00007d&f=huangli (accessed 8 June 2021).

Xue, H. Y. and Wu, A. M. (2014) *Nantong Has Become the First 'Capital of Longevity of the World' with the Average Life Expectancy of 80.71 Years Old* (Chinese version). Online. Available HTTP: http://district.ce.cn/zg/201405/29/t20140529_2895665.shtml (accessed 29 May 2021).

Yang, L. S., Wang, M. C. and Li, J. C. (2004) 'Study on Population Ageing and Social Protection of Targeted Population: The Case of Nantong', (Chinese version), *Population Journal*, 6: 49–54.

Zhang, B., Gu, A. P and Fan, R. (2021) 'The Effectiveness of the Long-Term Care Insurance System in Nantong after Five Years of Implementation and Its Implication', (Chinese version), *China Health Insurance*, 4: 15–18.

Zhang, M. (2015) 'Achieving Full Coverage of Social Insurance and Establishing a New Service System: A Survey on the Old-Age Insurance System in Nantong', (Chinese version), *World of Labour Security*, 2: 22–4.

Zhang, Y. (2015) 'Reduce the Medical and Nursing Burden of Disabled Patients', (Chinese version), *Nantong Daily*, 29 April. Online. Available HTTP: http://epaper.ntrb.com.cn/new/ntrb/html/2015-04/29/content_23123.htm (accessed 30 May 2021).

Zhang, Y. Z. and Feng, J. (2018) *Nantong City, Jiangsu Finds Solutions to the Problems of Caring Elders at Home and in the Community (Part 2)* (Chinese version). Online. Available HTTP: www.mca.gov.cn/article/xw/mtbd/201808/20180800010856.shtml (accessed 18 June 2021).

Zhu, C. X. (2012) *The Share of Persons Aged 65 and above in Total Population Reached 16.5 Percent in Nantong* (Chinese version). Online. Available HTTP: http://news.eastday.com/csj/2012-12-19/90276.html (accessed 30 May 2021).

7 The long-term care model in Shanghai

Introduction

Shanghai is a super-aged city in China. In 2013, Shanghai introduced a pilot home-based medical and nursing care scheme for older adults, which built a foundation for the creation of the long-term care insurance (LTCI) system in 2017. This chapter gives a detailed account of the development of LTCI in Shanghai. It evaluates the outcomes of LTCI in terms of five criteria: utilization of medical resources, cost, equity, quality of care, and financial sustainability. It finds that there is room for improvement in the quality of LTC services, the financial sustainability of LTCI, and the care for people with dementia (PWD). It suggests the Shanghai government learn from the experiences of Germany, Japan, and South Korea to facilitate fair distribution of LTC services to people in need, increase the supply of elder care workers, and enhance their level of competency. Further, the use of smart devices should be promoted to improve the quality of home care.

Background

Shanghai is located on 'the coast of the East China Sea between the mouth of the Yangtze River (Chang Jiang) to the north and the bay of Hangzhou to the south' (Boxer n.d.). It is the largest city in China with a population of over 24 million. It is 'a major industrial and commercial centre of China' (Boxer n.d.), 'the world's busiest container port' (World Maritime News 2020), and 'has been ranked among the top 3 global financial hubs, following New York and London' (Li 2020).

Shanghai has been facing the challenge of rapid population ageing. The average life expectancy in Shanghai rose from 75.5 in 1990 to 78.8 in 2000, 82.1 in 2010, and 83.7 in 2020 (Shanghai Municipal Health Commission 2020, Office of Shanghai Municipal Working Committee on Ageing *et al.* 2021). Shanghai was the first ageing society in China (Shi and Cui 2011: 206). It became an ageing society in 1979, with persons aged 65 and above making up 7.2 percent of its total population (Zhu 1999: 26). In 2005, Shanghai became an aged society, with the number of persons aged 65 and above accounting for 15 percent of its

DOI: 10.4324/9780429057199-7

total population (Shanghai Centre on Scientific Research on Ageing 2007). In 2017, Shanghai became a super-aged society, with the number of persons aged 65 and above accounting for about 21.8 percent of its total population (Shanghai Municipal Health Commission 2020).

As of 31 December 2020, the number of persons aged 65 and above reached over 3.82 million in Shanghai, which accounted for about 25.9 percent of the total population (Office of Shanghai Municipal Working Committee on Ageing *et al.* 2021). There were 3,080 persons aged 100 and above, of whom 2,288 were females and 792 were males (Office of Shanghai Municipal Working Committee on Ageing *et al.* 2021). It is estimated that the number of people aged 60 and above will reach 40 percent in Shanghai by 2030 (Gu 2020). However, the number of people aged 60 and above had already exceeded 40 percent of the total population in four districts in Shanghai. These included Hongkou (42.5%), Huangpu (41.7%), Putuo (41.1%), and Jing'an (40.1%) districts (Office of Shanghai Municipal Working Committee on Ageing *et al.* 2021: 8).

In Shanghai, many older adults age with disability. Shanghai had over 400,000 disabled elders in 2014 (Jie Fang Daily 2014). In 2015, Shanghai had about 636,500 disabled elders and elders with dementia, which accounted for 14.6 percent of the total number of persons aged 60 and above in the city ('The total number of disabled elders' n.d.). And 4.8 percent of 636,500 disabled elders and elders with dementia were fully disabled ('The total number of disabled elders' n.d.). Shanghai had about 400,000 to 450,000 disabled elders at the end of 2018, according to the calculation based on the 8 to 9 percent of the disability rate of elders in the city (The Paper 2020).

Shanghai has been facing the problem of rising 'empty-nesters'. 'Empty-nesters' (*kong chao lao ren*) refers to elders who are not living with their children, who are living alone, or who are living independently with their spouses (Liang *et al.* 2020: 361–2). They are 'vulnerable and usually experience the physical, psychological, and social problems associated with old age' (Gao *et al.* 2014: 1821). The number of 'empty-nesters' in Shanghai increased from about 0.71 million in 2004 (Yu 2008) to about 0.92 million in 2009 (Chen 2011), and about 0.99 million in 2015 (Office of Shanghai Chronicles 2015). In 2019, Shanghai had about 1.44 million 'empty-nesters', of whom 359,400 were people aged 80 and above, and 317,400 were elders who lived alone (Shanghai Municipal Health Commission 2020: 10).

Development of LTCI

The pilot home-based medical and nursing care scheme for older adults (2013)

The escalating growth of the elderly population in Shanghai led to an increasing demand for long-term care (LTC). In July 2013, Shanghai introduced a pilot home-based medical and nursing care scheme for older adults living in six subdistricts and towns in Pudong, Yangpu, and Changning Districts ('Policy

Interpretation' 2016). The pilot scheme covered older adults who, aged 70 and above, were Urban Employee Basic Medical Insurance (UEBMI) participants, had household registration (*hukou*) in Shanghai, and lived in subdistricts and towns where the pilot scheme was implemented ('Policy Interpretation' 2016). Older adults who wanted to obtain medical and nursing care services through the scheme could submit a written application together with the photocopies of their identity card, household registration record, medical insurance card, and medical history to the Community Affairs Service Center in their living districts ('Policy Interpretation' 2016). The application was then passed to the medical insurance centre for review. Once the application was accepted by the medical insurance centre, older adults would get a needs assessment according to the standards set by Shanghai Municipal Human Resources and Social Security Bureau and Shanghai Municipal Health Commission ('Policy Interpretation' 2016). Assessment content included the health and medical conditions of older adults and their self-care ability ('Policy Interpretation' 2016).

After the needs assessment, older adults would know about the level of care (*zhao gu ji bie*) they belonged to. Eligible older adults in care level two would receive three hours of services at home every week. Those in care level three or four would receive five hours of services at home every week. Those in care level five or six would receive seven hours of services at home every week. Although the scheme was called home-based medical and nursing care scheme, it actually also covered activities of daily living (ADLs) care. Services which were related to ADLs included changing bedsheets, washing face, combing hair, oral hygiene, perineal care, foot cleaning, dressing, assisting older adults to eat and drink, assist older adults to turn over in bed, assisted cough, toileting, incontinence care, pressure ulcer care, fingernail and toenail care, bathing, and home safety ('Policy Interpretation' 2016). Medical and nursing care services included blood glucose and vital signs monitoring, venous blood sampling, giving oral drugs, injection, nasogastric tube feeding, urinary catheterization, enema, and oxygen therapy ('Policy Interpretation' 2016). They were provided by nursing stations, community health centres, nursing homes, and outpatient clinics ('Policy Interpretation' 2016). The standard fee of renminbi (RMB) 65 was charged each time if the services were provided by medical care assistants and RMB 80 was charged each time if the services were provided by qualified nurses ('Policy Interpretation' 2016). The Social Pooling Fund (SPF) of the UEBMI would cover 90 percent of the fees, with the rest covered by the service recipient's individual Medical Savings Account (MSA) ('Policy Interpretation' 2016). The service recipient had to pay on his/her own if his/her individual MSA was unable to cover the service fees ('Policy Interpretation' 2016) (See Table 7.1).

In November 2014, the pilot scheme was extended to 28 subdistricts and towns in Pudong, Yangpu, Changning, Xuhui, and Putuo Districts ('Policy Interpretation' 2016). In January 2016, the pilot scheme was extended to the whole city. As of 30 June 2016, the pilot scheme provided LTC services for about 155,000 older adults ('Policy Interpretation' 2016). The pilot scheme built a foundation for the creation of the LTCI system in Shanghai (Liu 2018: 50).

Table 7.1 The pilot home-based medical and nursing care scheme for older adults (2013)

Description	To provide older adults with ADLs care, medical and nursing care at home		
Targeted population	Older adults aged 70 and above, who were Urban Employee Basic Medical Insurance (UEBMI) participants, had household registration (*hukou*) in Shanghai, and lived in six subdistricts and towns in Pudong, Yangpu, and Changning Districts		
Eligibility	Older adults in care level two and above		
Level of care	Two	Three or four	Five or six
Frequency of services	Three hours of services per week	Five hours of services per week	Seven hours of services per week
Service charges	[a] Qualified nurse: RMB 80 each time [b] Medical care assistant: RMB 65 each time The SPF of the UEBMI would cover 90% of the fees, with the rest covered by the service recipient's individual MSA. Out-of-pocket payment was required if the service recipient's individual MSA was unable to cover the service fees.		
Types of services	ADLs care	[1] Changing bedsheets [2] Washing face [3] Combing hair [4] Oral hygiene [5] Perineal care [6] Foot cleaning [7] Dressing [8] Assisting older adults to eat and drink [9] Assist older adults to turn over in bed [10] Assisted cough [11] Toileting [12] Incontinence care [13] Pressure ulcer care [14] Fingernail and toenail care [15] Bathing [16] Home safety	
	Medical and nursing care	[17] Blood glucose monitoring [18] Vital signs monitoring [19] Venous blood sampling [20] Giving oral drugs [21] Injection [22] Nasogastric tube feeding [23] Urinary catheterization [24] Enema [25] Oxygen therapy	

Source: Policy Interpretation of the Opinion on the Pilot Medical and Nursing Care Scheme for Older Adults in Shanghai (Chinese version) (2016). Online. Available HTTP: http://m.lc123.net/laws/2016-08-30/291483.html (accessed 5 April 2021).

Pilot measures for LTCI in Shanghai (2017)

The 2013 pilot home-based medical and nursing care scheme for older adults built a foundation for the creation of the LTCI system in Shanghai in 2017. In December 2016, the Shanghai municipal government issued *Pilot Measures for Long-term Care Insurance in Shanghai* (hereafter *the 2016 Pilot Measures*). According to the 2016 Pilot Measures, LTCI would be implemented first in Xuhui, Putuo, and Jinshan districts in January 2017 to provide ADLs care, medical care, and nursing care for people with long-term disability. It would then be implemented in the whole city starting from January 2018.

LTCI covered all the UEBMI participants as well as Urban and Rural Resident Basic Medical Insurance (URRBMI) participants aged 60 and above (Shanghai Municipal People's Government 2016a). According to Article 6 of *the 2016 Pilot Measures*, UEBMI participants, their employers, and URRBMI participants were required to pay LTCI premium. UEBMI participants were required to contribute 0.1 percent of their average monthly salary in the previous year to LTCI (Shanghai Municipal People's Government 2016a). Their employers were required to contribute 1 percent of their employees' average monthly salary in the previous year to LTCI (Shanghai Municipal People's Government 2016a). Retired UEBMI participants did not have to pay LTCI premium. For URRBMI participants, they were required to contribute about 15 percent of the total premium, with the rest of the premium being shared by the municipal and district finance in a 1:1 ratio (Shanghai Municipal People's Government 2016a). LTCI in Shanghai had two separate accounting systems: one for UEBMI participants and one for URRBMI participants (Shanghai Municipal People's Government 2016a). Nevertheless, Article 26 of the 2016 Pilot Measures stated that Article 6 would not be carried out during the pilot stage. This meant that the LTCI fund would not be funded by premium contribution from UEBMI participants, their employers, and URRBMI participants. Instead, it would be financed by fund transferred from the special account of the UEBMI (Shanghai Municipal People's Government 2016a). Starting from 1 January 2018, the LTCI fund for UEBMI participants would be financed by the SPF of the UEBMI, while the LTCI fund for URRBMI participants would be financed by the SPF of the URRBMI (Shanghai Municipal People's Government 2017).

Participants aged 60 and above and had household registration in Shanghai could submit a needs assessment application to see if they were eligible for receiving LTC services. They could submit the application through different channels such as Community Affairs Service Centers, Community Integrated Service Centres for the Elderly, online platforms, and mobile application (Shanghai Municipal People's Government 2016b). Once the district-level authority reviewed and accepted the application, it would entrust a designated third-party evaluation agency to send an evaluation team to the applicant's home to conduct the needs assessment. As of September 2020, there were 34 evaluation agencies and 9,000 evaluators in Shanghai (Xu 2020). Evaluators were doctors, nurses, or social workers (Hu 2018: 85). They had to receive training from the health and family planning department and pass the assessment before becoming an evaluator (Hu 2018). Due to insufficient number of evaluators, every district in the city had to mobilize doctors who worked in community health service centres to use their spare time to conduct needs assessment at the applicants' homes (Dai *et al.* 2019: 11).

According to *A Unified Needs Assessment Standard for Elder Care (Pilot)*, the evaluation team assessed the applicant's overall level of care needs based on two dimensions: the applicant's self-care ability and disease severity (Shanghai Municipal People's Government 2016b). Self-care ability consisted of three components, including 13 ADLs (e.g. eating, toileting), two instrumental activities of daily living (IADLs) (i.e. using transportation and handling finances), and cognitive abilities (i.e. orientation to time, orientation to space, short-term memory, and instant memory) (Shanghai Municipal People's Government 2016b). The corresponding weights of these three dimensions were 85 percent, 10 percent, and 5 percent respectively (Shanghai Municipal People's Government 2016b). Disease severity referred to 10 highly prevalent diseases among older population, including hypertension, chronic obstructive pulmonary disease (COPD), pneumonia, diabetes, Parkinson's disease, cerebral haemorrhage, cerebral infarction, advanced cancer, coronary artery disease, and lower extremity fractures (Shanghai Municipal People's Government 2016b). Each disease was assessed by four factors, including disease symptoms, signs, auxiliary examination, and medical complication, with a corresponding weight of 30 percent, 30 percent, 30 percent, and 10 percent respectively (Shanghai Municipal People's Government 2016b) (See Table 7.2).

The scores of the dimensions of self-care ability and disease severity would determine the level of care needed by the applicant. The score ranged from 0 to 100 points. The level of care was defined on seven levels: normal, level one, level two, level three, level four, level five, and level six (Shanghai Municipal People's Government 2016b). A LTC information system software would be used to calculate an overall score and indicate the level of care needed by the applicant (Shanghai Municipal Human Resources and Social Security Bureau and Shanghai Medical Health Insurance Office 2018). A higher assessment score translated to a higher level of care required.

In December 2019, an updated version of *A Unified Needs Assessment Standard for Elder Care (Pilot)* was implemented in Shanghai. The updated version showed that an applicant's overall level of care needs was still evaluated based on the two dimensions of the applicant's self-care ability and disease severity (Shanghai Municipal Health Commission *et al.* 2019). Self-care ability consisted of three components, including ADLs, IADLs, and cognitive ability. However, the corresponding weight of ADLs decreased from 85 percent to 65 percent, while the corresponding weight of cognitive ability increased from 5 percent to 25 percent (Shanghai Municipal Health Commission *et al.* 2019). The corresponding weight of IADLs remained the same. An applicant's self-care ability was assessed in a more comprehensive manner. The number of ADLs assessed increased from 13 to 20, while the number of IADLs assessed increased from 2 to 8 (Shanghai Municipal Health Commission *et al.* 2019). Meanwhile, the number of items to measure cognitive ability increased from 4 to 22 (Shanghai Municipal Health Commission *et al.* 2019). Dementia was added to the dimension of disease severity. Each disease was still assessed by four factors, including disease symptoms, signs, auxiliary examination, and medical complication, with

Table 7.2 A unified needs assessment standard for elder care (pilot) in 2016

Dimensions	Components	Weightage
Self-care ability	13 ADLs	85%
	[1] Faecal incontinence (Yes/No)	
	[2] Urinary incontinence (Yes/No)	
	[3] Hand/face washing	
	[4] Combing hair	
	[5] Toileting	
	[6] Eating	
	[7] Standing up from a seated position	
	[8] Sitting on a chair	
	[9] Walking on level ground	
	[10] Putting on/taking off clothes	
	[11] Putting on/taking off trousers	
	[12] Walking up and down the stairs	
	[13] Bathing	
	Two IADLs:	10%
	[1] Using transportation	
	[2] Handling finances	
	Four types of cognitive abilities:	5%
	[1] Orientation to time	
	[2] Orientation to space	
	[3] Short-term memory	
	[4] Instant memory	
Disease severity	10 highly prevalent diseases among older population:	Each disease was assessed by four factors:
	[1] Hypertension	[1] Disease symptoms (30%)
	[2] Chronic obstructive pulmonary disease (COPD)	[2] Signs (30%)
	[3] Pneumonia	[3] Auxiliary examination (30%)
	[4] Diabetes	[4] Medical complication (10%)
	[5] Parkinson's disease	
	[6] Cerebral haemorrhage	
	[7] Cerebral infarction	
	[8] Advanced cancer	
	[9] Coronary artery disease	
	[10] Lower extremity fractures	

Source: Shanghai Municipal People's Government (2016b) *Opinions on Comprehensively Promoting the Establishment of a Unified Needs Assessment System for Elder Care* (Chinese version). Online. Available HTTP: http://law.esnai.com/view/181979/ (accessed 15 April 2021).

a corresponding weight of 30 percent, 30 percent, 30 percent, and 10 percent respectively (Shanghai Municipal Health Commission *et al.* 2019) (See Table 7.3). The updated version indicated that the government paid attention to the impact of cognitive impairment or dementia on care needs of older adults.

The evaluation team must finish the needs assessment within 15 working days. Based on the assessment result, the evaluation team suggested which type of LTC service would be suitable for the applicant and provided the name of the LTC service provider in the assessment report (Shanghai Municipal Human Resources

Table 7.3 A unified needs assessment standard for elder care (pilot) in 2019

Dimensions	Components	Weightage
Self-care ability	*20 ADLs	65%
	[1] Turning over in bed	
	[2] Standing up from the lying position	
	[3] Sitting on a chair	
	[4] Standing up from a seated position	
	[5] Standing on level ground for 10 seconds	
	[6] Walking on level ground	
	[7] Need assistance during the sit to stand transfer (Yes/No)	
	[8] Need assistance when eating (yes/No)	
	[9] Brushing teeth	
	[10] Hand/face washing	
	[11] Combing hair	
	[12] Putting on/taking off clothes	
	[13] Putting on/taking off trousers	
	[14] Bathing	
	[15] Urinary incontinence (Yes/No)	
	[16] Faecal incontinence (Yes/No)	
	[17] Visual acuity	
	[18a] Make and receive phone calls	
	[18b] Hearing	
	[19] Paralysis (hand/leg)	
	[20] Joint mobility	
	(e.g. neck, shoulder, knees)	
	*Eight IADLs	10%
	[1] Cooking	
	[2] Doing household chores	
	[3] Walking up and down the stairs	
	[4a] Going out but not knowing how to go back home	
	[4b] Frequency of going out	
	[5] Using transportation	
	[6] Go shopping	
	[7] Handling finance	
	[8] Take oral medicine	
	22 types of cognitive abilities	25%
	*Examples:	
	[1] What is your name?	
	[2] How old are you?	
	[3] What is the current season?	
	[4] Name three unrelated objects (i.e. ball, national flag, and tree). Then ask the older adult to repeat all three objects after 30 seconds.	

(*Continued*)

Table 7.3 (Continued)

Dimensions	Components	Weightage
	[5] What is the (year) (month) (day)? What time is it now?	
	[6] Where are you?: (province) (city) (street) (hospital) (floor)	
	[7] Ask the older adult to begin with 100 and count backwards by 7. Stop after 5 subtractions (93, 86, 79, 72, 65).	
	[8] Ask the older adult to recall the three objects previously stated (in Question 4).	
Disease severity	11 highly prevalent diseases among older population: [1] Hypertension [2] COPD [3] Pneumonia [4] Diabetes [5] Parkinson's disease [6] Cerebral haemorrhage [7] Cerebral infarction [8] Advanced cancer [9] Coronary artery disease [10] Lower extremity fractures [11] Dementia	Each disease was assessed by four factors: [1] Disease symptoms (30%) [2] Signs (30%) [3] Auxiliary examination (30%) [4] Medical complication (10%)

Source: Shanghai Municipal Health Commission, Shanghai Civil Affairs Bureau and Shanghai Municipal Medical Insurance Bureau (2019) *A Unified Needs Assessment Standard for Elder Care, Version 2.0 (Pilot)* (Chinese version). Online. Available HTTP: http://wsjkw.sh.gov.cn/gjhztgahz/20191220/4ee7499b3f2f4fa699a1b04880404d93.html (accessed 20 April 2021).

* Survey Form for the Unified Needs Assessment of Elder Care in Shanghai (Chinese version). Online. Available HTTP: www.wjx.cn/jq/87409560.aspx (accessed 20 April 2021).

and Social Security Bureau and Shanghai Medical Health Insurance Office 2018). After finishing the needs assessment, the evaluation team would submit both the assessment report and the Notification of the LTCI Needs Assessment Result to the district-level authority. Then, the district-level authority would notify the applicant of the assessment result. In principle, the assessment result was valid for a maximum of two years (Shanghai Municipal People's Government 2016b). The older adults should apply for the needs assessment again within 60 days prior to the expiration date of the assessment result (Shanghai Municipal People's Government 2018). During the validity period, however, the older adult could submit a request for reassessment if his or her health condition had changed (Shanghai Municipal People's Government 2016b).

Standard needs assessment fee had to be jointly shared by the applicant and district finance (Shanghai Municipal People's Government 2016b). However, fee reduction or fee waiver could be available for older adults who had financial hardship (Shanghai Municipal People's Government 2016b). In January 2018, standard needs assessment fee was RMB 200 each time (Shanghai Municipal Human Resources and Social Security Bureau and Shanghai Medical Health Insurance Office 2018; Shanghai Municipal Price Bureau *et al.* 2018). Starting from 1 January 2018, LTCI would cover 80 percent of the needs assessment fee, with the remainder paid by the applicant out of pocket (Shanghai Municipal People's Government 2017; Shanghai Municipal Human Resources and Social Security Bureau and Shanghai Medical Health Insurance Office 2018). For older adults who came from low-income family or were Minimum Living Standard Guarantee (*dibao*) recipients, they did not pay for the needs assessment fee out of pocket because the fee would be fully subsidized by district finance (Shanghai Civil Affairs Bureau *et al.* 2018). Retired cadres, old Red Army, and disabled military personnel were exempted from paying the needs assessment fee (Shanghai Municipal Medical Insurance Bureau 2019). The designated evaluation agency, after recording such fee, would apply to the district medical insurance centre for settlement (Shanghai Municipal Medical Insurance Bureau 2019). The district medical insurance centre would review the application and report the result of the preliminary review to Shanghai Municipal Medical Insurance Management Centre. Shanghai Municipal Medical Insurance Management Centre then decides the appropriate payment to the designated evaluation agency based on the reviewing result (Shanghai Municipal Medical Insurance Bureau 2019). Older adults could receive LTC services if they were in care level two and above.

There were three types of LTC services, including community home care, nursing home care, and inpatient medical and nursing care. First, community home care provided older adults with ADLs care, medical care, and nursing care in the comfort of their own home. Staff from elder care institutions, nursing stations, nursing homes, outpatient clinics, and community health centres made regular home visits to provide community home care for older adults. Each home visit lasted one hour. The standard fee of RMB 80 was charged each hour if the community home care services were provided by nurse practitioners, RMB 65 if the services were provided by elder care workers, and RMB 40 if the services were provided by other nursing care staff (Hu 2018: 87). The frequency of home care depended on the level of care. Older adults in care level two or three would receive home care services three times a week while older adults in care level four would receive home care services five times a week (Shanghai Municipal People's Government 2016a). Older adults in care level five or six would receive home care services seven times a week (Shanghai Municipal People's Government 2016a). They were encouraged by the government to receive home care services through financial and non-financial incentives. They could choose to receive a cash subsidy of RMB 40 or an extra hour of home care service every month if they continued to receive community home care for more than one month, but less than six months (Shanghai Municipal People's Government 2016a). They could choose to receive a cash subsidy of RMB 80 or two more hours of home care services every month if they continue to receive community home care for more than six months (Shanghai Municipal People's Government 2016a) (See Table 7.4).

Table 7.4 Community home care in Shanghai

Description	To provide older adults with ADLs care, medical care, and nursing care in the comfort of their own home		
Eligibility	Older adults in care level two and above		
Level of care	Two or three	Four	Five or six
Frequency of services	Three one-hour services per week	Five one-hour services per week	Seven one-hour services per week
Service charges	[a] Nurse practitioners: RMB 80 per hour [b] Elder care workers: RMB 65 per hour [c] Other nursing care staff: RMB 40 per hour		
Financial and non-financial incentives	[1] For older adults in care level five or six and who continued to receive community home care for more than one month, but less than six months: – a cash subsidy of RMB 40 or – an extra hour of home care service every month [2] For older adults in care level five or six and who continued to receive community home care for more than six months: – a cash subsidy of RMB 80 – two more hours of home care services every month		

Source: Shanghai Municipal People's Government (2016a) *Pilot Measures for Long-term Care Insurance in Shanghai* (Chinese version). Online. Available HTTP: http://law.esnai.com/view/179508/ (accessed 12 April 2021).
Hu, S. (2018) 'Pilot Study on Long-term Care Insurance System in Shanghai: Status, Problems and Suggestions', (Chinese version), *Journal of East China University of Science and Technology* (Social Science Edition), 4: 84–91.

Second, nursing home care provided older adults with residential care, ADLs care, medical care, and nursing care. Older adults who received nursing home care had to pay RMB 20 per day if they were in care level two or three, RMB 25 per day if they were in care level four, and RMB 30 per day if they were in care level five or six (Hu 2018).

Both community home care and nursing home care included 42 service items, which could be divided into two categories: ADLs care and common medical and nursing care. Among these 42 service items, 27 belonged to ADLs care while 15 belonged to common medical and nursing care (See Table 7.5).

A document titled *Long-term Care Insurance Service Standards and Norms* was published to provide detailed step-by-step instructions on how to carry out these 42 services (Shanghai Civil Affairs Bureau *et al.* 2016). In Shanghai, the government focused on promoting community home care while nursing home care was treated as a supplementary LTC service (Shanghai Civil Affairs Bureau *et al.* 2016). Third, inpatient medical and nursing care was provided by nursing homes, community health centres, and Grade II hospitals for their older patients (Shanghai Municipal People's Government 2016a).

Table 7.5 A list of service items that are inside the scope of community home care and nursing home care

Category	Service item	Frequency
ADLs care	[1] Facial cleansing, brushing hair	3 times/day
	[2] Hair washing	1–2 time(s)/week
	[3] Fingernail and toenail care	If necessary
	[4] Hand-washing and foot-washing	1–2 time(s)/day
	[5] Warm sponge bath	1 time/day
	[6] Bathing	If necessary
	[7] Assist in eating and drinking	3–5 times/day
	[8] Oral care	2 times/day
	[9] Assist elders with dressing	3–5 times/day
	[10] Bed making	2 times/day
	[11] Excretion care	5–7 times/day
	[12] Incontinence care	If necessary
	[13] Toileting in bed	If necessary
	[14] Manual removal of faeces	If necessary
	[15] Day care (e.g. oral care, facial cleaning, brushing hair, dressing, hand-washing, bed making)	1 time/day
	[16] Night care (e.g. oral care, facial cleaning, hand-washing, foot-washing, changing clothes)	1 time/day
	[17] Perineal care	2 times/day
	[18] Medication management	If necessary
	[19] Aid sputum expectoration	If necessary
	[20] Help elders move in bed	If necessary
	[21] Choose suitable mobility aids (e.g. wheelchair) to help elders move around	If necessary
	[22] Apply ointment to elders' skin	If necessary
	[23] Safety care (e.g. fall prevention)	1 time/day
	[24] Self-care ability training (e.g. personal hygiene, wearing shoes)	If necessary
	[25] Pressure ulcer prevention and care	If necessary
	[26] Indwelling urinary catheter care	If necessary
	[27] Colostomy bag care	If necessary
Common medical and nursing care	[28] Rectal suppository administration	If necessary
	[29] Nasogastric tube feeding	If necessary
	[30] Assist elders with oral medication	1–4 time(s)/day
	[31] External cooling in the management of fever	If necessary
	[32] Vital signs monitoring	If necessary
	[33] Oxygen therapy	If necessary
	[34] Enema	If necessary
	[35] Urethral catheterization (female)	If necessary
	[36] Blood glucose monitoring	If necessary
	[37] Wound care dressings for pressure ulcers	If necessary

(*Continued*)

Table 7.5 (Continued)

Category	Service item	Frequency
	[38] Venous blood sample collection	If necessary
	[39] Intramuscular injection	If necessary
	[40] Subcutaneous injection	If necessary
	[41] Ostomy care	If necessary
	[42] Management of Peripherally Inserted Central Catheter (PICC)	If necessary

Source: Shanghai Civil Affairs Bureau et al. (2016) *Notification on Printing and Distributing a List of Long-term Care Insurance Service Items and Related Service Standards and Norms (Trial Implementation)* (Chinese version). Online. Available HTTP: www.yanglao.com.cn/article/56456.html (accessed 15 April 2021).

The LTCI coverage rate varied among different types of LTC services. The LTCI fund covered 90 percent of the community home care fees, with the remainder paid by care recipients out of pocket (Ma and He 2019). It covered 85 percent of the nursing home care fees, with the remainder paid by care recipients out of pocket (Ma and He 2019). LTC provided in hospitals 'is reimbursed according to the beneficiaries' health insurance status, that is, either UEBMI or URRBMI' (Feng *et al.* 2020: 113081). According to the UEBMI document, the SPF of the UEBMI would reimburse inpatient fees that exceeded the payment threshold (Shanghai Municipal People's Government 2000). The payment threshold ranged from 5–10 percent of Shanghai employees' average annual salary in the previous year, depending on whether the participants were incumbent or retired employees (Shanghai Municipal People's Government 2000). The reimbursement rate was 85 percent for incumbent employees and 92 percent for retired employees (Shanghai Municipal People's Government 2000). The ceiling of the SPF was capped at four times Shanghai employees' average annual salary in the previous year (Shanghai Municipal People's Government 2000). An additional fund (*fu jia ji jin*) would cover 80 percent of inpatient expenses that exceed the ceiling of the SPF, with the remainder paid by the participants on their own (Shanghai Municipal People's Government 2000). According to the latest URRBMI document, the URRBMI fund would reimburse inpatient fees that exceed the payment threshold of RMB 50 in Grade I medical institutions, RMB 100 in Grade II medical institutions, and RMB 300 in Grade III medical institutions (Shanghai Municipal People's Government 2020). The reimbursement rate was 90 percent for eligible participants aged 60 and above if they stayed in Grade I medical institutions, 80 percent for eligible participants aged 60 and above if they stayed in Grade II medical institutions, and 70 percent for eligible participants aged 60 and above if they stayed in Grade III medical institutions (Shanghai Municipal People's Government 2020).

Government subsidies would be given to very old people, people with severe disability, or URRBMI participants who were Minimum Living Standard Guarantee (*dibao*) recipients to help cover their out-of-pocket (OOP) expenses incurred by LTC services (Shanghai Municipal People's Government 2016a). For older adults from the *dibao* family, their OOP expenses incurred by LTC services would be fully subsidized (Shanghai Civil Affairs Bureau *et al.* 2018). For older adults from the low-income family, half of their OOP expenses incurred by LTC services would be subsidized (Shanghai Civil Affairs Bureau *et al.* 2018). Subsidies would be shared by the municipal and district finance in a 1:1 ratio (Shanghai Civil Affairs Bureau *et al.* 2018). In addition, favourable treatment was given to retired cadres, old Red Army, and disabled military personnel. They were exempted from paying expenses incurred by LTC services. The designated LTC service provider, after recording such expenses, would apply to the district medical insurance centre for settlement (Shanghai Municipal Medical Insurance Bureau 2019). The district medical insurance centre would review the application and report the result of the preliminary review to Shanghai Municipal Medical Insurance Management Centre. Shanghai Municipal Medical Insurance Management Centre then decided if it would appropriate the payment to the designated LTC service provider based on the reviewing result (Shanghai Municipal Medical Insurance Bureau 2019).

Designated LTC service providers in Shanghai

In Shanghai, LTC services are provided by medical institutions, elder care organizations, and community elder care organizations (Shanghai Municipal Human Resources and Social Security Bureau *et al.* 2016). Medical institutions refer to nursing hospitals, nursing stations, community health centres, and outpatient clinics that have obtained the Practice License for Medical Institution (Shanghai Municipal Human Resources and Social Security Bureau *et al.* 2016). Elder care organizations refer to organizations that have obtained the Permit for Establishing Elder Care Institution (Shanghai Municipal Human Resources and Social Security Bureau *et al.* 2016). Community elder care organizations refer to those that have obtained Non-profit Organization Registration Certificate (Shanghai Municipal Human Resources and Social Security Bureau *et al.* 2016).

Medical institutions, elder care organizations, and community elder care organizations can voluntarily apply to the district medical insurance centre for becoming designated LTC service providers if they meet the establishment and practice standards stipulated in the national and local regulations, meet the staffing requirements of LTCI, have a sound service management system, and have a computer management system that can handle insurance settlement online and corresponding management and operational personnel (Shanghai Municipal Human Resources and Social Security Bureau *et al.* 2016). Their application and supporting documents would be reviewed by the district medical insurance centre. Once the district medical insurance centre accepts the application, it would send a work team to the medical institution or the elder care organization to conduct a site assessment. Then, it submits the assessment result and relevant documents to Shanghai Municipal Medical Insurance Management Centre to make the final decision. Medical institutions and elder care organizations would be chosen by Shanghai Municipal Medical Insurance Management Centre as designated LTC service providers if they can provide LTC services with reasonable prices and good quality and have standardized management (Shanghai Municipal Human Resources and Social Security Bureau *et al.* 2016).

Service agreements which are generally valid for two years would be signed between Shanghai Municipal Medical Insurance Management Centre and the chosen medical institutions and elder care organizations (Shanghai Municipal Human Resources and Social Security Bureau *et al.* 2016). Before expiration of service agreements, Shanghai Municipal Medical Insurance Management Centre would assess the performance of designated LTC service providers in fully executing the promised services stated in service agreements (Shanghai Municipal Human Resources and Social Security Bureau *et al.* 2016). It would renew service agreements with only designated LTC service providers which pass the performance assessment. As of September 2020, there were 1,173 designated LTC service providers in Shanghai (Xu 2020). Among these designated LTC service providers, 646 of them were designated elder care organizations, 320 of them were designated community elder care organizations, and 207 of them were designated medical institutions (Shanghai Municipal Veteran Bureau 2020).

Evaluating the outcomes of LTCI

Since the implementation of LTCI, Shanghai has seen an increase in the number of beneficiaries. As of end October 2017, 14,000 out of 25,000 older adults who submitted application were eligible for receiving community home care and nursing home care (Shanghai Observer 2017). In November 2018, the number of older adults receiving LTC services was about 186,000 (Tian 2019). As of July 2019, 305,000 older adults received community home care and 111,000 older adults received nursing home care (Shanghai Observer 2019). As of June 2020, 324,000 older adults received community home care and 67,000 older adults received nursing home care (Xu 2020). In March 2021, the number of older adults receiving LTC services reached over 500,000 (Shanghai Observer 2021a). The average age of LTCI beneficiaries receiving home care was 80.1 years old, while the average age of LTCI beneficiaries receiving institutional care was 85 years old (Xu 2020). From January to October 2018, the LTCI expenditure was RMB 706 million (Tian 2019). As of July 2019, the LTCI expenditure was RMB 1.27 billion, of which RMB 940 million was payment for community home care, RMB 300 million was payment for nursing home care, and RMB 30 million was needs assessment fee (Shanghai Observer 2019). The outcomes of LTCI in Shanghai can be evaluated in terms of five criteria: utilization of medical resources, cost, equity, quality of care, and sustainability.

Better utilization of medical resources

The implementation of LTCI in Shanghai helps utilize medical resources in a better way. A recent study which used the administrative patient-level data in

Shanghai in 2016 and 2017 found that the implementation of LTCI led to the substitution of LTC for hospitalization and health improvement (Feng *et al.* 2020: 113081). The length of stay in LTC facilities significantly increased by about 55 percent while the length of inpatient stay decreased by 41 percent (Feng *et al.* 2020: 113081). Meanwhile, inpatient expenditures, medical insurance expenditures, and outpatient visits per month decreased by 17.7 percent, 11.4 percent, and 8.2 percent respectively (Feng *et al.* 2020: 113081). Besides, the study found that the implementation of LTCI had a greater effect on inpatient care and expenditures among older people aged over 80 years old (Feng *et al.* 2020: 113081). One possible explanation was that older people had more severe disability and had lower IADLs performance (Feng *et al.* 2020). They had greater demand for LTC. Through a cost–benefit analysis, the study also found that every extra RMB 1 spent in LTCI could lead to a decrease of RMB 8.6 in medical insurance expenditures (Feng *et al.* 2020: 113081). In sum, the implementation of LTCI promoted more older adults to receive more care services in LTC facilities than medical services in hospitals, which drove the lower inpatient expenditures on average (Feng *et al.* 2020: 113081). It helped promote better utilization of medical resources and 'improve the allocation of health insurance funds' (Feng *et al.* 2020: 113081).

Cost

In Shanghai, LTCI can greatly reduce the financial costs borne by care recipients and their family members because it covers 85–90 percent of LTC service fees, with the remainder paid by care recipients. As of 17 September 2018, the number of hours disabled elders receiving community home care had been accumulated over 6.31 million and the number of days elders receiving nursing home care had been over 13.18 million (The Development Research Centre of Shanghai Municipal People's Government 2020). This helped directly reduce the economic burden of older adults and their caregivers by RMB 131.1 million (The Development Research Centre of Shanghai Municipal People's Government 2020). Besides, LTCI can save a large amount of medical insurance fund. A study by Feng *et al.* (2020) found that the benefit of decreased medical insurance payment after the implementation of LTCI in Shanghai was substantially greater than the cost of implementing LTCI. Through the cost–benefit analysis, Feng *et al.* (2020) estimated that the cost of implementing LTCI was about RMB 14.3 million. Nevertheless, the implementation of LTCI could save about RMB 123 million of medical insurance fund due to the reduction in inpatient admission and the reduction in reimbursement expenditure per day (Feng *et al.* 2020). To elaborate further, LTCI led to a substitution effect, which transferred older adults in need of LTC services from tertiary hospitals to LTC facilities (Feng *et al.* 2020). The inpatient expenditure per day in LTC facilities in the city was RMB 502.45, which was about one-sixth of that in tertiary hospitals (Feng *et al.* 2020). Meanwhile, reimbursement expenditure per day in LTC facilities in Shanghai was RMB 418.82, which was about 5.2 times less than that of in tertiary hospitals (Feng *et al.* 2020). Hence, the implementation of LTCI could reduce older adults' reliance on tertiary hospitals to receive LTC, thereby saving medical insurance fund (Feng *et al.* 2020).

Equity

At present, LTCI beneficiaries are restricted to UEBMI and URRBMI participants who are aged 60 and above and who are in care level two and above. Disabled people aged below 60 are unable to enjoy LTCI. Besides, the current LTC services that focus on providing ADLs care, medical care, and nursing care fail to meet the needs of PWD (Ma and He 2019). Existing studies found that the need of PWD to manage behavioural problems, their need to engage in daily individualized activities and care, their emotional needs/personhood, and social needs must not be ignored in LTC (Cadieux *et al.* 2013: 728). Besides, the needs of people with mild dementia differ greatly from those with moderate or advanced dementia (Cadieux *et al.* 2013). For example, people with mild dementia may 'need cues and reminders to help with memory' ('Early-Stage Caregiving' n.d.) and need caregivers to help create 'a daily routine which promotes quality sleep and engagement with others' ('Early-Stage Caregiving' n.d.). But people with advanced dementia may require around-the-clock assistance with daily personal care or hospice care ('Stages of Alzheimer's' n.d.). Unmet needs are both a source of increased disruptive behaviours and reduced quality of life (QoL) of PWD (Cadieux *et al.* 2013: 723).

The needs assessment also fails to accurately identify the level of care needed by older adults (Chen and Hao 2020). An applicant's overall level of care needs is evaluated based on two dimensions: the applicant's self-care ability and disease severity (Shanghai Municipal Health Commission *et al.* 2019). The need assessment that takes into account an applicant's disease severity leads to applicants who had rich disease history but high self-care ability getting a higher level of care than applicants who had little or no medical history but low self-care ability (Chen and Hao 2020; Dai *et al.* 2019). For example, the levels of care obtained by stroke patients and patients with diabetes can be five and above, while the levels of care obtained by bedridden patients and PWD were four and two respectively (Hu 2018: 87). In reality, however, more manpower, time, and energy are needed to care for bedridden and people in the middle and severe stages of dementia (Hu 2018: 87). Since the needs assessment does not precisely indicate the level of care needed by applicants, some applicants may be unable to obtain the LTC care they need.

Quality of care

In Shanghai, there is a need for improving the quality of home care as well as the quality of care in nursing homes. In 2018, there was a survey examining 93 disabled elders' satisfaction with community home care and nursing home care in Xuhui, Putuo, and Jinshan districts (Dai and Jin 2019). The survey result found that disabled elders were highly satisfied with ADLs care (scored 4.27 out of 5) (Dai and Jin 2019). In particular, a majority of respondents were 'very satisfied with' and 'satisfied with' safety care (81%), day care (78%), and assistance services (75%) (Dai and Jin 2019). But the respondents' satisfaction with perineal care was the lowest (59%) because elder care workers failed to provide such care thoroughly with patience (Dai and Jin 2019). Besides, the survey result found that disabled elders' satisfaction with medical and nursing care was the lowest (scored 3.98 out of 5) (Dai and Jin 2019). In particular, disabled elders were not satisfied with enema administration, urethral catheterization, nasogastric tube feeding, oxygen therapy, and ostomy care due to elder care workers' insufficient knowledge and skills to perform these tasks (Dai and Jin 2019). Also, the survey result found that uneven distribution of LTC facilities and resources among three districts affected disabled elders' satisfaction with LTC services. The levels of disabled elders' satisfaction with LTC service in Xuhui and Putuo district were respectively 2.34 times and 1.81 times higher than that of in Jinshan district (Dai and Jin 2019). This was because both Xuhui and Putuo districts had more developed public transport systems and more LTC facilities than Jinshan district. They could deliver LTC services to disabled elders more easily. As a suburban district, Jinshan district was 11 times bigger than Xuhui and Putuo districts but had no subway services (Dai and Jin 2019). Jinshan district had only 38 organizations providing LTC while Xuhui and Putuo districts had respectively 55 and 53 organizations providing LTC (Dai and Jin 2019). Due to insufficient LTC facilities and less convenient public transportation, disabled elders in Jinshan district may find it difficult to obtain good quality LTC services, which in turn affected their satisfaction with LTC services.

Another study which examined the view of 2,059 older adults on LTC services in Shanghai found that 98.2 percent of them were satisfied with ADLs care, while only 18.8 percent of them were satisfied with medical and nursing care services (The Development Research Center of Shanghai Municipal People's Government 2020). There were inadequate medical and nursing care services due to several reasons. First, nursing stations preferred providing ADLs care because of lower cost and insufficient nurse practitioners (The Development Research Center of Shanghai Municipal People's Government 2020). The current LTC charge was insufficient to cover the cost of providing medical and nursing care services (The Development Research Center of Shanghai Municipal People's Government 2020). Second, nursing stations could avoid the risks of having medical disputes with older adults and save the trouble of disposing medical wastes if they did not provide medical and nursing care services (The Development Research Center of Shanghai Municipal People's Government 2020). Some family members of older adults thought that it was a waste of money to pay RMB 80 for community home care services provided by nurse practitioners when nurse practitioners mainly provided ADLs care but barely provided medical and nursing care (Li 2018: 87). They could have paid RMB 65 to let elder care workers provide the same service (Li 2018). Third, some of the medical and nursing care services such as ostomy care and management of PICC can hardly be provided by nurses at home due to an unhygienic environment (Hu 2018: 87). In fact, a recent study has found that among 33 nursing stations in Shanghai, only about 42 percent of them could provide 42 services items which included both ADL care and common medical and nursing care, about 21 percent could provide 27 services items belonging to ADLs care, about 12 percent could provide only some services items belonging to ADLs care, and about 9 percent were not clear about what kind of home care services they could provide for older adults (Cheng 2020: 50).

At present, both home community care and nursing home care are unable to meet the demands from disabled elders because they have yet to provide targeted, personalized, and diversified services (Zhan 2018). Some severely disabled elders who need the company of caregivers all the time find that one-hour service provided by community home care per visit is too short (Shanghai Municipal Veteran Bureau 2020). The one-hour home care service was unable to meet some of the older adults' demand for turning over in bed multiple times every day because the elder care worker could help older adults turn over in bed only one time (Li 2018: 28). Some LTC recipients hope that the insurance can cover IADLs such as cooking, cleaning, and shopping (Shanghai Municipal Veteran Bureau 2020). For older residents in nursing homes, most of them have multiple chronic illnesses and are partially or fully disabled (Huang 2019). Their QoL needs to be enhanced by receiving medical care, rehabilitation treatment, and health management services (Huang 2019). However, most of the nursing homes are unable to recruit and retain sufficient qualified healthcare professionals who prefer to work in hospitals (Huang 2019). They can hire only retired medical professionals to provide medical care, rehabilitation treatment, and health management services for older residents (Huang 2019).

In fact, a severe shortage of LTC workers and LTC workers' inadequate knowledge and skills in Shanghai pose obstacles to improving the quality of home care and the quality of care in nursing homes. In Shanghai, there are over 90 elder care training institutions and vocational colleges (Shanghai Observer 2019). In order to become a LTC worker, one must obtain a job qualification certificate (*shang gang zheng*) through receiving an eight-day training organized by the Ministry of Civil Affairs and then passing the examination (Cao 2020: 15). The number of LTC workers has increased over time. But it has failed to meet the government's target of having 100,000 registered LTC workers by December 2020 (Gang Wo Education 2020) and could barely meet the growing demand caused by the ageing population. In particular, the shortage of LTC workers in rural areas is more serious because LTC workers prefer to work in urban areas for better salary, better living environment, and more convenient transportation (Zhan 2018). As of November 2018, there were about 32,000 LTC workers, including licensed practical nurses and personal care workers (Tian 2019). In August 2019, there were about 50,000 LTC workers in designated LTC service providers (Shanghai Observer 2019). Among these LTC workers, about 35,000 of them provided home care while 15,000 of them provided institutional care (Shanghai Observer 2019). In September 2020, there were 63,000 LTC workers in Shanghai (Xu 2020). On average, every LTC worker had to care for about eight older adults every day (Shanghai Municipal Veteran Bureau 2020). In some local districts, however, a LTC worker cared for too many older adults. For example, a LTC worker in a nursing station in Putuo district had to care for 10 older adults (Zhan 2018). In Jiading district, a LTC worker had to provide community home care services for 63 older adults (Liu 2018: 51). Work overload and increased burden on LTC workers may lead to poor physical health (e.g. chronic pain in lower back) and burnout, increase the risks of injuries, and reduce productivity.

In Shanghai, LTC workers have to work long hours and rarely take time off (Xinhua Insight 2015). They work an average of 56 hours per week (Xiao Xiang Morning Post 2020a). But they receive lower pay than healthcare workers or psychologists and lack other welfare benefits (Cao 2020: 16). The average monthly salary for LTC workers was RMB 5,064 (Xiao Xiang Morning Post 2020a). It was much lower than the average monthly salary of employees in Shanghai, which was RMB 9,580 in 2019 (China Economic Net 2020). In some suburban areas, however, the monthly salary for LTC workers was just RMB 2,700 (Xinhua Insight 2015). In addition, difficult working conditions, low social status, and the lack of employment prospect lead to LTC workers leaving the sector easily (Cao 2020). LTC workers in Shanghai worked for the same organization only for an average of 12.6 months (Xiao Xiang Morning Post 2020a). High turnover in the LTC sector reduced the productivity of delivering care.

The LTC sector in Shanghai can hardly recruit young people. Many current LTC workers are older females with very low education level. In terms of gender, about 91 percent of LTC workers were females (60 Plus 2020). In terms of age, about 60 percent of LTC workers were aged 51 and above, about 34 percent of LTC workers were between the ages of 41 and 50, about 4.9 percent of LTC workers were between the ages 31 and 40, about 0.81 percent of LTC workers were between the ages of 21 and 30, and about 0.15 percent of LTC workers were aged 20 and below (60 Plus 2020). In terms of education level, about 87 percent of LTC workers had lower secondary education and below (60 Plus 2020). Some of them were even illiterate (Cao 2020). Low education level or illiteracy may reduce the efficiency of delivering care or the quality of care. For example, some illiterate LTC workers in nursing homes had to rely on other LTC workers or nurse directors to help them write down the health conditions (e.g. flu, insomnia, constipation) of older residents (Xinhua Insight 2015). Another example was that some LTC workers who came from rural villages lacked sufficient medical and nursing knowledge to read a vital sign monitor and make instant and precise judgement based on the data collected from the vital signs monitor (Xiao Xiang Morning Post 2020b). Due to low education level and poorer learning capacity (Cao 2020), many LTC workers find it difficult to receive vocational training and take an examination. Their motivation to learn more job-related knowledge and skills is low.

The need for more LTC workers in Shanghai is a structural issue. The government strives to meet the target of having 85,000 registered LTC workers in the city by 2022 (Xiao Xiang Morning Post 2020b). In August 2020, the Shanghai government introduced a new training subsidy policy to incentivize LTC workers aged below 60 to receive occupational skills training (Qian 2020). It set up a prescribed subsidy standard according to the occupation and skill level obtained by the LTC workers: RMB 1,780 for junior care worker (Level 5); RMB 1,820 for intermediate care worker (Level 4); RMB 2,740 for advanced care worker (Level 3); and RMB 3,560 for both technician (Level 2) and advanced technician (Level One) (Qian 2020). LTC workers can get an 80 percent subsidy from the government after finishing the vocational training, passing the examination, and getting a certificate (Qian 2020). But it is yet to know if this financial incentive can successfully attract more LTC workers to receive training, which in turn enhance the quality of LTC workers.

In order to improve the quality of home care, the Medical Insurance Bureau in Jing'an district in 2021 introduced a smart device which used biometric technologies (e.g. sound wave) to record how LTC workers deliver home care to older adults (Shanghai Observer 2021b). LTC workers in Jing'an district are asked to wear this device on their shoulders when they deliver home care services to care recipients (Shanghai Observer 2021b). Once the LTC worker arrives at the care recipient's place, he/she unlocks the device using face recognition (Shanghai Observer 2021b). Then, the device records audio during the care delivery process (Shanghai Observer 2021b). All audio can be listened and played back by the quality supervision service system in the back end in real time (Shanghai Observer 2021b). Algorithms are used to analyse the audio data to detect any inappropriate behaviours from LTC workers and evaluate care recipients' satisfaction with home care services (Shanghai Observer 2021b). It is expected that over 2,600 LTC workers would wear this digital device to deliver home care services by the second quarter of 2021 (Shanghai Observer 2021b).

In recent years, the Shanghai government has encouraged commercial insurance companies to develop private LTC coverage products so that individuals can subscribe the product to obtain more personalized LTC services (Shanghai Municipal People's Government 2019). But introducing private LTCI in the city is not as easy as it may seem. At present, 'LTC insurance market is limited in most countries, although the recognition and the need for a market is strong' (OECD 2020a: 16). Factors explaining why the private LTCI is small include asymmetric information (e.g. adverse selection and moral hazard) in the private LTC insurance market, premium mark-up by insurers, individuals' myopia in planning for the financial risk associated with LTC, competing financial obligations and priorities faced by individuals, and the presence of the public LTCI (OECD 2011: 252–3). 'Typically, private LTC insurance arrangements develop around a country's public LTC system, either to complement available public coverage, or provide benefits where there is no public LTC coverage' (OECD 2011: 248). Evidence in overseas countries suggests that voluntary private LTC insurance would mainly 'serve the segment of the population with relatively higher income and accumulated assets' (OECD 2011: 259). In Shanghai, the introduction of private LTCI and the provision of more personalized LTC services require more investments in LTC facilities, manpower, and new technologies.

Sustainability

Although the Shanghai government stated in *the 2016 Pilot Measures* that employers, UEBMI and URRBMI participants should make premium contribution to LTCI, it has yet to implement this funding policy. One possible explanation is that the government does not want to increase the financial burden of employers and employees. Employers are required by the Social Insurance Law of the People's Republic of China to make financial contribution to five types of social insurances, including old-age insurance, basic medical insurance, work injury insurance, unemployment insurance, and maternity insurance (Standing Committee of the National People's Congress 2010). Meanwhile, employees are required by the Social Insurance Law to make financial contribution to old-age insurance, basic medical insurance, and unemployment insurance (Standing Committee of the National People's Congress 2010). To avoid increasing the financial burden of employers and employees, the Shanghai government relies on the SPF of two basic medical insurance funds (i.e. the UEBMI and the URRBMI) to fund LTCI. However, this may affect the financial stability and sustainability of the LTCI system (Chen and Hao 2020). The expenditures of the two basic medical insurance funds will increase over time due to an increase in the number of older adults. Older adults have a higher morbidity rate, consultation rate, and hospitalization rate than younger people, which implies higher medical expenditures for this age group (Ai 2018). For example, the medical expense of retired employees in Shanghai was 4.3 times higher than that of incumbent employees (Xu 2005: 56). It may lead to a decrease in the surplus of the SPF of the UEBMI and a deficit in the UEBMI fund in the long run (Ai 2018). If the UEBMI fund is not financially sustainable in the long run, it may not be able to provide sufficient financial resources to fund LTCI. The financial sustainability of LTCI is not guaranteed under this circumstance.

Recommendations

The growth of ageing population in Shanghai will lead to the rise in demand for LTC. It is important for the government to ensure the financial sustainability and quality of LTC services so that different needs of older adults can be met. In order to ensure the financial sustainability of LTCI, LTCI should be created as a scheme independent of medical insurance. The government can consider adjusting the contribution rate of old-age insurance, basic medical insurance, unemployment insurance, and other types of social insurance (Chen and Hao 2020: 112) so that employers and employees can contribute to LTCI without increasing their financial burden.

To provide LTC services that can meet the needs of older adults, the government should improve the needs assessment. The needs assessment can be more comprehensive and accurate by reducing the weightage of disease severity (Chen and Hao 2020) while adding other components to the needs assessment to determine individual care needs. The government can learn from Germany, which 'has operated one of the longest-running public programs providing universal support for the cost of long term services and supports' (Nadash *et al.* 2018: 588). In Germany, eligibility assessment aims to assess individual LTC needs based on his or her level of autonomy, awarding points along six parameters: self-care (e.g. eating, drinking), mobility (e.g. climbing stairs), structuring everyday life and social contacts (e.g. arranging the daily routine), cognitive and communication skills, behaviours and psychological problems (e.g. defence against nursing procedures, nightly restlessness), and mastering of and dealing independently with therapy or illness-related requirements (Nadash *et al.* 2018; The Federal Ministry of Health, Germany 2017: 6–7). These parameters help determine individual care assistance more appropriately and facilitate fair distribution of LTC services to people in need.

More older adults can benefit from LTCI if the government can remove the age limit for those enjoying LTCI. At present, only UEBMI and URRBMI participants aged 60 and above can receive LTC if they are in care level two and above. Those who develop disability at younger ages can only wait to receive LTC until they reach 60. It is suggested that LTCI should break age limits so that more people with disability can enjoy LTC (Ma and He 2019: 111). The Shanghai government can learn from Japan, which allows both 'primary insured people' and 'secondary insured people' to receive LTC (Tsutsumi n.d.). In Japan, 'primary insured people' are those aged 65 and above requiring LTC regardless of what makes them need LTC (Tsutsumi n.d.: 23). 'Secondary insured people' are those aged between 40 and 64 being eligible for receiving LTC if their need for LTC is caused by age-related diseases (Tsutsumi n.d.: 23). The Shanghai government can consider categorizing UEBMI and URRBMI participants aged 60 and above as 'primary insured people' and UEBMI and URRBMI participants aged between 40 and 59 as 'secondary insured people'. 'Primary insured people' are eligible for receiving LTC if they are in care level two and above. 'Secondary insured people' are eligible for receiving LTC if they have disability, or their disability is caused by age-related diseases. However, if younger UEBMI and URRBMI participants can receive LTC, the government should ensure the financial sustainability of LTCI by asking UEBMI and URRBMI participants to make financial contribution to LTCI or looking for multiple sources of finance to support LTCI. The government can also improve PWDs' access to LTCI benefits by providing more services targeted to PWD. These services can include home-based night care, cognitive training, and cognitive rehabilitation. They can help improve the physical and mental well-being of PWD.

Multiple ways can be adopted by the government to improve the quality as well as increase the supply of LTC workers. First, the government can consider learning from the Republic of Korea (ROK), which has 'a national certification system for LTC workers to ensure quality of care' (United Nations Economic and Social Commission for Asia and the Pacific 2015: 17). In the ROK, those who become certified elder care worker must complete 240 hours of training (theory 80 hours, practice 80 hours, and apprenticeship 80 hours) and pass the qualification examination (United Nations Economic and Social Commission for

Asia and the Pacific 2015: 17). A more structured and comprehensive training programme and certification help enhance workforce performance, increase salary, and worker retention rate. Second, more specific training programmes can be offered to incumbent LTC workers. They can increase the level of competency among LTC workers involved in performing specific tasks such as the use of oxygen delivery equipment and providing support to frail older adults receiving palliative care (OECD 2020b: 81–2). For example, geriatric care training can be offered to nurses and other elder care workers so that they can acquire important knowledge in healthcare for specific conditions of older adults, such as dementia, and skills in complex disease management and rehabilitation (OECD 2020b: 67). Third, paid leaves can be provided to elder care workers to motivate them to enrol in on-the-job training (Fujisawa and Colombo 2009: 35). Fourth, recruitment strategies which target recent unemployed or divorced homemakers can be adopted to increase the supply of LTC workers (Fujisawa and Colombo 2009: 36). For example, the government can consider learning from the German Federal Employment Agency (FEA), which finances training programmes in elderly care professions for unemployed workers (Dauth and Lang 2019: 544). Unemployed workers can be qualified as semi-skilled elderly care assistants if they receive short training which provides them with basic care knowledge (Dauth and Lang 2019: 544). Alternatively, they 'can participate in retraining, which takes 3 years and yields a vocational degree as an elderly care nurse' (Dauth and Lang 2019: 544).

Conclusion

To conclude, the implementation of LTCI in Shanghai leads to better utilization of medical resources, save medical insurance fund, and greatly reduce the financial costs borne by care recipients and their family members. However, the government needs to remove the age limit of LTCI, provide LTC services targeting PWD, increase the supply and improve the quality of LTC workers, improve the quality of LTC services, and ensure the financial sustainability of LTCI in the long run. Looking forward, more people in Shanghai will have access to LTC and enjoy better quality of LTC services.

References

60 Plus (2020) *Report on Elder Care Services Market in Shanghai 2020* (Chinese version). Online. Available HTTP: www.sohu.com/a/417244542_120000154 (accessed 8 May 2021).

Ai, H. (2018) 'Ageing, Policy Change and the Fiscal Balance of the Social Pooling Fund of the Urban Employee Basic Medical Insurance in Shanghai: Using System Dynamic Simulation', *Chinese Health Resources*, 21 (2): 133–9.

Boxer, B. (n.d.) *Shanghai*. Online. Available HTTP: www.britannica.com/place/Shanghai (accessed 27 May 2021).

Cadieux, M., Garcia, L. J. and Patrick, J. (2013) 'Needs of People with Dementia in Long-Term Care: A Systematic Review', *American Journal of Alzheimer's Disease & Other Dementias*, 28 (8): 723–33.

Cao, X. Y. (2020) 'Study on the Mobility of Elder Care Workers in Shanghai under the Long-Term Care Insurance Policy', *Statistics and Management*, 60: 14–18.

Chen, L. (2011) '"Empty-nesters" Accounted for One-Third of the Total Number of Elderly in Shanghai', (Chinese version), *Shanghai Morning Post*, 23 January. Online. Available HTTP: http://sh.sina.com.cn/news/s/2011-01-23/0934170576.html?from=wap (accessed 4 April 2021).

Chen, Q. Q. and Hao, Y. (2020) 'Problems and Countermeasures in the Pilot Program of Long-Term Care Insurance System in Shanghai', (Chinese version), *Scientific Development*, 1: 108–13.

Cheng, Q. D. (2020) 'Unbalanced Game and Countermeasures in Home Care Service under Long-Term Care Insurance System', *Journal of Xinyang Agriculture and Forestry University*, 30 (1): 46–52.

China Economic Net (2020) *The Average Monthly Salary of Employees in Shanghai in 2019 Was Renminbi 9,580* (Chinese version). Online. Available HTTP: https://baijiahao.baidu.com/s?id=1670914330905103304&wfr=spider&for=pc (accessed 10 May 2021).

Dai, R. M., He, S. Y., Jiang, M., Wang, Y., Bai, G. and Luo, L. (2019) 'Implementing the Long-Term Care Insurance System in Shanghai: Experience and Problems', (Chinese version), *Medicine and Society*, 32 (2): 9–13.

Dai, W. and Jin, S. (2019) 'Disabled Elders' Satisfaction with Long-Term Care Service and Its Influencing Factors in Shanghai', (Chinese version), *Disability Research*, 3 (35): 30–8.

Dauth, C. and Lang, J. (2019) 'Can the Unemployed Be Trained to Care for the Elderly? The Effects of Subsidized Training in Elderly Care', *Health Economics*, 28: 543–55.

The Development Research Centre of Shanghai Municipal People's Government (2020) *A Study on Shanghai Further Improving the Long-Term Care Insurance System* (Chinese version). Online. Available HTTP: www.fzzx.sh.gov.cn/zdkt_2018/20200117/0053-10525.html (accessed 13 May 2021).

'Early-Stage Caregiving' (n.d.) Online. Available HTTP: www.alz.org/help-support/caregiving/stages-behaviors/early-stage (accessed 19 May 2021).

The Federal Ministry of Health, Germany (2017) *Peer Review on "Germany's Latest Reforms of the Long-Term Care System"*. Online. Available HTTP: https://ec.europa.eu/social/BlobServlet?docId=18964&langId=en (accessed 19 May 2021).

Feng, J., Wang, Z. and Yu, Y. (2020) 'Does Long-Term Care Insurance Reduce Hospital Utilization and Medical Expenditures? Evidence from China', *Social Science & Medicine*, 258: 113081.

Fujisawa, R. and Colombo, F. (2009) *The Long-Term Care Workforce: Overview and Strategies to Adapt Supply to a Growing Demand*. OECD Health Working Papers, No. 44. OECD Publishing. Online. Available HTTP: http://envejecimiento.csic.es/documentos/documentos/fujisawa-longterm-01.pdf (accessed 22 May 2021).

Gang Wo Education (2020) *Certificate for Long-Term Care Workers in Shanghai* (Chinese version). Online. Available HTTP: www.sohu.com/a/429371917_120373504 (accessed 8 May 2021).

Gao, Y., Wei, Y., Shen, Y., Tang, Y. and Yang, J. (2014) 'China's Empty Nest Elderly Need Better Care', *Journal of the American Geriatrics Society*, 62 (9): 1821.

Gu, J. (2020) 'The Number of Elderly Will Account for 40 Percent of the Total Number of People in Shanghai by 2030', (Chinese version), *Shanghai Observer*, 30 July. Online. Available HTTP: www.jfdaily.com/staticsg/res/html/web/newsDetail.html?id=274443 (accessed 4 April 2021).

Hu, S. (2018) 'Pilot Study on Long-Term Care Insurance System in Shanghai: Status, Problems and Suggestions', (Chinese version), *Journal of East China University of Science and Technology (Social Science Edition)*, 4: 84–91.

Huang, Q. (2019) 'The Release of Shanghai Nursing Home Guide', (Chinese version), *Xinmin Weekly*, 26 May. Online. Available HTTP: https://baijiahao.baidu.com/s?id=1634601058090043945&wfr=spider&for=pc (accessed 9 May 2021).

Jie Fang Daily (2014) 'The Number of Disabled Elders Reached over 400,000 in Shanghai', (Chinese version), *Jie Fang Daily*, 25 November. Online. Available HTTP: www.chinadaily.com.cn/dfpd/sh/2014-11/25/content_18974920.htm (accessed 4 April 2021).

Li, Q. (2018) *Study on the Quality of Long-Term Care Services in Shanghai* (Chinese version). Master Thesis, Shanghai: East China Normal University.

Li, T. (2020) *Shanghai Now Third in Ranking of Global Financial Centers*. Online. Available HTTP: https://plataformamedia.com/en/2020/09/29/shanghai-now-third-in-ranking-of-global-financial-centers/ (accessed 27 May 2021).

Liang, Y., Niu, X. and Lu, P. (2020) 'The Aging Population in China: Subjective Well-Being of Empty Nesters in Rural Eastern China', *Journal of Health Psychology*, 25 (3): 361–72.

Liu, T. J. (2018) 'A Study on the Long-Term Care Insurance in Shanghai', (Chinese version), *Economic Research Guide*, 28: 50–1.

Ma, M. and He, J. (2019) 'Analysis the Practice and Problems of Long-Term Care Insurance in Shanghai', (Chinese version), *Scientific Development*, 7: 109–13.

Nadash, P., Doty, P. and von Schwanenflügel, M. (2018) 'The German Long-Term Care Insurance Program: Evolution and Recent Developments', *The Gerontologist*, 58 (3): 588–97.

OECD (2011) *Help Wanted? Providing and Paying for Long-Term Care*. Online. Available HTTP: www.oecd.org/els/health-systems/help-wanted-9789264097759-en.htm (accessed 17 May 2021).

OECD (2020a) *Long-Term Care and Health Care Insurance in OECD and Other Countries*. Online. Available HTTP: www.oecd.org/daf/fin/insurance/Long-Term-Care-Health-Care-Insurance-in-OECD-and-Other-Countries.pdf (accessed 17 May 2021).

OECD (2020b) *Who Cares? Attracting and Retaining Care Workers for the Elderly*, *OECD Health Policy Studies*, Paris: OECD Publishing. Available HTTP: https://doi.org/10.1787/92c0ef68-en (accessed 20 May 2021).

Office of Shanghai Chronicles (2015) *Elder Life* (Chinese version). Online. Available HTTP: www.shtong.gov.cn/dfz_web/DFZ/Info?idnode=196691&tableName=userobject1a&id=298288 (accessed 4 April 2021).

Office of Shanghai Municipal Working Committee on Ageing, Shanghai Municipal Health Commission, Shanghai Municipal Statistics Bureau and Shanghai Municipal Centre for Senior Citizens Program Development (2021) *Statistics on Demographics and Programs of Senior Citizens in Shanghai* (Chinese version). Online. Available HTTP: http://wsjkw.sh.gov.cn/cmsres/78/783845a354ae4b69a6fb076f932960ac/e316f0cf068719ae4b0e46b4520001c4.pdf (accessed 8 May 2021).

The Paper (2020) 'Shanghai Would Promulgate Legislation on Elder Care Services and Focus on Providing Long-Term Care for Disabled Elders and Elders with Dementia', (Chinese version), *The Paper*, 5 March. Online. Available HTTP: https://baijiahao.baidu.com/s?id=1660309734730635016&wfr=spider&for=pc (accessed 4 April 2021).

'Policy Interpretation of the Opinion on the Pilot Medical and Nursing Care Scheme for Older Adults in Shanghai', (Chinese version) (2016) Online. Available HTTP: http://m.lc123.net/laws/2016-08-30/291483.html (accessed 5 April 2021).

Qian, P. J. (2020) 'Shanghai Announced a New Policy to Evaluate the Skills of Long-Term Care Workers', (Chinese version), *Workers' Daily*, 7 August. Online. Available HTTP: http://acftu.people.com.cn/n1/2020/0807/c67502-31813932. html (accessed 9 May 2021).

Shanghai Centre on Scientific Research on Ageing (2007) *The 2006 Statistics on Ageing Population and Eldercare Industry in Shanghai* (Chinese version). Online. Available HTTP: http://ylgw.shweilao.cn/cms/cmsDetail?uuid=4a8692c9-bf50-4f9d-8bd7-a7bb8527ec82 (accessed 4 April 2021).

Shanghai Civil Affairs Bureau, Shanghai Municipal Commission of Health and Family Planning, Shanghai Municipal Human Resources and Social Security Bureau and Shanghai Medical Health Insurance Office (2016) *Notification on Printing and Distributing a List of Long-Term Care Insurance Service Items and Related Service Standards and Norms (Trial Implementation)* (Chinese version). Online. Available HTTP: www.yanglao.com.cn/article/56456.html (accessed 21 April 2021).

Shanghai Civil Affairs Bureau, Shanghai Municipal Finance Bureau and Shanghai Municipal Human Resources and Social Security Bureau (Shanghai Medical Health Insurance Office) (2018) *Notification on Subsidies to Cover Out-of-Pocket Expenses Incurred by Long-Term Care Insurance in the City* (Chinese version). Online. Available HTTP: http://k.sina.com.cn/article_5617251953_14ed076710190049mv. html?cre=tianyi&mod=pcpager_china&loc=37&r=9&doct=0&rfunc=100&tj=no ne&tr=9 (accessed 24 April 2021).

Shanghai Municipal Health Commission (2020) *The 2019 Statistics on Ageing Population and Eldercare Industry in Shanghai* (Chinese version). Online. Available HTTP: http://wsjkw.sh.gov.cn/cmsres/04/04e3d13e15ec433ab29ad39aae669 30d/6264cec00d12ea2848b1a86f48440f93.pdf (accessed 4 April 2021).

Shanghai Municipal Health Commission, Shanghai Civil Affairs Bureau and Shanghai Municipal Medical Insurance Bureau (2019) *A Unified Needs Assessment Standard for Elder Care, Version 2.0 (Pilot)* (Chinese version). Online. Available HTTP: http://wsjkw.sh.gov.cn/gjhztgahz/20191220/4ee7499b3f2f4fa699a1b048804 04d93.html (accessed 20 April 2021).

Shanghai Municipal Human Resources and Social Security Bureau and Shanghai Medical Health Insurance Office (2018) *Rules for Implementing and Managing a Unified Needs Assessment and for Elder Care (Pilot)* (Chinese version). Online. Available HTTP: http://rsj.sh.gov.cn/tylbx_17284_17284/20200617/ t0035_1390123.html (accessed 17 April 2021).

Shanghai Municipal Human Resources and Social Security Bureau, Shanghai Medical Health Insurance Office, Shanghai Municipal Commission of Health and Family Planning and Shanghai Civil Affairs Bureau (2016) *Ways to Manage Designated Long-Term Care Insurance Service Providers in Shanghai (Trial Implementation)* (Chinese version). Online. Available HTTP: https://m.chashebao.com/shanghai/ ziliao/17076.html (accessed 24 April 2021).

Shanghai Municipal Medical Insurance Bureau (2019) *Notification on Printing and Distributing "Shanghai Long-Term Care Insurance Settlement Measures" (Trial Implementation)* (Chinese version). Online. Available HTTP: http://service.shanghai. gov.cn/XingZhengWenDangKuJyh/XZGFDetails.aspx?docid=REPORT_ NDOC_006179 (accessed 21 April 2021).

Shanghai Municipal People's Government (2000) *Urban Employee Basic Medical Insurance in Shanghai* (Chinese version). Online. Available HTTP: http://law.51labour.com/lawshow-4276-1.html (accessed 10 May 2021).

Shanghai Municipal People's Government (2016a) *Pilot Measures for Long-Term Care Insurance in Shanghai* (Chinese version). Online. Available HTTP: http://law.esnai.com/view/179508/ (accessed 12 April 2021).

Shanghai Municipal People's Government (2016b) *Opinions on Comprehensively Promoting the Establishment of a Unified Needs Assessment System for Elder Care* (Chinese version). Online. Available HTTP: http://law.esnai.com/view/181979/ (accessed 15 April 2021).

Shanghai Municipal People's Government (2017) *Notification on Revising Pilot Measures for Long-Term Care Insurance in Shanghai* (Chinese version). Online. Available HTTP: www.shanghai.gov.cn/nw41430/20200823/0001-41430_54809.html (accessed 20 April 2021).

Shanghai Municipal People's Government (2018) *Measures of a Unified Needs Assessment System and Service Management for Elder Care in Shanghai* (Chinese version). Online. Available HTTP: www.askci.com/news/chanye/20180126/113247116966.shtml (accessed 16 April 2021).

Shanghai Municipal People's Government (2019) *Notification on Printing and Distributing the Implementation Plan for Deepening Elderly Care Services in Shanghai* (Chinese version). Online. Available HTTP: www.yanglaocn.com/shtml/20190604/1559602050119363.html (accessed 13 May 2021).

Shanghai Municipal People's Government (2020) *Notification on Printing and Distributing Procedures of Urban and Rural Resident Basic Medical Insurance in Shanghai* (Chinese version). Online. Available HTTP: www.shanghai.gov.cn/nw12344/20210105/0099fc847579431e85dc33e8fd3626e7.html (accessed 10 May 2021).

Shanghai Municipal Price Bureau, Shanghai Municipal Commission of Health and Family Planning and Shanghai Medical Health Insurance Office (2018) *Notification on Charges for the Long-Term Care Insurance Needs Assessment (Trial Implementation)* (Chinese version). Online. Available HTTP: http://m.lc123.net/laws/2018-02-06/324417.html (accessed 21 April 2021).

Shanghai Municipal Veteran Bureau (2020) *Long-Term Care Insurance Can Protect Disabled Elders in a Better Way* (Chinese version). Online. Available HTTP: www.shlgbj.gov.cn/view/6310 (accessed 24 April 2021).

Shanghai Observer (2017) 'Shanghai Will Implement a Pilot Long-Term Care Insurance Scheme in the Whole City: Older Adults Can Receive Home Care Services', (Chinese version), *Shanghai Observer*, 27 December. Online. Available HTTP: https://sh.qq.com/a/20171227/005417.htm (accessed 20 May 2021).

Shanghai Observer (2019) 'This Year the Long-Term Care Insurance Expenditure Reached RMB 1.27 Billion and 410,000 People Benefited from the Long-Term Care Insurance', (Chinese version), *Shanghai Observer*, 20 August. Online. Available HTTP: http://sh.sina.com.cn/zw/c/2019-08-20/detailzw-ihytcern2113232.shtml (accessed 25 April 2021).

Shanghai Observer (2021a) 'The Sixth Type of Social Insurance: About 500,000 People in Shanghai Have Benefitted from Long-Term Care Insurance', (Chinese version), *Shanghai Observer*, 8 March. Online. Available HTTP: https://sghexport.shobserver.com/html/baijiahao/2021/03/08/376940.html (accessed 25 April 2021).

Shanghai Observer (2021b) 'Jing'an District in Shanghai Will Use Smart Devices to Monitor All the Community Home Care Services by June 2021', (Chinese version), *Shanghai Observer*, 18 February. Online. Available HTTP: https://sghexport. shobserver.com/html/baijiahao/2021/02/18/362570.html (accessed 9 May 2021).

Shi, Y. and Cui, Y. (2011) 'The Current Situation of Population Ageing and the Development Trend of Elder Care Facilities in Shanghai', (Chinese version), *Huazhong Architecture*, 29 (8): 206–9.

'Stages of Alzheimer's' (n.d.) Online. Available HTTP: www.alz.org/alzheimers-dementia/stages (accessed 19 May 2021).

Standing Committee of the National People's Congress (2010) *The Social Insurance Law of the People's Republic of China.* Online. Available HTTP: www.mohrss.gov. cn/gjhzs/GJHZzhengcewenjian/201506/t20150625_212401.html (accessed 19 May 2021).

Tian, X. (2019) *About 186,000 Elders in Shanghai Benefited from the Long-Term Care Insurance* (Chinese version) Online. Available HTTP: www.gov.cn/xinwen/ 2019-02/01/content_5363149.htm (accessed 25 April 2021).

'The Total Number of Disabled Elders and Elders with Dementia in Shanghai Was over 630,000', Chinese version (n.d.) Online. Available HTTP: www.day-care.cn/ nd.jsp?id=139 (accessed 4 April 2021).

Tsutsumi, Shuzo (n.d.) *Long-Term Care Insurance in Japan: Understanding the Ideas behind Its Design.* Online. Available HTTP: www.jica.go.jp/english/our_work/ thematic_issues/social/c8h0vm0000f4pxgh-att/insurance.pdf (accessed 19 May 2021).

United Nations Economic and Social Commission for Asia and the Pacific (2015) *Long-Term Care of Older Persons in the Republic of Korea.* Online. Available HTTP: www.unescap.org/sites/default/d8files/knowledge-products/SDD%20 Working%20Paper%20Ageing%20Long%20Term%20Care%20ROK%20v1-2.pdf (accessed 20 May 2021).

World Maritime News (2020) 'Shanghai Remains World's Top Container Port', *World Maritime News*, 16 January. Online. Available HTTP: www.offshore-energy. biz/shanghai-remains-worlds-top-container-port/ (accessed 27 May 2021).

Xiao Xiang Morning Post (2020a) 'Shanghai Strives to Have 85,000 Long-Term Care Workers by 2022', Chinese version, *Xiao Xiang Morning Post*, 29 July. Online. Available HTTP: https://baijiahao.baidu.com/s?id=1673531507813540590&w fr=spider&for=pc (accessed 8 May 2021).

Xiao Xiang Morning Post (2020b) 'Shanghai Needs to Attract More Talented People to Join the Long-Term Care Sector', (Chinese version), *Xiao Xiang Morning Post*, 1 November. Available HTTP: https://baijiahao.baidu.com/s?id=168211085726 5466854&wfr=spider&for=pc (accessed 9 May 2021).

Xinhua Insight (2015) *An Acute Shortage of Long-Term Care Workers in Shanghai* (Chinese version). Online. Available HTTP: www.sohu.com/a/34818571_114 812 (accessed 9 May 2021).

Xu, J. (2020) *Shanghai Moves towards Refined Management of Long-Term Care Insurance: As of June 2020, a Total of 391,000 Disabled Elders Had Received Long-Term Care Services* (Chinese version). Online. Available HTTP: https://baijiahao.baidu. com/s?id=1678986737215505329&wfr=spider&for=pc (accessed 24 April 2021).

Xu, Li (2005) 'An Analysis on Challenges Brought by Population Aging to the Basic Medical Insurance Fund and Policy Reponses: The Case Study of Shanghai', *Inquiry into Economic Issues*, 12: 56–60.

Yu, H. (2008) 'The Process of Population Ageing in Shanghai: Challenges and Countermeasures', (Chinese version), *Shanghai Journal of Economics*, 3: 78–88.

Zhan, S. W. (2018) 'Shanghai Has Implemented Long-Term Care Insurance for One Month! How to Achieve the Goals? How to Apply for Long-Term Care Insurance', (Chinese version), *East Day*, 1 February. Online. Available HTTP: www.sohu.com/a/220349472_391463 (accessed 8 May 2021).

Zhu, G. H. (1999) 'Population Ageing in Shanghai: Trend, Problems and Countermeasures', (Chinese version), *Population and Family Planning*, 2: 26–8.

8 Conclusion

Introduction

China's success in providing universal coverage of health insurance has been praised as an exemplar for other nations (Yip *et al.* 2012: 840). It is, therefore, of great interest to both academics and policymakers to see if the same would be true for long-term care (LTC). This chapter recapitulates the development of LTC financing and delivery in China in terms of its general approach, its merits, as well as issues arising from some of the major recent initiatives and the 2019 coronavirus diseases (COVID-19) pandemic. Recommendations for the Chinese government to improve the financing and delivery of LTC and implications of China's long-term care insurance (LTCI) reform for other countries and regions are made towards the end.

The general approach to LTC

China's population is rapidly ageing. The impressive economic growth over the past decades is a relatively recent phenomenon. 'Incomes are rapidly rising, but still low when compared to more advanced economies' (Riley 2013). Hence, many older adults throughout the country are still poor with little savings. Findings from a landmark survey showed that 23 percent of older adults in China were below the poverty line, 38 percent reported having disability, and 32 percent reported having poor health (Riley 2013). Meanwhile, changed circumstances over the decades – the previous one-child policy, massive migration of younger persons to urban areas, the increasing cost of care, and longer life expectancy – have rendered the traditional care approach that relies on family members impractical and ineffective.

Previous chapters show that the Chinese government is acutely aware of the situation. This resulted in the implementation of LTCI in the country. The strategy of the Chinese government is to initially provide LTC coverage to people who are participants of the employment-based health insurance scheme and then extend the coverage to other segments of population at a later stage. This enables rapid development of a LTCI system, taking advantage of the infrastructure developed under the near-universal health insurance system.

The pilot cities selected for implementing LTCI are highly heterogeneous in terms of geographic location, the level of economic development, wealth,

DOI: 10.4324/9780429057199-8

ethnic composition, and other demographic characteristics to ensure the general adaptability at the national level. For example, Shanghai and Qingdao are major metropolitan centres in the eastern coast, while Shihezi is a sub-prefecture-level city in Northern Xinjiang. Local variations for implementing the pilot LTCI are allowed within the general guidelines. This approach is similar to the one chosen for developing the national health insurance system and has proven to be successful in terms of extending insurance coverage, eventually, to the entire population, in a relatively short period of time (Yu 2015). It also allows fine-tuning of the insurance scheme at a later stage based on the experience gained from the successes and failures of different pilot cities.

LTC services are provided by public and private organizations, including for-profit organizations. This allows a more rapid supply of the needed services once the insurance is rolled out. All the designated LTC service providers must pass the assessment conducted by their local insurance authority which dictates quality standards, fee arrangements, and other requirements. LTCI enrollees can seek services from only designated LTC service providers, if they wish to have the service fees reimbursed by LTCI.

Merit of this approach

The current approach adopted by the Chinese government is a clear departure from the residual approach it adopted to care for older adults. It now seeks to finance LTC by using an insurance system, which is a step towards eventual universal coverage. It seeks to also standardize the financing and provision of LTC by issuing broad guidelines that define the parameters including the target population, the types of services covered, the co-payment ratio, and quality assurance systems. The approach is an incremental one, not a 'big bang' one. It takes advantage of the existing infrastructure developed for the financing of healthcare to finance LTC, thereby facilitating a more rapid implementation of LTCI.

The general guidelines allow local variations. Meanwhile, they include parameters to ensure minimum standards, affordability for the population, and sustainability of the insurance scheme. Given the huge variations in terms of wealth and other demographic characteristics of the various parts of the country, the approach is clearly a sensible one.

An insurance-based approach can provide funding for a wide range of LTC services in a more rapid manner. It is generally much more difficult for government to raise taxes to fund LTC. LTC services funded through taxes are often constrained by insufficient funding resources and/or narrow eligibility of the target population (Yang *et al.* 2016: 1399).

Challenges of implementing LTCI in China

An analysis on the LTCI schemes in 15 pilot cities shows that there are several challenges facing the central and local governments when implementing LTCI.

Long-term sustainability

All insurance schemes and tax-based schemes are pay-as-you-go financing systems. They are viable only if the ratio of contributors to benefit recipients remains more or less constant over time. In ageing societies, the working population, who are contributors, is shrinking. The elderly population, who are benefit recipients, is growing. The scheme can remain viable only if the contributors agree to contribute more. Hence, population ageing strains the financial sustainability of a pay-as-you-go financing system in ageing societies (Borsch-Supan *et al.* 2016: 788) because 'fewer young contributors to the system will have to finance a large number of old beneficiaries' (Borsch-Supan *et al.* 2016: 788). Only capital-funded schemes and savings schemes, whereby the population or the government accumulates assets for future use, can overcome such problems in ageing societies.

Having the LTCI scheme as an extension of the health insurance scheme is, therefore, more problematic. Medical inflation caused by new medicines, treatments, and technology tends to be very high ('The Mystery behind Medical Inflation' 2018) and can easily render health insurance schemes non-viable, even without population ageing. LTCI schemes relying heavily on fund transferred from the cumulative surplus of a health insurance scheme on a regular basis is not going to be realistic, especially for countries experiencing an increase in old-age dependency ratio.

The health insurance schemes of cities with relatively high economic growth, a high percentage of working middle-class population, and a high per capita income are likely to be in good financial health, at least for the current moment. These well-off cities can use the surplus in their health insurance schemes to fund LTCI without additional contributions from LTCI enrollees, at least at the initial phase of implementing LTCI. But not all cities are in such a privileged position when their health insurance schemes are already under severe financial pressure. Analyses in Chapter 4 on LTCI schemes in 15 pilot cities indicate that some schemes will have problems in meeting the expenses as defined by the minimum requirements of the national guidelines, even at the early stage. Even for cities which currently have surplus in their health insurance schemes and can meet the LTC expenses, their financial position is likely to change as the population ages. This is because they have fewer working persons contributing to the premium while having more older adults requiring both healthcare and LTC. Reliance on surpluses from the health insurance scheme to finance LTC is obviously not sustainable. Having a more diversified source of income for the LTCI scheme is absolutely necessary.

Coverage

Not requiring cities to provide LTCI to persons outside the formal employment sector is also undesirable. Many persons under this category 'tend to work with low pay' (Fang *et al.* 2009: 3), have little savings, 'less social protection' (Fang *et al.* 2009: 3), reside in rural areas, and are, in general, in greater need for assistance than those in the formal employment sector. Some well-off cities have extended the coverage of LTCI to persons enrolled under the Urban Resident Basic Medical Insurance (URBMI) or Urban and Rural Resident Basic Medical Insurance (URRBMI) scheme. However, cities that have not done so tend to have a less developed economy, lower per capita incomes, and more vulnerable older adults. Hopefully, the limited coverage of LTCI in such cities is just a temporary situation rather than a permanent feature. The case study on Qingdao, Nantong, and Shanghai suggests that near-universal coverage has been achieved in these three cities, with high enrolment for both the employee and resident schemes, although the benefits provided to those outside the Urban Employee Basic Medical Insurance (UEBMI) system are generally less generous and comprehensive.

Equity

The national guidelines on co-payment and on some eligibility criteria are likely to cause hardship for some older adults. Additional assistance from the government on the means-testing basis is highly desirable to ensure that those who fall outside the normal eligibility net but have genuine need and lack financial means would not be shut out of the system. Some form of central or provincial government assistance to the less wealthy localities to assist such needy individuals are necessary. Meanwhile, the differences between the benefits enjoyed by UEBMI enrollees and the benefits enjoyed by URBMI or URRBMI enrollees have created equity problems and should be addressed.

Supply issues

Having adequate supply of different types of LTC facilities and trained manpower is important to ensure that eligible beneficiaries do not have to wait for unacceptably long periods of time before obtaining care. It is also important that eligible beneficiaries have choices and are not forced to receive poor quality of care simply because of inadequate supply of high-quality LTC facilities.

The national guidelines explicitly indicate the preference for home care and community-based care over residential care. It is encouraging to note that from the case study of Qingdao, Nantong, and Shanghai, home care has become the dominant form of LTC in these three cities. Highly affordable home care services appear to be readily available, especially in the urban areas, taking up in excess of 80 percent of all LTC services. In rural areas, however, it appears to be a bit more problematic to provide LTC services. The government can consider providing greater incentives such as government start-up grants for service providers that wish to set up services in the underserved areas.

Specialized services and institutions for people with dementia (PWD) are available in Qingdao and Nantong. It is reassuring to find that the authorities in these two cities recognize the need to have a separate system to handle PWD that may require 24/7 supervision due to having behavioural issues and not have them group together with those requiring only physical assistance. But the degree of specialization in terms of services for people experiencing different stages of dementia appears to be crude at the current stage. As regards Shanghai, there is room for improvement in the care for PWD.

The problem of manpower shortage is particularly serious in rural areas. Manpower shortages in the LTC sector is a common problem worldwide. It cannot be easily resolved, given the decrease in the number of working-age persons and the relatively low wages that generally prevail in the sector.

Quality

The national guidelines require local authorities to have regulations and requirements relating to LTC personnel training and licensing of LTC facilities to ensure service quality. As the guidelines stipulate only general principles, each city develops its own standards and practices in quality assurance regulations. All cities have licensing systems for medical and LTC institutions. With the introduction of LTCI, however, more standards and requirements have been laid down by government agencies for designated LTC service providers to follow. All the designated LTC service providers are assessed and rated regularly by the insurance authorities. The ratings are made public. Financial penalties would be imposed on designated LTC service providers which fail to meet the minimum standards and the revocation of designation can result for repeated underperformers.

Evidence from the three case studies shows that differences in terms of standards and practices across localities can be very substantial, resulting in big variations in quality. In general, LTC beneficiaries are more satisfied with activities for daily living (ADLs) care, and less satisfied with the more skilled nursing services, owning to the shortage of skilled personnel. Quality problems are more common in rural areas. Since high-quality providers tend to charge more, LTC beneficiaries with low income seek care from poor quality providers. LTCI, for the most part, pays service providers on either fee-for-service or per-diem basis. These forms of payment often drive providers to cut costs so as to maximize profit and have little incentive to deliver person-centred care.

Cost

It is expected that LTC expenses will go up with the introduction of LTCI. Free informal care is being substituted for formal care that is paid by LTCI. However, LTCI has the potential to divert care from the expensive acute care sector to the most cost-effective LTC sector, thereby reducing the overall costs of health and LTC.

The three case study cities show that the implementation of LTCI led to a drastic decrease in medical expenses for LTCI beneficiaries. Without LTCI, many disabled older adults would have been left in acute hospitals where the cost of stay is far more expensive than the cost of stay in LTC facilities or home care in these cities.

Insights from the COVID-19 pandemic

The weaknesses of the health and LTC systems of many countries have been acutely exposed by the COVID-19 pandemic. Data from China demonstrated that older adults were most at risk from COVID-19 (Stevis-Gridneff *et al.* 2020). Estimates of COVID-19 infection fatality ratio was 7.8 percent for persons aged above 80 in China, as compared with COID-19 infection ratio of about 0.66 percent for the general population (Verity *et al.* 2020: 673).

The over reliance of older adults on hospitals for services has left many with chronic conditions without care for months. Non-urgent surgeries, psycho-geriatric consultations, physiotherapy sessions were all cancelled for extended periods of time. While these might not be life-saving interventions, their pro-longed postponement could lead to further deterioration of the illness, affecting quality of life (QoL). Older adults in nursing homes have been particularly hard hit during the pandemic. The Ministry of Civil Affairs (MCA) issued various guidelines and orders to stop the spread of virus in nursing homes (Ng and Xu 2020). Nursing homes 'were put under total lockdown: no one was allowed in and out' (Ng and Xu 2020). All community-run elder care services such as meal planning, cleaning, meals-on-wheels, and adult day cares were halted (Ng and Xu 2020). With visitors banned in all hospitals and nursing homes to control the spread of the virus, almost all dying patients died in isolation, away from their loved ones (Hixenbaugh and Solon 2020).

The Chinese government's emphasis on the development of home care as the dominant form of LTC is definitely desirable in the face of the pandemic. While home care has definite advantages over residential-based care during the pan-demic, it is unclear whether the authorities have ways to deliver care and other services to older adults, especially the severely disabled ones, in their homes in a safe and uninterrupted manner. Besides, it is unclear whether there were mea-sures to safeguard the mental and social well-being of homebound and bedridden older adults during lockdowns.

In China, the current fragmented, hospital-centred and treatment-dominated healthcare system (Wang *et al.* 2018) 'should be transformed to a system based on primary care, where health providers are closely connected and coordinated to offer continuing and integrated care' (Meng *et al.* 2019). Only the establishment of a strong primary healthcare system can support the medical needs of older adults residing in their own homes.

Is the approach likely to succeed?

Given China's track record in achieving universal health insurance coverage within a relatively short period of time, there is a good chance that this will also be the case for LTC. The database for the target population is already available for the entire country, as LTCI enrollees are the current enrollees of the health insurance schemes. The infrastructure for collection and disbursement of LTCI is similar to that of the health insurance system, reducing the time and cost of setting up the system. The schemes in the pilot cities, on the whole, appear to be working well. The scope of the services covered by LTCI is reasonably comprehensive, with home care playing a major part.

There is a clear mandate from the central government to develop LTCI in China. Local governments are well known to be efficient on matters deemed as priority by the central government. Despite the pandemic, high rate of economic growth appears to have been revived, thus strengthening the fiscal capacity of the government to provide the necessary investment and subsidies.

Finally, ageing issues have in recent years generated huge public concerns and expectations in China. The initiative of implementing LTCI in the country should be highly popular. Experience from Japan suggests that LTCI contributions 'have become a new revenue source to which people appear to be more willing to contribute than paying higher consumer taxes' (Ikegami 2019: 465).

Recommendations for improving the financing and delivery of LTC in China

The early chapters show that LTCI is developed in a major way across the country. However, common problems have also appeared. The following are suggestions to deal with some of the more common issues.

Sustainability: The question of financial sustainability should be taken seriously. The heavy reliance on transferring money from the health insurance schemes without additional contributions from any other parties needs to be rectified. A more diversified source of income for the LTCI scheme is absolutely necessary. Creating a multiple party contribution system – from enrollees, employers, health insurance fund, the government, and charity (e.g. lottery) – is a good starting point. Studies should be conducted on the feasibility of supplementing the aforementioned LTC income sources with some form of savings or capital-funded schemes, whereby an individual or the government accumulates assets for future use. Future fund and individual savings account schemes are reliable ways to ensure financial sustainability of LTCI in the long run in ageing societies. While this is logical, it is very unpopular as this approach is seen as double taxing the younger working population – paying taxes and contributing to the pay-as-you-go scheme for the current older population and accumulating capital for their own future needs. Very few countries can implement such schemes in a substantive manner.

Workforce: Ensuring an adequate supply of LTC workforce is crucial. Government investing more in the LTC workforce development and training should be given high priority, including the creation of a new breed of LTC professionals, with a generalist training. Incentives should be provided by the government to encourage individuals to undertake such training. The pay structure for LTC jobs should be reviewed to ensure that it is reasonable to attract sufficient numbers to the occupation. The greater use of volunteers should be encouraged and facilitated by systems such as time-banking as in the case of Nantong.

Quality: Enhancing the quality of LTC is always important, especially for fledgling systems. Having more uniform standards across the country, benchmarking them with international accreditation practices would be helpful.

Currently, LTC providers are paid on a fee-for-service or per diem basis, which does not provide incentives for providers to deliver high-quality care to older adults. Having some pay-for-performance elements as part of the pay package should be explored – for example, bonus for improvement of the functional status of the client and for achieving high interRAI score that measures QoL of older adults such as their autonomy, care, comfort, and safety (InterRAI n.d.).

China is well known for rapid adoption of technology. More pervasive use of technology to assure or enhance LTC quality would be highly desirable. As described earlier in the case study of Shanghai, the Jing'an district in 2021 introduced a smart device which used biometric technologies to record how LTC workers deliver home care to older adults (Shanghai Observer 2021b). Such innovative practices should be more widely adopted in other parts of Shanghai and the country.

Implications of China's LTCI reform for other countries

China is facing serious population ageing and is 'getting old before getting rich' (Kuhn 2020). Its attempt to provide universal LTCI is commendable. Its experience can provide important lessons and inspirations to middle- and low-income countries facing similar problems.

First, the strategy of starting with providing LTCI coverage for people in formal employment sector and gradually expanding to other residence and to rural areas seems to be pragmatic. Second, the strategy of not requiring additional contributions from different stakeholders is conducive to the rapid launching of the LTCI scheme. Third, the strategy of starting with less generous benefits is also wise. Experience from Japan suggests that once a benefit becomes an entitlement, it would be difficult to take it back (Ikegami 2019). As a result, the Japanese government's efforts to contain LTC costs, including reducing provider fees, reducing benefits, raising the eligibility criteria, and increasing the coinsurance rate, had only marginal effects (Ikegami 2019: 462–4). Fourth, the strategy of providing home care as the dominant form of LTC is highly desirable. The set-up cost for home care provision is relatively low. It allows more older adults to age in place. It is cost-effective. It can save huge amount of money for the government or the medical insurance fund by reducing unnecessary and inappropriate hospital stay.

The Chinese approach is, of course, not perfect. The potential problems and suggestions for corrections are clearly presented in the preceding paragraphs. Nevertheless, the goal to provide LTC coverage to all older adults in an expeditious manner is a lofty one and should be a common goal for all countries and regions that still do not have universal coverage of LTC services. Such an initiative needs to be pursued imminently if the United Nations' Sustainable Development Goal 3 (SDG3) of ensuring healthy lives and promoting well-being for all at all ages (United Nations n.d.) is to be attained.

References

Borsch-Supan, A., Härtl, K. and Leite, D. N. (2016) 'Social Security and Public Insurance', in J. Piggott and A. Woodland (eds.) *Handbook of the Economics of Population Aging (Volume 1B)*. Amsterdam: Elsevier, pp. 781–863.

Fang, C., Du, Y. and Wang, M. (2009) *Employment and Inequality Outcomes in China*. Online. Available HTTP: www.oecd.org/employment/emp/42546043. pdf (accessed 16 July 2021).

Hixenbaugh, M. and Solon, O. (2020) *Death in the Age of Coronavirus: A Daughter Fights to Say Goodbye to Her Mother*. Online. Available HTTP: www.nbcnews.com/news/us-news/death-age-coronavirus-daughter-fights-say-goodbye-her-mother-n1180576 (accessed 16 July 2021).

Ikegami, N. (2019) 'Financing Long-Term Care: Lessons from Japan', *International Journal of Health Policy and Management*, 8 (8): 462–66.

InterRAI (n.d.) *Instruments Overview*. Online. Available HTTP: www.interrai.org/long-term-care-facilities.html (accessed 17 July 2021).

Kuhn, R. L. (2020) 'Is China Getting Old before Getting Rich?', *CGTN*, 29 September. Online. Available HTTP: https://news.cgtn.com/news/3149544d7930575 a306c5562684a335a764a4855/index.html (accessed 16 July 2021).

Meng, Q., Mills, A., Wang, L. and Han, Q. (2019) 'What Can We Learn from China's Health System Reform?', *BMJ*, 365: l2349.

The Mystery behind Medical Inflation (2018) Online. Available HTTP: www.axa globalhealthcare.com/en/wellbeing/global-access/the-mystery-behind-medical-inflation/ (accessed 16 July 2021).

Ng, L. Y. and Xu, F. (2020) *Eldercare during the Covid-19 Pandemic: China and Singapore – Pt. 2*. Online. Available HTTP: https://onlineacademiccommunity.uvic. ca/globalsouthpolitics/2020/07/01/eldercare-during-the-covid-19-pandemic-china-and-singapore-pt-2/ (accessed 16 July 2021).

Riley, C. (2013) 'New Portrait of China's 185 Million Seniors', *CNN*, 31 May. Online. Available HTTP: https://money.cnn.com/2013/05/31/news/economy/china-elderly/ (accessed 16 July 2021).

Shanghai Observer (2021b) 'Jing'an District in Shanghai Will Use Smart Devices to Monitor All the Community Home Care Services by June 2021', (Chinese version), *Shanghai Observer*, 18 February. Online. Available HTTP: https://sghexport.shob server.com/html/baijiahao/2021/02/18/362570.html (accessed 9 May 2021).

Stevis-Gridneff, M., Apuzzo, M. and Pronczuk, M. (2020) 'When COVID-19 Hit, Many Elderly Were Left to Die', *The New York Times*, 8 August. Online. Available HTTP: www.nytimes.com/2020/08/08/world/europe/coronavirus-nursing-homes-elderly.html (accessed 16 July 2021).

United Nations (n.d.) *Sustainable Development Goals*. Online. Available HTTP: www. un.org/sustainabledevelopment/ (accessed 16 July 2021).

Verity, R., Okell, L. C., Dorigatti, I., Winskill, P., Whittaker, C. and Imai, N. (2020) 'Estimates of the Severity of Coronavirus Disease 2019: A Model-Based Analysis', *The Lancet Infectious Diseases*, 20 (6): 669–77. Online. Available HTTP: www.

thelancet.com/journals/laninf/article/PIIS1473-3099(20)30243-7/fulltext (accessed 16 July 2021).

Wang, X., Sun, X., Birch, S., Gong, F., Valentijn, P., Chen, L., Zhang, Y., Huang, Y. and Yang, H. (2018) 'People-Centred Integrated Care in Urban China', *Bulletin of the World Health Organization*, 96 (12): 843–52.

Yang, W., He, A. J., Fang, L. and Mossialos, E. (2016) 'Financing Institutional Long-Term Care for the Elderly in China: A Policy Evaluation of New Models', *Health Policy and Planning*, 31: 1391–401.

Yip, W. C., Hsiao, W. C., Chen, W., Hu, S., Ma, J. and Maynard, A. (2012) 'Early Appraisal of China's Huge and Complex Health-Care Reforms', *The Lancet*, 379: 833–42.

Yu, H. (2015) 'Universal Health Insurance Coverage for 1.3 Billion People: What Accounts for China's Success?', *Health Policy*, 119 (9): 1145–52.

Index

Note: Page numbers in **bold** indicate a table on the corresponding page.

Printed in the USA
CPSIA information can be obtained
at www.ICGtesting.com
LVHW020711190923
758533LV00006B/675